Microsoft® 365 PowerPoint®

Microsoft® 365 PowerPoint®

2nd Edition

by Doug Lowe

Microsoft® 365 PowerPoint® For Dummies®, 2nd Edition

Published by: **John Wiley & Sons, Inc.**, 111 River Street, Hoboken, NJ 07030-5774, www.wiley.com

Copyright © 2025 by John Wiley & Sons, Inc. All rights reserved, including rights for text and data mining and training of artificial technologies or similar technologies.

Media and software compilation copyright © 2025 by John Wiley & Sons, Inc. All rights reserved, including rights for text and data mining and training of artificial technologies or similar technologies.

Published simultaneously in Canada

No part of this publication may be reproduced, stored in a retrieval system or transmitted in any form or by any means, electronic, mechanical, photocopying, recording, scanning or otherwise, except as permitted under Sections 107 or 108 of the 1976 United States Copyright Act, without the prior written permission of the Publisher. Requests to the Publisher for permission should be addressed to the Permissions Department, John Wiley & Sons, Inc., 111 River Street, Hoboken, NJ 07030, (201) 748-6011, fax (201) 748-6008, or online at http://www.wiley.com/go/permissions.

Trademarks: Wiley, For Dummies, the Dummies Man logo, Dummies.com, Making Everything Easier, and related trade dress are trademarks or registered trademarks of John Wiley & Sons, Inc. and may not be used without written permission. Microsoft 365 and PowerPoint are trademarks or registered trademarks of Microsoft Corporation. All other trademarks are the property of their respective owners. John Wiley & Sons, Inc. is not associated with any product or vendor mentioned in this book. *Microsoft® 365 PowerPoint® For Dummies®*, 2nd Edition, is an independent publication and is neither affiliated with, nor authorized, sponsored, or approved by, Microsoft Corporation.

LIMIT OF LIABILITY/DISCLAIMER OF WARRANTY: THE PUBLISHER AND THE AUTHOR MAKE NO REPRESENTATIONS OR WARRANTIES WITH RESPECT TO THE ACCURACY OR COMPLETENESS OF THE CONTENTS OF THIS WORK AND SPECIFICALLY DISCLAIM ALL WARRANTIES, INCLUDING WITHOUT LIMITATION WARRANTIES OF FITNESS FOR A PARTICULAR PURPOSE. NO WARRANTY MAY BE CREATED OR EXTENDED BY SALES OR PROMOTIONAL MATERIALS. THE ADVICE AND STRATEGIES CONTAINED HEREIN MAY NOT BE SUITABLE FOR EVERY SITUATION. THIS WORK IS SOLD WITH THE UNDERSTANDING THAT THE PUBLISHER IS NOT ENGAGED IN RENDERING LEGAL, ACCOUNTING, OR OTHER PROFESSIONAL SERVICES. IF PROFESSIONAL ASSISTANCE IS REQUIRED, THE SERVICES OF A COMPETENT PROFESSIONAL PERSON SHOULD BE SOUGHT. NEITHER THE PUBLISHER NOR THE AUTHOR SHALL BE LIABLE FOR DAMAGES ARISING HEREFROM. THE FACT THAT AN ORGANIZATION OR WEBSITE IS REFERRED TO IN THIS WORK AS A CITATION AND/OR A POTENTIAL SOURCE OF FURTHER INFORMATION DOES NOT MEAN THAT THE AUTHOR OR THE PUBLISHER ENDORSES THE INFORMATION THE ORGANIZATION OR WEBSITE MAY PROVIDE OR RECOMMENDATIONS IT MAY MAKE. FURTHER, READERS SHOULD BE AWARE THAT INTERNET WEBSITES LISTED IN THIS WORK MAY HAVE CHANGED OR DISAPPEARED BETWEEN WHEN THIS WORK WAS WRITTEN AND WHEN IT IS READ.

For general information on our other products and services, please contact our Customer Care Department within the U.S. at 877-762-2974, outside the U.S. at 317-572-3993, or fax 317-572-4002. For technical support, please visit https://hub.wiley.com/community/support/dummies.

Wiley publishes in a variety of print and electronic formats and by print-on-demand. Some material included with standard print versions of this book may not be included in e-books or in print-on-demand. If this book refers to media that is not included in the version you purchased, you may download this material at http://booksupport.wiley.com. For more information about Wiley products, visit www.wiley.com.

Library of Congress Control Number is available from the publisher.

ISBN 978-1-394-29236-3 (pbk); ISBN 978-1-394-29238-7 (ebk); ISBN 978-1-394-29237-0 (ebk)

SKY10094788_123024

Contents at a Glance

Introduction 1

Part 1: Getting Started with PowerPoint 5
CHAPTER 1: Welcome to PowerPoint 7
CHAPTER 2: Taking the Backstage Tour 31
CHAPTER 3: Editing Slides 45
CHAPTER 4: Working in Outline View 65
CHAPTER 5: Proofing Your Presentations 73
CHAPTER 6: Don't Forget Your Notes! 83
CHAPTER 7: Show Time! 91

Part 2: Creating with Copilot 107
CHAPTER 8: Getting Started with Copilot 109
CHAPTER 9: Using Copilot in PowerPoint 123
CHAPTER 10: Perfecting Your Prompts 131

Part 3: Creating Great-Looking Slides 137
CHAPTER 11: All about Fonts and Text Formatting 139
CHAPTER 12: Designing Your Slides 155
CHAPTER 13: Animating Your Slides 169
CHAPTER 14: Masters of the Universe Meet the Templates of Doom 189

Part 4: Embellishing Your Slides 211
CHAPTER 15: Inserting Pictures 213
CHAPTER 16: Drawing on Your Slides 239
CHAPTER 17: Charting for Fun and Profit 259
CHAPTER 18: Working with SmartArt 281
CHAPTER 19: Lights! Camera! Action! (Adding Sound and Video) 293
CHAPTER 20: Adding Tables to Your Slides 307

Part 5: Working with Others 317
CHAPTER 21: Collaborating on Presentations 319
CHAPTER 22: Exporting Your Presentation to Other Formats 337

Part 6: The Part of Tens..345
CHAPTER 23: Ten PowerPoint Commandments..............................347
CHAPTER 24: Ten (or So) Tips for Creating Readable Slides.............351
CHAPTER 25: Ten Ways to Keep Your Audience Awake...................357

Index..361

Table of Contents

INTRODUCTION 1
    About This Book 1
    Foolish Assumptions 2
    Icons Used in This Book 2
    Beyond the Book 3
    Where to Go from Here 3

PART 1: GETTING STARTED WITH POWERPOINT 5

CHAPTER 1: Welcome to PowerPoint 7
    What in the Sam Hill Is PowerPoint? 7
    Getting PowerPoint 9
    Introducing PowerPoint Presentations 11
    Understanding Presentation Files 12
    What's in a Slide? 13
    Starting PowerPoint 14
    Creating a Blank Presentation 15
    Navigating the PowerPoint Interface 16
    Unraveling the Ribbon 18
    The View from Here Is Great 19
    Editing Text 19
    Making It Pretty 21
    Adding a New Slide 22
    Moving from Slide to Slide 24
    Displaying Your Presentation 25
    Saving Your Work 26
    Closing a Presentation 26
    Getting Help 27
    Exiting PowerPoint 28

CHAPTER 2: Taking the Backstage Tour 31
    Welcome to Backstage View 32
    Considering Themes and Templates 34
    Saving Your Presentation 37
        Saving to a location on your computer 38
        Saving to OneDrive 39
        Saving a copy of a presentation 41
    Opening a Presentation 41
    Pinning a Presentation for Easy Access 43

CHAPTER 3: Editing Slides 45
Moving from Slide to Slide 46
Working with Objects 46
  Selecting objects 47
  Resizing or moving an object 48
Editing a Text Object 51
Selecting Text 52
Using Cut, Copy, and Paste 53
Duplicating an Object 54
Using the Clipboard Task Pane 55
Oops! I Didn't Mean It (The Marvelous Undo Command) 55
Working with Slide Layouts 56
Deleting a Slide 58
Duplicating a Slide 59
Finding Text 59
Replacing Text 61
Rearranging Your Slides in Slide Sorter View 62

CHAPTER 4: Working in Outline View 65
Calling Up the Outline 65
Selecting and Editing an Entire Slide 67
Selecting and Editing One Paragraph 67
Promoting and Demoting Paragraphs 68
Adding a New Paragraph 69
Adding a New Slide 69
Moving Text Up and Down 70
Collapsing and Expanding the Outline 71

CHAPTER 5: Proofing Your Presentations 73
Checking Spelling as You Go 74
Spell-Checking After the Fact 75
Using the Thesaurus 77
Capitalizing Correctly 78
Using the AutoCorrect Feature 79

CHAPTER 6: Don't Forget Your Notes! 83
Understanding Notes 84
Adding Notes to a Slide 85
Adding an Extra Notes Page for a Slide 86
Adding a New Slide from Notes Page View 87
Printing Notes Pages 87
Displaying Notes on a Separate Monitor 88

CHAPTER 7: Show Time! 91
    The Quick Way to Print 92
    Printing from Backstage View 92
        Printing more than one copy 93
        Changing printers 93
        Printing part of a document 94
        Using Print Preview 95
    Setting Up a Slide Show 95
    Starting a Slide Show 97
    Working in Presenter View 97
    Controlling Your Presentation with the Keyboard and Mouse 99
    Using Presentation Tools 100
        Using the Laser Pointer feature 101
        Scribbling on your slides 102
    Rehearsing Your Slide Timings 103
    Using Custom Shows 104
        Creating a custom show 104
        Showing a custom show 105
        Hiding slides 106

PART 2: CREATING WITH COPILOT 107

CHAPTER 8: Getting Started with Copilot 109
    What Is Microsoft Copilot? 110
    Choosing Between the Free and Paid Versions of Copilot 112
    Using the Free Version of Copilot 113
    Accessing the Free Version of Copilot 114
        Using the Copilot app 114
        Using Copilot in Bing 115
        Using the Edge sidebar 117
    Refining Copilot's Response 117
    Getting Copilot's Content into PowerPoint 118
    Creating a Picture with Copilot 119

CHAPTER 9: Using Copilot in PowerPoint 123
    Creating a Presentation with Copilot 124
    Using the Copilot Sidebar 127
    Using the Copilot Sidebar to Change a Picture 128

CHAPTER 10: Perfecting Your Prompts 131
    Stating the Goal 132
    Being Specific 132
    Providing Context 133

Laying Out Your Expectations 133
Keeping Copilot Honest 134
Structuring Your Prompts 135
Prompting Etiquette 135
Keep Trying! 136

PART 3: CREATING GREAT-LOOKING SLIDES 137

CHAPTER 11: All about Fonts and Text Formatting 139
Changing the Look of Your Text 140
    Changing the size of characters 142
    Choosing text fonts..................................... 143
    Adding color to your text 143
    Adding shadows.. 144
Big Picture Text Formatting 144
    Biting the bulleted list................................... 145
    Creating numbered lists 147
    Setting tabs and indents................................. 148
    Spacing out... 149
    Lining things up 150
    Making columns.. 151
Creating Fancy Text with WordArt 151

CHAPTER 12: Designing Your Slides 155
Looking at the Design Tab 155
Working with Themes...................................... 156
    Applying themes 157
    Using theme colors 158
    Using theme fonts 162
    Applying theme effects.................................. 162
Changing the Slide Size..................................... 163
Applying Background Styles................................. 164
    Using a gradient fill 165
    Using other background effects 167
Using the Designer to Improve Your Slides...................... 168

CHAPTER 13: Animating Your Slides 169
Using the Transitions Tab................................... 169
    Creating a slide transition 170
    Using the Morph transition effect.......................... 173
Using the Animations Tab 175
    Using advanced animations.............................. 176
    Adding an effect....................................... 179

More about animating text 182
Timing your animations 185

CHAPTER 14: Masters of the Universe Meet the Templates of Doom 189

Working with Masters 190
  Modifying the slide master 191
  Modifying the handout master 196
  Modifying the notes master 197
Using Masters 198
  Overriding the master text style 198
  Hiding background objects 199
Using Headers and Footers 200
  Adding a date, number, or footer to slides 200
  Adding a header or footer to notes or handout pages . 202
  Editing the header and footer placeholders directly . 202
Yes, You Can Serve Two Masters 202
  Creating a new slide master 202
  Applying masters 204
  Preserving your masters 204
Restoring Lost Placeholders 206
Working with Templates 207
  Creating a new template 207
  Creating a presentation based on a template 208
Working with Presentation Sections 209

PART 4: EMBELLISHING YOUR SLIDES 211

CHAPTER 15: Inserting Pictures 213

Exploring the Many Types of Pictures 214
  Bitmap pictures 214
  Victor, give me a vector 215
Inserting Pictures in Your Presentation 216
  From the web 216
  From your computer 219
  From the stock library 220
Moving, Sizing, Stretching, and Cropping Pictures 222
Adding Style to Your Pictures 224
  Applying a picture border 225
  Applying picture effects 225
  Applying artistic effects 226
  Removing picture backgrounds 227
Correcting Sharpness, Brightness, Contrast, and Color . 230

Compressing Your Pictures 232
Working with 3D Models 233
    Morphing a 3D model 235
    Using animated 3D models 236

CHAPTER 16: Drawing on Your Slides 239

Some General Drawing Tips 239
    Zooming in 239
    Displaying the ruler, gridlines, and guides 240
    Sticking to the color scheme 241
    Saving frequently 241
    Remembering Ctrl+Z 241
Drawing Simple Objects 242
    Drawing straight lines 243
    Drawing rectangles, squares, ovals, and circles 244
Creating Other Shapes 244
    Drawing a shape 245
    Drawing a polygon or free-form shape 246
    Drawing a curved line or shape 248
    Creating a text box 249
Styling Your Shapes 250
    Setting the shape fill 250
    Setting the shape outline 250
    Applying shape effects 252
Flipping and Rotating Objects 252
    Flipping an object 252
    Rotating an object 90 degrees 253
    Using the rotate handle 253
Drawing a Complicated Picture 254
    Changing layers 254
    Line 'em up 255
    Using the grids and guides 256
    Group therapy 257

CHAPTER 17: Charting for Fun and Profit 259

Understanding Charts 260
Adding a Chart to Your Presentation 261
    Adding a new slide with a chart 261
    Adding a chart to an existing slide 265
    Pasting a chart from Excel 266
Changing the Chart Type 266
Working with Chart Data 267

       Switching rows and columns 267
       Changing the data selection 269
       Editing the source data 269
       Refreshing a chart 270
   Changing the Chart Layout 270
   Changing the Chart Style 271
   Embellishing Your Chart 273
   Using Treemap and Sunburst Charts 276
   Using Map Charts 278

CHAPTER 18: Working with SmartArt 281

   Understanding SmartArt 281
   Creating a SmartArt Diagram 284
   Tweaking a SmartArt Diagram 286
   Editing the SmartArt Text 287
   Working with Organization Charts 289
       Adding boxes to a chart 290
       Deleting chart boxes 290
       Changing the chart layout 291

CHAPTER 19: Lights! Camera! Action! (Adding Sound and Video) 293

   Adding Sound to a Slide 294
       Investigating sound files 294
       Inserting an audio sound object 295
       Setting audio options 297
   Adding Video to Your Slides 299
       Finding a video to add to your presentation 299
       Inserting a video clip 300
       Setting video options 301
   Compressing Media 305

CHAPTER 20: Adding Tables to Your Slides 307

   Creating a Table in a Content Placeholder 307
   Inserting a Table on a Slide 309
   Drawing a Table 310
   Adding Style to a Table 312
   Working with the Layout Tab 314

PART 5: WORKING WITH OTHERS 317

CHAPTER 21: Collaborating on Presentations 319

   Understanding Collaboration 319
   Working with OneDrive 321

Managing OneDrive features............................324
Sharing a OneDrive presentation 326
Working with Teams..330
Collaborating in Real Time................................333
Using Comments...334

CHAPTER 22: Exporting Your Presentation to Other Formats 337
Creating a PDF File 338
Crafting a Video...340
Using the Record Tab......................................341
Recording a Slide Show 342

PART 6: THE PART OF TENS....................................345

CHAPTER 23: Ten PowerPoint Commandments 347
I. Thou Shalt Frequently Savest Thy Work 347
II. Thou Shalt Storeth Each Presentation in Its Proper Folder......348
III. Thou Shalt Not Abuseth Thy Program's Formatting Features....348
IV. Thou Shalt Not Stealeth Copyrighted Materials 348
V. Thou Shalt Abideth by Thine Color Scheme, Auto-Layout, and Template..349
VI. Thou Shalt Not Abuse Thine Audience with an Endless Array of Cute Animations or Funny Sounds 349
VII. Keep Thy Computer Gurus Happy..........................349
VIII. Thou Shalt Backeth Up Thy Files Day by Day...............349
IX. Thou Shalt Fear No Evil, for Ctrl+Z Is Always with Thee........350
X. Thou Shalt Not Panic 350

CHAPTER 24: Ten (or So) Tips for Creating Readable Slides 351
Try Reading the Slide from the Back of the Room 351
Avoid Small Text 352
No More Than Five Bullets, Please 352
Avoid Excessive Verbiage Lending to Excessively Lengthy Text That Is Not Only Redundant But Also Repetitive and Reiterative..352
Use Consistent Wording....................................352
Avoid Unsightly Color Combinations 353
Watch the Line Endings 354
Keep the Background Simple 354
Use Only Two Levels of Bullets 354
Avoid Bullets Altogether If You Can 354
Keep Charts and Diagrams Simple..........................355

CHAPTER 25: Ten Ways to Keep Your Audience Awake 357
    Don't Forget Your Purpose. 357
    Don't Become a Slave to Your Slides 358
    Don't Overwhelm Your Audience with Unnecessary Detail 358
    Don't Neglect Your Opening 358
    Be Relevant. 359
    Don't Forget the Call to Action. 359
    Practice, Practice, Practice 359
    Relax!. 360
    Expect the Unexpected. 360
    Don't Be Boring 360

INDEX 361

Introduction

Welcome to *Microsoft 365 PowerPoint For Dummies*, 2nd Edition, the book written especially for people who are lucky enough to use the latest and greatest version of PowerPoint and want to find out just enough to finish that presentation that was due yesterday.

Did you give up on PowerPoint a long time ago because all your presentations looked like they'd been recycled from the '90s? Have you often wished that you could create presentations that drive home your point with simple and concise illustrations that don't look silly, cheesy, or just plain awful? Do you find PowerPoint too difficult to use? Do you long for the good old days of flip charts and dry-erase markers?

If you answered yes to any of these questions, you're holding the perfect book right here in your formerly Magic Marker-stained hands. Help is here, within these humble pages.

This book talks about PowerPoint in everyday — and often irreverent — terms. No lofty prose here. I have no Pulitzer expectations for this book. My goal is to make an otherwise dull and lifeless subject at least tolerable — and maybe even kind of fun.

About This Book

This isn't the kind of book that you pick up and read from start to finish as though it were a cheap novel. If I ever see you reading it at the beach, I'll kick sand in your face. This book is more like a reference — the kind of book you can pick up, turn to just about any page, and start reading. It has 25 chapters, each covering a specific aspect of using PowerPoint — such as printing, animating your slides, or using clip art.

You don't have to memorize anything in this book. It's a need-to-know book: You pick it up when you need to know something. Need to know how to create an organization chart? Pick up the book. Need to know how to override the slide master? Pick up the book. After you find what you're looking for, put it down and get on with your life.

Within this book, you may note that some web addresses break across two lines of text. If you're reading this book in print and you want to visit one of these web pages, simply key in the web address exactly as it's noted in the text, pretending as though the line break doesn't exist. If you're reading this as an e-book, you've got it easy — just click the web address to be taken directly to the web page.

Foolish Assumptions

I make only three assumptions about you:

- » You use a computer.
- » It's a Windows computer, not a Mac. PowerPoint requires at least Windows 10. (PowerPoint works on Macs as well, and it works almost the same. But this book is designed primarily for Windows users.)
- » You use or are thinking about using PowerPoint.

Nothing else. I don't assume that you're a computer guru who knows how to change a controller card or configure memory for optimal use. These types of computer chores are best handled by people who like computers. My hope is that you're on speaking terms with such a person. Do your best to stay there.

Icons Used in This Book

As you're reading all this wonderful prose, you occasionally see icons in the margins. They draw your attention to important information, and here's what they mean:

Pay special attention to this icon — it tells you that some particularly useful tidbit is at hand (perhaps a shortcut or a way of using a command that you may not have considered).

Danger! Danger! Danger! Stand back, Will Robinson! You won't cause death or destruction to anyone with PowerPoint, but this icon warns you of anything that could cause you to lose work or otherwise want to tear your hair out.

Did I tell you about the memory course I took? Paragraphs marked with this icon simply point out details that are worth committing to memory.

Watch out! Some technical drivel is just around the corner. Read it only if you have your pocket protector firmly attached.

Beyond the Book

In addition to what you're reading right now, this product also comes with a free access-anywhere Cheat Sheet that includes a variety of shortcuts for everything from formatting and editing to slide shows and more. To get this Cheat Sheet, simply go to www.dummies.com and type **PowerPoint For Dummies Cheat Sheet** in the Search box.

Where to Go from Here

Yes, you can get there from here. With this book in hand, you're ready to charge full speed ahead into the strange and wonderful world of desktop presentations. Browse the table of contents and decide where you want to start. Be bold! Be courageous! Be adventurous! Above all else, have fun!

1
Getting Started with PowerPoint

IN THIS PART . . .

Get a bird's-eye view of PowerPoint and what you can do with it.

Open and save files.

Edit the content on PowerPoint slides, from the text itself to text objects to other types of objects, such as clip art or drawn shapes.

Work in Outline view so you can focus on your presentation's main points and subpoints without worrying about appearance.

Proof your presentation with PowerPoint and avoid embarrassing mistakes.

Create speaker notes to help you get through your presentation.

Finish the final preparations by printing copies of your slides, notes, and handouts; setting up a projector; and actually delivering your presentation.

> **IN THIS CHAPTER**
> » Discovering PowerPoint
> » Firing up PowerPoint
> » Making sense of the PowerPoint screen and the Ribbon
> » Creating a new presentation
> » Saving and closing your work
> » Getting help
> » Getting out of PowerPoint

Chapter **1**

Welcome to PowerPoint

This chapter is a grand and gala welcoming ceremony for PowerPoint, Microsoft's popular slide-presentation program.

This chapter is sort of like the opening ceremony of the Olympics, in which all the athletes parade around the stadium and people make speeches in French. In much the same way, this chapter marches PowerPoint around the stadium so you can get a bird's-eye view of what the program is and what you can do with it. I make a few speeches but not in French (unless, of course, you're reading the French edition of this book).

What in the Sam Hill Is PowerPoint?

PowerPoint is a program that comes with Microsoft 365, which includes Word, Excel, and Outlook, too.

You know what Word is — it's the world's most-loved and most-hated word-processing program, and it's perfect for concocting letters, term papers, and great

American novels. I'm thinking of writing one as soon as I finish this book. Excel is a spreadsheet program used by bean counters the world over. Outlook is that program you use to read your email. But what the heck is PowerPoint? Does anybody know or care? (And as long as I'm asking questions, who in Sam Hill was Sam Hill? If you really want to know, check out the sidebar "Who in the Sam Hill was Sam Hill?")

PowerPoint is a presentation program, and it's one of the coolest programs I know. It's designed to work with a big-screen TV or a projector to display presentations that will bedazzle your audience members and instantly sway them to your point of view, even if you're selling real estate on Mars, season tickets for the Las Vegas Raiders, or a new tax increase in an election year. If you've ever flipped a flip chart, you're going to love PowerPoint.

Here are some of the many uses of PowerPoint:

- **Business presentations:** PowerPoint is a great timesaver for anyone who makes business presentations, whether you've been asked to speak in front of hundreds of people at a shareholders' convention, a group of sales reps at a sales conference, or your own staff or coworkers at a business meeting.

- **Sales presentations:** If you're an insurance salesperson, you can use PowerPoint to create a presentation about the perils of not owning life insurance and then use your laptop or tablet computer to show it to hapless clients at your local Cheesecake Factory.

- **Lectures:** PowerPoint is useful for teachers or conference speakers who want to reinforce the key points in their lectures with slides.

- **Homework:** PowerPoint is a great program to use for certain types of homework projects, like those big history reports that count for half your grade.

- **Church:** People use PowerPoint in churches to display song lyrics on big screens so everyone can sing along or to display sermon outlines so everyone can take notes. If your church still uses hymnals or prints the outline in the bulletin, tell the minister to join the 21st century.

- **Information stations:** You can use PowerPoint to set up a computerized information kiosk that people can walk up to and use. For example, you can create a museum exhibit about the history of your town or set up a trade-show presentation to provide information about your company and products.

- **Online presentations:** PowerPoint can even help you set up a presentation that you can share in an online meeting or videoconference so people can join in on the fun without having to leave the comfort of their own homes or offices.

WHO IN THE SAM HILL WAS SAM HILL?

Copilot can easily help you with research and answer questions for you, including questions like "Who in the Sam Hill was Sam Hill?"

I've always loved the term *Sam Hill* because it seems so quaint. But I've never understood the origins of the phrase. So, I decided to ask Copilot. Specifically, I put in the question "Who in the Sam Hill was Sam Hill?" and here's how Copilot replied:

1. **Sam Hill** is an American English slang phrase that serves as a euphemism or minced oath for "the devil" or "hell" personified. You might hear it used in expressions like, "What in the Sam Hill is that?" The exact origin of this phrase is a bit mysterious, but here are some possibilities:

2. **Euphemism for the Devil:** Some believe it comes from Samiel, the name of the Devil in *Der Freischütz*, an opera by Carl Maria von Weber performed in New York City in 1825.

3. **Store Owner in Arizona:** There was a mercantile store owner named Sam Hill in Arizona. People used the phrase to describe odd or unusual things, much like the diverse inventory found in his store. The original Sam Hill Mercantile building still stands in Prescott, Arizona.

4. **Politician in Connecticut:** An article from 1889 mentioned a Mr. Sam Hill who represented Guilford, Connecticut, in the legislature. This might be the source of the popular Connecticut adjuration to "Give 'em Sam Hill."

5. **Surveyor in Michigan:** Samuel W. Hill, a surveyor associated with the Keweenaw Peninsula area, could be another origin. His foul language led to his name becoming a euphemism for swear words.

So, in summary, Sam Hill remains a colorful and enigmatic figure in linguistic history!

Now you know who Sam Hill was or at least might have been!

For more information about using Copilot to help you craft your PowerPoint presentations, turn to Chapter 8.

Getting PowerPoint

There are several ways you can gain access to PowerPoint:

>> **Subscribe to Microsoft 365.** Microsoft 365 is a cloud-based subscription service that lets you use various products that are part of the Microsoft 365

suite. The main advantages of subscribing to Microsoft 365 are that you pay a low monthly or yearly fee (as low as $6.99 per month), you always get the latest updates for free, and you can install the software on all your devices and sign in to Microsoft 365 on as many as five of them at the same time.

» **Buy a copy of Office 2024.** You can buy Office 2024 for about twice the price of an annual subscription. The advantage is that you own the software outright; the disadvantage is that you don't get free updates.

» **Use the free online version of PowerPoint.** The free online version of PowerPoint has limited features. I don't recommend this option because a subscription to PowerPoint isn't very expensive. But if you want to check it out, go to www.microsoft.com/en-us/Microsoft-365/free-office-online-for-the-web.

My preferred method, and the one Microsoft recommends, is to subscribe to Microsoft 365. If you opt to go the subscription route, you'll find that there are several plans to choose from:

» **Home:** Intended for home or personal use. This is the option usually chosen by families or students. There are two Home subscription options:

- **Personal:** Can be used by just one user
- **Family:** Can be used by up to six users

» **Business:** Intended for small businesses. Technically, you can support up to 300 users with a Business subscription, but most businesses with more than 50 employees should use an Enterprise subscription instead. There are three Business subscription options:

- **Basic:** The Basic edition does not include the desktop version of PowerPoint or the other Microsoft 365 applications. It only includes an online version that provides most, but not all, of the features of the desktop version.
- **Standard:** The Standard edition provides both the online and desktop versions of PowerPoint and the other Microsoft 365 applications.
- **Premium:** The Premium edition provides advanced security features.

» **Enterprise:** Designed for businesses of any size. The two most popular Enterprise subscription plans that include PowerPoint are

- **E3:** Includes both online and desktop versions of Microsoft 365 applications (including PowerPoint, of course), as well as email hosting.
- **E5:** Includes more security features than E3.

You may find yourself confused about the name *Microsoft 365*. For decades, PowerPoint has been part of a suite called *Microsoft Office*. When Office became part of a cloud suite, the name became *Office 365*. Office 365 still exists and is part of Microsoft 365. But the official new name of the entire suite is *Microsoft 365*, sometimes abbreviated to just *M365*. Throughout this book, I use the newer name, Microsoft 365, but you can call it Office 365 if you want. That's what I still call it when Microsoft isn't listening.

Introducing PowerPoint Presentations

PowerPoint is similar to a word-processing program such as Word, except that it's geared toward creating presentations rather than documents. A presentation is kind of like those Kodak Carousel slide projector trays that your grandpa filled with 35mm slides from the time he took the family to the Grand Canyon. The main difference is that, with PowerPoint, you don't have to worry about dumping all the slides out of the tray and figuring out how to get them back into the right order.

If you have no idea what a Kodak Carousel slide projector is, look it up. It was one of the coolest inventions of the 1960s. Just about everyone's dad had one or wanted one.

Word documents consist of one or more pages; PowerPoint presentations consist of one or more *slides*. Each slide can contain text, graphics, animations, videos, and other information. You can easily rearrange the slides in a presentation, delete slides that you don't need, add new slides, or modify the contents of existing slides.

Unlike in Word, content on a slide in PowerPoint does not flow from one slide to the next. Each slide is self-contained. If you put too much text on a slide, PowerPoint doesn't spill the text onto the next slide. Instead, it automatically makes the text small so that it will fit on the slide.

You can use PowerPoint both to create your presentations and to actually present them.

You can use several different types of media to actually show your presentations:

» **Computer screen:** Your computer screen is a suitable way to display your presentation when you're showing it to just one or two other people.

» **Big-screen TV:** If you have a big-screen TV that can accommodate computer input, it's ideal for showing presentations to medium-size audiences — say, 10 to 12 people in a small conference room.

- » **Computer projector:** A computer projector projects an image of your computer monitor onto a screen so that large audiences can view it.
- » **Online meeting screen share:** You can easily show your presentation by using the screen-sharing feature of your favorite videoconferencing platform. That way, all of your audience doesn't have to be in the same place at the same time.
- » **Printed or PDF pages:** You can distribute a printed copy of your entire presentation to each member of your audience. Or, you can save the slides as a single PDF file and distribute the PDF file to your audience. (When you print your presentation, you can print one slide per page, or you can print several slides per page to save paper.)

Understanding Presentation Files

A presentation is to PowerPoint what a document is to Word or a workbook is to Excel. In other words, a presentation is a file that you create with PowerPoint. Each presentation that you create is saved on your computer's hard drive as a separate file.

PowerPoint presentations have the special extension .pptx added to the ends of their filenames. For example, Sales Conference.pptx and History Day.pptx are both valid PowerPoint filenames. When you type the filename for a new PowerPoint file, you don't have to type the .pptx extension — PowerPoint automatically adds the extension for you. Windows may hide the .pptx extension, in which case a presentation file named Conference.pptx often appears as just Conference.

TECHNICAL STUFF

Versions of PowerPoint prior to 2007 saved presentations with the extension .ppt instead of .pptx. The x at the end of the newer file extension denotes that the new file format is based on an Office Open XML standard data format that makes it easier to exchange files among different programs. Although you can still save files in the old .ppt format, I don't recommend it — you'll lose many of the newer capabilities of PowerPoint if you do.

PowerPoint is set up initially to save your presentation files in the Documents folder, but you can store PowerPoint files in any folder on your OneDrive or any local or network-accessible disk location.

What's in a Slide?

PowerPoint presentations comprise one or more slides. Each slide can contain text, graphics, and other elements. A number of PowerPoint features work together to help you easily format attractive slides:

- **Slide layouts:** Every slide has a slide layout that controls how information is arranged on the slide. A slide layout is simply a collection of one or more placeholders, which set aside an area of the slide to hold information. Depending on the layout that you choose for a slide, the placeholders can hold text, graphics, clip art, sound or video files, tables, charts, graphs, diagrams, or other types of content.

- **Background:** Every slide has a background, which provides a backdrop for the slide's content. The background can be a solid color; a blend of two colors; a subtle texture, such as marble or parchment; a pattern, such as diagonal lines, bricks, or tiles; or an image. Each slide can have a different background, but you usually want to use the same background for every slide in your presentation in order to provide a consistent look.

- **Transitions:** Transitions control the visual effect that is employed when moving from one slide to the next. The norm is to have the next slide instantly replace the previous slide with no splashy effects. But if you want, you can have one slide dissolve into the next, or new slides can push slides out of the way, or you can make it look like the wind has blown away the old slide to reveal the next slide. In all, there are nearly 50 transition effects you can choose from.

- **Themes:** Themes are combinations of design elements, such as color schemes and fonts, that make it easy to create attractive slides that don't look ridiculous. You can stray from the themes if you want, but you should do so only if you have a better eye than the design gurus who work for Microsoft.

- **Slide masters:** Slide masters are special slides that control the basic design and formatting options for slides in your presentation. Slide masters are closely related to layouts — in fact, each layout has its own slide master that determines the position and size of basic title and text placeholders; the background and color scheme used for the presentation; and font settings, such as typefaces, colors, and sizes. In addition, slide masters can contain graphic and text objects that you want to appear on every slide. You can edit the slide masters to change the appearance of all the slides in your presentation at once. This helps to ensure that the slides have a consistent appearance.

All the features described in the preceding list work together to control the appearance of your slides in much the same way that style sheets and templates control the appearance of Word documents. You can customize the appearance of individual slides by adding any of the following elements:

» **Title and body text:** Most slide layouts include placeholders for title and body text. You can type any text that you want into these placeholders. By default, PowerPoint formats the text according to the slide master, but you can easily override this formatting to use any font, size, style (like bold or italic), or text color that you want.

» **Text boxes:** You can add text anywhere on a slide by drawing a text box and then typing text. Text boxes enable you to add text that doesn't fit conveniently in the title or body text placeholders.

» **Shapes:** You can use PowerPoint's drawing tools to add a variety of shapes to your slides. You can use predefined AutoShapes, such as rectangles, circles, stars, arrows, and flowchart symbols. Alternatively, you can create your own shapes by using basic line, polygon, and freehand drawing tools.

» **Illustrations:** You can illustrate your slides by inserting clip art, photographs, and other graphic elements. PowerPoint comes with a large collection of clip art pictures you can use, and Microsoft provides an even larger collection of clip art images online. And, of course, you can insert photographs from your own picture library.

» **Charts and diagrams:** PowerPoint includes a slick diagramming feature called *SmartArt* that enables you to create several common types of diagrams, including organization charts, cycle diagrams, and others. In addition, you can insert pie charts, line charts, bar charts, and many other chart types.

» **Video and sound:** You can add sound clips or videos to your slides. You can also add background music or a custom narration.

» **Animations:** Animations put the various elements on an individual slide into motion. One common use of animation is to make text appear on the slide with movement to capture your audience's attention. But you can apply animation to any element on a slide.

Starting PowerPoint

Here's the procedure for starting PowerPoint:

1. **Get ready.**

   Light some votive candles. Take two Tylenol. Put on a pot of coffee. Play *The Tortured Poets Department* on low in the background.

2. **Press the Windows key on your keyboard.**

   The Windows key is the one that has the fancy Windows flag printed on it. On most keyboards, it's located between the Alt and Tab keys. When you press this button, the Start page appears; here, you see a list of your commonly used applications in large tiles.

3. **Click the PowerPoint tile (shown in the margin).**

   That's all there is to it — PowerPoint starts up in a flash.

   TIP If you hate clicking through menus but don't mind typing, another way to start PowerPoint is to press your keyboard's Windows key (usually found between the Ctrl and Alt keys), type the word **PowerPoint**, and press Enter.

Creating a Blank Presentation

When you start PowerPoint, it greets you with the screen shown in Figure 1-1. This screen lets you create a blank presentation, create a presentation based on one of several templates supplied by PowerPoint, or open an existing presentation.

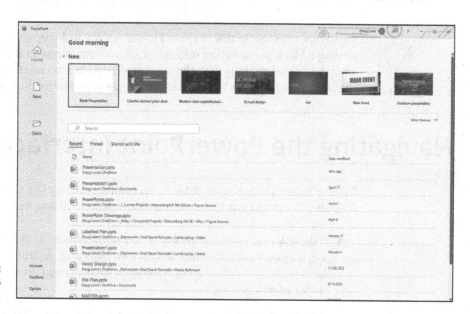

FIGURE 1-1: PowerPoint's opening screen.

For the purposes of this chapter, double-click Blank Presentation to get started with a new presentation, as shown in Figure 1-2.

CHAPTER 1 **Welcome to PowerPoint** 15

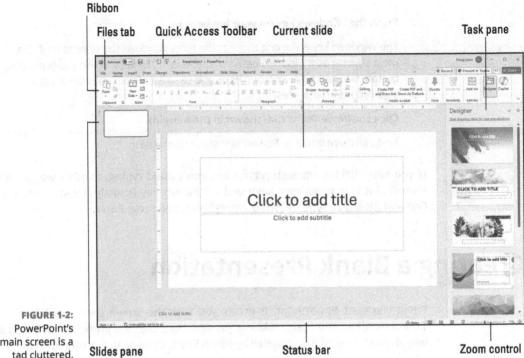

FIGURE 1-2: PowerPoint's main screen is a tad cluttered.

Throughout the rest of this chapter, I introduce you to some simple techniques for turning a blank presentation into an actual presentation with real content. I recommend following along with the numbered steps in later sections of this chapter so you can get a feel for how to create a simple presentation in PowerPoint.

Navigating the PowerPoint Interface

Refer to Figure 1-2 to see the basic PowerPoint screen in all its cluttered glory. The following list points out the more important parts of this screen:

» **Ribbon:** Across the top of the screen, just below the Microsoft PowerPoint title, is PowerPoint's main user-interface gadget, called the *Ribbon*. The deepest and darkest secrets of PowerPoint are hidden on the Ribbon. Wear a helmet when exploring it.

The exact appearance of the Ribbon varies a bit depending on the size of your monitor. On smaller monitors, PowerPoint may compress the Ribbon a bit by using smaller buttons and arranging them differently (for example, stacking them on top of one another instead of placing them side by side).

16 PART 1 **Getting Started with PowerPoint**

For more information about working with the Ribbon, see the section "Unraveling the Ribbon," later in this chapter.

» **File tab:** The first tab on the Ribbon is called the File tab, which switches PowerPoint into Backstage view where you can perform various functions such as opening and saving files, creating new presentations, printing, and other similar chores. For more information about using the File tab, turn to Chapter 2.

» **Quick Access Toolbar:** Just above the Ribbon is the *Quick Access Toolbar,* or QAT for short. Its sole purpose is to provide a convenient resting place for the PowerPoint commands you use most often.

Initially, the QAT contains just three commands: Save, Undo, and Redo. However, you can add more commands if you want. To add any button to the QAT, right-click the command and choose Add to Quick Access Toolbar. You can also find a pull-down menu at the end of the QAT that lists several frequently used commands. You can use this menu to add these common commands to the QAT.

» **Current slide:** Smack dab in the middle of the screen is where your current slide appears. (Note that on a tablet, the Title section of this slide may read "Tap to Add Title" rather than "Click to Add Title.")

» **Slides pane:** To the left of the slide is an area that shows thumbnail icons of your slides. You can use this area to easily navigate to other slides in your presentation.

» **Task pane:** To the right of the slide is an area called the *task pane.* The task pane is designed to help you complete common tasks quickly. In Figure 1-2, the task pane contains the Design Ideas feature, which suggests some design possibilities for your blank presentation. The Design Ideas task pane always appears when you create a new presentation. For more information about using it, please refer to Chapter 12.

» **Status bar:** At the very bottom of the screen is the *status bar,* which tells you the slide that's currently displayed (for example, Slide 1 of 1). You'll also find buttons that let you switch to different view modes. Figure 1-2 shows PowerPoint in its standard mode, which is called Normal.

You can configure the status bar by right-clicking anywhere on it; you see a list of options that you can select or deselect to determine which elements appear on the status bar.

» **Zoom control:** PowerPoint automatically adjusts its zoom factor so that you can zoom in or out to see your slides in their entirety or close up. You can change the size of your slide by using the zoom control slider that appears at the lower right of the window.

TIP
You'll never get anything done if you feel you have to understand every pixel of the PowerPoint screen before you can do anything. Don't worry about the stuff you don't understand. Just concentrate on what you need to know to get the job done, and worry about the bells and whistles later.

Unraveling the Ribbon

The Ribbon is Microsoft's primary user-interface gadget. Across the top of the Ribbon is a series of tabs. You can click one of these tabs to reveal a set of controls specific to that tab. For example, Figure 1-2 (earlier in this chapter) shows the Ribbon with the Home tab selected. Figure 1-3 shows the Ribbon with the Insert tab selected.

FIGURE 1-3:
The Ribbon with the Insert tab selected.

Initially, the Ribbon displays the tabs described in Table 1-1.

In addition to these basic tabs, additional tabs appear from time to time. For example, if you select a picture, a Picture Tools tab appears with commands that let you manipulate the picture.

The commands on a Ribbon tab are organized into groups. Within each group, most of the commands are simple buttons that are similar to toolbar buttons in earlier versions of PowerPoint.

TABLE 1-1   The Basic Tabs on the Ribbon

Tab	Actions You Can Perform
File	Open, close, print, and share presentations.
Home	Create and format slides.
Insert	Insert various types of objects on slides.
Draw	Doodle on your slides using various types of pens or markers.
Design	Tweak the layout of a slide.
Transitions	Change the transition effects that are applied when you switch from one slide to the next.

Tab	Actions You Can Perform
Animations	Add animation effects to your slides.
Slide Show	Present your slide show.
Record	Create a recording of a presentation.
Review	Proof and add comments to your presentation.
View	Change the view.
Help	Get help, training, and support information.

The View from Here Is Great

Near the right edge of the status bar is a series of four View buttons. These buttons enable you to switch among the various *views*, or ways of looking at your presentation. Table 1-2 summarizes what each View button does.

TABLE 1-2   The View Buttons

Button	What It Does
	Switches to Normal view, which shows your slide, outline, and notes all at once. This is the default view for PowerPoint.
	Switches to Slide Sorter view, which enables you to easily rearrange slides and add slide transitions and other special effects.
	Switches to Reading view, which displays your slide show within a window.
	Switches to Slide Show view, which displays your slides in full-screen mode. This is the view you use when you're actually giving your presentation.

Editing Text

In PowerPoint, slides are blank areas that you can adorn with various objects. The most common type of object is a *text placeholder*, a rectangular area that's specially designated for holding text. Other types of objects include shapes, such as circles or triangles; pictures imported from clip art files; and graphs.

Most slides contain two text objects: one for the slide's title and the other for its body text. However, you can add more text objects if you want, and you can remove the body text or title text object. You can even remove both to create a slide that contains no text.

TIP

Whenever you move the cursor over a text object, the cursor changes from an arrow to an *I-beam*, which you can use to support bridges or build aircraft carriers. Seriously, when the cursor changes to an I-beam, you can click the mouse and start typing text.

When you click a text object, a box appears around the text, and an insertion pointer appears at the spot where you clicked. PowerPoint then becomes like a word-processing program. Any characters that you type are inserted into the text at the insertion pointer location. You can press Delete or Backspace to demolish text, and you can use the arrow keys to move the insertion pointer around in the text object. If you press Enter, a new line of text begins within the text object.

When a text object contains no text, a placeholder message appears in the object. For example, a title text object displays the message Click to add title. Other placeholders display similar messages. The placeholder message magically vanishes when you click the object and begin typing text.

TIP

If you start typing without clicking anywhere, the text that you type is entered into the title text object — assuming that the title text object doesn't already have text of its own. If the title text object is not empty, any text that you type (with no text object selected) is simply ignored.

After you finish typing text, press Esc or click anywhere outside the text object.

In Chapter 3, you find many details about playing with text objects. But let's get started developing a blank presentation. Follow these steps:

1. **Click anywhere in the Click to Add Title placeholder on the blank presentation's title slide.**

2. **Type the following text:** Let's Have a Thumb War!

   That's right: In this chapter, you're going to create a simple PowerPoint presentation that explains the rules of the classic game of Thumb War.

3. **Click anywhere in the Click to Add Subtitle placeholder.**

4. **Type** The World's Least Barbaric Form of War.

You've now completed a simple title slide for your presentation, as shown in Figure 1-4.

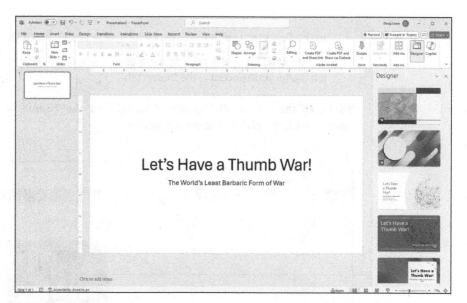

FIGURE 1-4: The completed title slide for the Thumb War presentation.

Making It Pretty

In Parts 3 and 4 of this book, I show you many different ways to create great-looking slides. However, you don't have to wait until then to apply some basic style to your presentation. Earlier, I mention that the Designer task pane is always available to help you improve the look of your PowerPoint slides. The Ribbon also includes a Design tab that lets you select which of several design themes should apply to your presentation. You use these features to improve the look of the Thumb War presentation:

1. **Select the Design tab on the Ribbon.**

   You see a list of various PowerPoint themes, along with several variants for each theme. Each theme has a name, which you can see by hovering the mouse over the theme.

2. **Select the Ion theme (the sixth theme from the left on the Design tab, assuming that you've maximized PowerPoint to fill the screen).**

   The Ion theme applies various formatting elements to your presentation, including a nice teal background, white text, and a simple red graphic box near the upper right of each slide for a fancy look.

3. **In the Variants section of the Design tab, click the purple variant (third from the left).**

   This changes the colors for the Ion theme to a lovely collection of purple tones.

CHAPTER 1 Welcome to PowerPoint 21

4. **In the Designer task pane, select which slide design you'd like to apply.**

    The Designer task pane presents several alternate designs based on the Purple Ion theme you selected in the Design tab.

That's all there is to it! Figure 1-5 shows how the Thumb Wars presentation appears with the purple Ion theme applied.

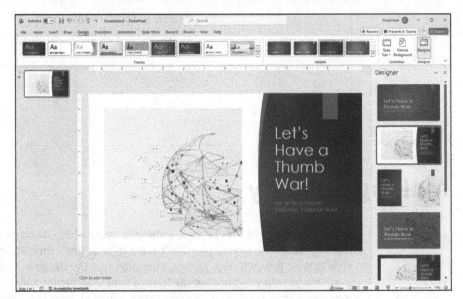

FIGURE 1-5:
The Thumb Wars presentation with the purple Ion theme.

Adding a New Slide

A presentation with just one slide isn't much of a presentation. Fortunately, PowerPoint gives you numerous ways to add more slides to your presentation. You add a second slide to the Thumb War presentation by following these steps:

1. **Press Ctrl+M to insert a new slide.**

    If you're allergic to keyboard shortcuts, you can click the New Slide button on the Home tab (shown in the margin).

    Either way, a new slide appears, as shown in Figure 1-6. Notice that the new slide adopts the Purple Ion design theme that you chose in the preceding section.

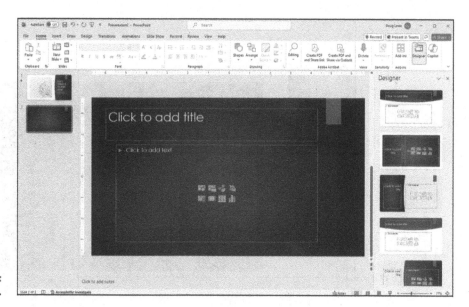

FIGURE 1-6: A new slide.

2. **Click anywhere in the Click to Add Title placeholder and type the following text:** The Rules Are Simple.

3. **Click anywhere in the Click to Add Text placeholder and type the following text, pressing the Enter key between each item:**

    - Clasp each other's hands with four fingers.
    - Use your thumbs to tap each other's index fingers, alternating left to right while chanting, "1, 2, 3, 4, Let's Have a Thumb War!"
    - The war is on! Try to trap your opponent's thumb under yours.
    - Victory is yours when you trap your opponent's thumb long enough to say, "1, 2, 3, 4, I Won the Thumb War!"

TIP

Note that you don't have to enter the bullet symbols — PowerPoint automatically adds a new bulleted paragraph when you press the Enter key.

Congratulations! You've successfully added a second slide to your presentation, as shown in Figure 1-7.

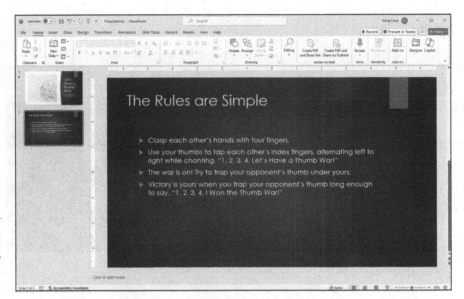

FIGURE 1-7:
The completed second slide of the Thumb War presentation.

Moving from Slide to Slide

Now that your presentation has more than one slide, you need to know how to move forward and backward through your presentation. Here are some of the most popular methods:

- **Click one of the double-headed arrows at the bottom of the vertical scroll bar.** Doing so moves you through the presentation one slide at a time.
- **Press the Page Up or Page Down key.** Using these keys also moves one slide at a time.
- **Use the scroll bar.** When you drag the box in the scroll bar, a tooltip appears to display the number and title of the current slide. Dragging the scroll bar is the quickest way to move directly to any slide in your presentation.
- **In the list of slides on the left side of the window, click the thumbnail for the slide that you want to display.** If the thumbnails aren't visible, click the Slides tab above the outline.

Displaying Your Presentation

When your masterpiece is ready, you can show it on the screen. Just follow these steps:

1. **Select the Slide Show tab on the Ribbon and then, in the Start Slide Show group, click the From Beginning button (shown in the margin).**

   There are several shortcuts to this command. You can also start the show by pressing F5 or by clicking the Slide Show button, located with the other view buttons in the lower-right corner of the screen.

   The first slide fills the screen, as shown in Figure 1-8.

FIGURE 1-8: When you start the slide show, the title slide fills the screen.

2. **Press Enter to advance to the next slide.**

   You can keep pressing Enter to call up the next slide in the presentation. If you don't like using the Enter key, you can use the spacebar instead.

   If you want to go back a slide, press Page Up.

3. **Press Esc when you're done.**

   You don't have to wait until the last slide is shown. If you find a glaring mistake in a slide or you just get bored, you can press Esc at any time to return to Normal view.

For the complete lowdown on showing your presentation, turn to Chapter 7.

Saving Your Work

Saving a presentation in PowerPoint is the same as saving a file in any other Microsoft 365 program: You just use the Save command, found on the File menu or in the QAT. The first time you save a new file, you have to provide a filename. After that, saving your presentation updates the existing presentation with any changes you've made since the last time the file was saved.

Note that if your presentation is saved to OneDrive storage, the AutoSave feature is activated. When AutoSave is on, your presentations are automatically saved as you work.

You can find more information about various options for saving your presentation in Chapter 2.

Closing a Presentation

Having finished and saved your presentation, you've come to the time to close it. Closing a presentation is kind of like gathering your papers, putting them neatly in a file folder, and returning the folder to its proper file drawer. The presentation disappears from your computer screen. Don't worry: It's tucked away safely on your hard drive where you can get to it later if you need to.

To close a file, click the Close button at the upper right of the PowerPoint window. Alternatively, you can choose File ⇨ Close, or use the keyboard shortcut Ctrl+W. But clicking the Close button is the easiest way to close a file.

TIP

You don't have to close a file before exiting PowerPoint. If you exit PowerPoint without closing a file, PowerPoint graciously closes the file for you. The only reason you may want to close a file is if you want to work on a different file and you don't want to keep both files open at the same time.

If you've made changes since the last time you saved the file, PowerPoint offers to save the changes for you. Click Save to save the file before closing, or click Don't Save to abandon any changes that you made to the file.

If you close all the open PowerPoint presentations, you may discover that most of the PowerPoint commands have been rendered useless. (They're grayed out on the menu.) Fear not. If you open a presentation or create a new one, the commands return to life.

Getting Help

The ideal way to use PowerPoint would be to have a PowerPoint expert sitting patiently by your side, answering your every question with a straightforward response, gently correcting you when you make silly mistakes, and otherwise minding their own business. All you'd have to do is occasionally toss the expert a Twinkie and let them outside once a day.

Short of that, the next best thing is to find out how to coax PowerPoint itself into giving you the answers you need. Fortunately, PowerPoint includes a nice built-in Help feature that can answer your questions. No matter how deeply you're lost in the PowerPoint jungle, help is never more than a few mouse clicks or keystrokes away.

As with everything else in Microsoft 365, more than one method is available for calling up help when you need it. The easiest thing to do would be to yell, "Skipper!" in your best Gilligan voice. Otherwise, you have the following options:

» Press F1 or click the Help button, located at the left edge of the Help tab on the Ribbon. This activates PowerPoint's main Help system, as shown in Figure 1-9.

» Whenever a dialog box is displayed, you can click the question mark button in the upper-right corner of the dialog box to summon help.

» When you hover the mouse over an item in the Ribbon, a tooltip appears that explains what the item does. Many of these tooltips include the phrase "Press F1 for more help." In that case, you can press F1 to get help specific to that item.

The Help tab in Figure 1-9 offers several ways to access the help you need. Here are the various ways you can work your way through PowerPoint's Help feature:

» **Help window links:** You can click any of the links that appear on the Help tab to display help on a particular topic. For example, if you click Pictures and Charts, you'll find a page of useful information about working with pictures and charts.

» **Search:** If you can't find what you're looking for, try entering a word or phrase in the Search box and clicking the Search button. This displays a list of topics that pertain to the word or phrase you entered.

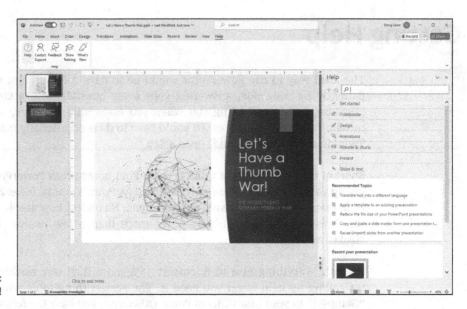

FIGURE 1-9:
Help!

>> **Back button:** You can retrace your steps by clicking the Help window's Back button. You can use the Back button over and over again, retracing all of your steps if necessary.

>> **Home button:** Takes you back to the Help home page.

Other icons on the Help tab on the Ribbon let you contact Microsoft Support, leave feedback on a feature of PowerPoint that you like or that frustrates you, view training opportunities to help you learn PowerPoint quickly, and view new features.

TIP

If you have access to Microsoft Copilot, it can also help you create slides or even entire presentations. For more information, refer to Part 2 of this book.

Exiting PowerPoint

Had enough excitement for one day? Use either of these techniques to shut down PowerPoint:

>> Click the X box at the upper-right corner of the PowerPoint window.

>> Press Alt+F4.

Bam! PowerPoint is history.

You should know a couple things about exiting PowerPoint (or any application):

>> **PowerPoint doesn't let you abandon ship without first considering whether you want to save your work.** If you've made changes to any presentation files and you haven't saved them, PowerPoint offers to save the files for you. Lean over and plant a big fat kiss right in the middle of your monitor — PowerPoint just saved you your job.

>> **Never, ever, never, ever turn off your computer while PowerPoint or any other program is running.** Although PowerPoint can often recover presentations that were damaged by an ungraceful shutdown, it's still a good idea to always exit PowerPoint and all other programs that are running *before* you turn off your computer.

IN THIS CHAPTER

» Getting backstage

» Creating new presentations with themes and templates

» Saving presentations

» Opening existing presentations

» Pinning your favorite presentations

Chapter 2
Taking the Backstage Tour

My wife, Kristen, and I attend plays at the Oregon Shakespeare Festival in Ashland, Oregon, every summer. A few years back, we took the special backstage tour. It was absolutely fascinating, revealing all kinds of nifty secrets worthy of a Dan Brown novel.

PowerPoint has a backstage as well. It's officially called Backstage view. In Backstage view, you can create new presentations or open existing presentations. In addition, you can print, share, or export presentations. And you can make changes to your Microsoft 365 account or adjust PowerPoint's myriad options.

This chapter presents an overview of Backstage view, focusing on the features that let you create and save presentations.

Okay, the only secret I learned on the backstage tour at Ashland that was really worthy of a Dan Brown novel is about Psalm 46 in the King James translation of the Bible, which was published in 1611 — when William Shakespeare turned 46. If you count 46 words from the start of the Psalm, you get the word *Shake*. And if you count 46 words backward from the end of the Psalm, you get the word *Spear*. Which clearly means that there's a treasure buried directly beneath the stage in Ashland's outdoor theater. Next year, I'm taking a shovel.

Welcome to Backstage View

You've already seen Backstage view: It opens automatically when you start PowerPoint (see Figure 2-1).

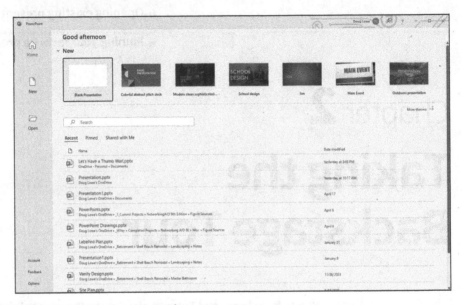

FIGURE 2-1:
Backstage view is displayed when you launch PowerPoint.

Backstage view has three main pages:

>> **Home:** Lets you create a new blank presentation or a presentation using a small selection of predefined themes and templates. From this page, you can also open recently used presentations. (For a refresher on these features, see Chapter 1.)

>> **New:** Provides additional options for creating presentations based on themes and templates. (For more information, see the section "Considering Themes and Templates," later in this chapter.)

>> **Open:** Lets you open recently used presentations or search for other existing presentations on your computer or online. (For more information, see the section "Opening a Presentation," later in this chapter.)

If you already have a presentation open in PowerPoint, you can flip to Backstage view at any time by selecting the File tab. This displays a slightly different version of Backstage view (see Figure 2-2). In addition to the standard Home, New, and Open pages, this version of Backstage view has the following options to choose from:

- **Get Add-ins:** Lets you install add-ins, which add additional functions to PowerPoint.

- **Info:** Displays interesting information about the current presentation.

- **Save a Copy:** Creates a copy of the current presentation using a different filename or folder location. (For more information, see the section "Saving a copy of a presentation," later in this chapter.)

- **Print:** Lets you print your presentation. (You can find more information about printing in Chapter 7.)

- **Share:** Lets you share your presentation with other people. (You can find more information about sharing presentations in Chapter 21.)

- **Export:** Lets you save your presentation in an alternate format, such as a PDF file or a video file. (For more information, see Chapter 22.)

- **Close:** Closes the current presentation.

FIGURE 2-2: Backstage view with a presentation open.

Considering Themes and Templates

Creating a presentation completely from scratch can be a daunting task. Fortunately, PowerPoint provides a huge collection of themes and templates you can use to get started. What are themes and templates, and what's the difference? Glad you asked:

>> **A *theme* is a collection of formatting elements, including colors, fonts, background elements, and other formatting options.** Themes let you quickly create presentations that look good. And if you aren't satisfied with the look of your presentation, you can easily change the theme on the fly.

Figure 2-3 shows a slide with four different themes.

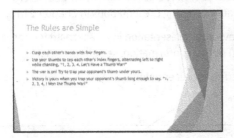

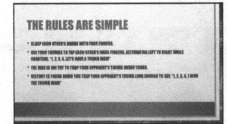

FIGURE 2-3: A theme can dramatically change the appearance of a slide.

>> **A *template* is a theme plus boilerplate content.** Templates are designed to help get you started with a specific type of presentation, such as a sales presentation, a quarterly report, or a design proposal. Unlike themes, you can't apply a template to an existing presentation. To do so would overwrite the content you've created for your presentation with the content in the template. (Turn to Chapter 12 to find out more about templates.)

To create a new presentation from a theme or template, click New in Backstage view. This summons the New page, as shown in Figure 2-4.

FIGURE 2-4:
Creating a presentation from a theme or template.

At the top of the New page, you find a few suggested themes and templates. If none of the suggestions suits your fancy, you can browse or search for just the right theme or template from among the hundreds provided by PowerPoint.

To search for a theme or template, enter a search word or phrase in the Search box and press Enter or click the magnifying glass. You can also select one of PowerPoint's suggested searches, which include Presentations, Themes, Education, Charts, Diagrams, Business, and Infographics.

Figure 2-5 shows the results of a search for "Themes." If you don't see anything you like, click Back to return to the New page or refine your search by changing the text in the Search box and pressing Enter.

If you find a theme or template you like, follow these steps to create a presentation from the theme:

1. **Click the theme or template.**

   The window shown in Figure 2-6 appears.

2. **If you want, use the More Images control to view how different types of slides will appear with the theme or template.**

   Click > or < to move forward or backward through the list of available slide images.

   Note that for templates, using the More Images control will show you the slides that will be inserted into your presentation when you create the template. For themes, slides won't actually be inserted into the presentation.

Click Create (shown in the margin) to create the presentation.

CHAPTER 2 Taking the Backstage Tour 35

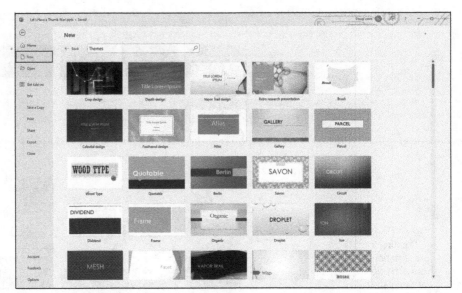

FIGURE 2-5:
Searching for a theme.

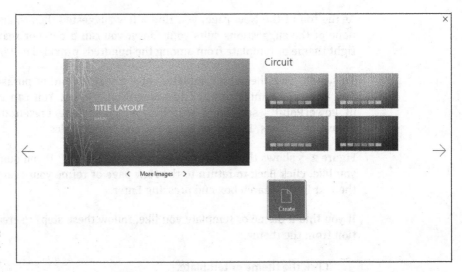

FIGURE 2-6:
Selecting a theme.

TIP

You can force any theme or template to appear in the list of suggestions at the top of the New pane by right-clicking the theme and choosing Pin to List. To remove a theme or template from the list, right-click it and choose Remove from List.

Saving Your Presentation

When you've spent hours creating the best presentation since God gave Moses the Ten Commandments, it's time to save your work to a file.

Like everything else in PowerPoint, you have at least four ways to save a document:

- » Click the Save button on the Quick Access Toolbar (QAT).
- » Select the File tab to switch to Backstage view, and then choose Save.
- » Press Ctrl+S.
- » Press Shift+F12.

If you haven't yet saved the file, you're redirected to the Save a Copy page in Backstage view (see Figure 2-7). Here, you have several options for selecting where you'd like to save the presentation:

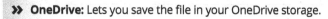
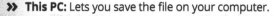

- » **Recent:** Lets you choose from locations where you've recently stored presentation files.
- » **OneDrive:** Lets you save the file in your OneDrive storage.
- » **This PC:** Lets you save the file on your computer.
- » **Add a Place:** Lets you add other cloud locations so you can find them easily.
- » **Browse:** Lets you browse directly to the location where you want to save the file.

Here are a few other thoughts to ponder when saving your presentation files:

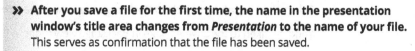

TIP

- » **After you save a file for the first time, the name in the presentation window's title area changes from *Presentation* to the name of your file.** This serves as confirmation that the file has been saved.
- » **Put on your thinking cap when assigning a name to a new file.** The filename is how you'll recognize the file later on, so pick a meaningful name that suggests the file's contents.
- » **Don't work on your file for hours at a time without saving it.** I've learned the hard way to save my work every few minutes. You never know when the power will go out or your computer will unexpectedly self-destruct. Get into the habit of saving every few minutes, especially after making a significant change to a presentation, such as adding a covey of new slides or making a gaggle of complicated formatting changes.

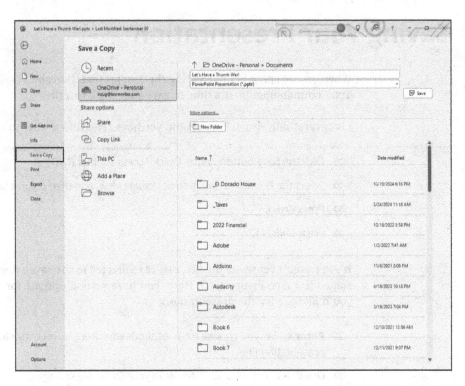

FIGURE 2-7:
Save a Copy in Backstage view.

The following sections walk you through how to save your file on your computer and in OneDrive, as well as how to save a copy of your presentation.

Saving to a location on your computer

Here's how to save a new file to a location on your computer:

1. **Select the File tab to switch to Backstage view, and then choose Save.**

   You'll be taken to the Save As page in Backstage view (refer to Figure 2-7).

2. **Click Browse.**

   The Save As dialog box appears (see Figure 2-8).

3. **Navigate to the folder in which you'd like to save the presentation.**

   If necessary, click New Folder to create a new folder for the presentation.

FIGURE 2-8:
The Save As dialog box.

4. **If the proposed filename isn't right, change the filename to suit your needs.**

   PowerPoint proposes the Title text on the first slide as the filename.

5. **Click Save.**

   Voilà! Your file is saved.

Saving to OneDrive

One of the best features of Microsoft 365 is OneDrive, which provides an online location for you to save your files. Microsoft 365 subscriptions give you a whopping 1TB of OneDrive storage!

OneDrive storage is organized much like the storage on your local hard drive: You can create folders to organize your files, and you can nest folders within folders as deep as you want.

When you save a file to your OneDrive account, you can later retrieve it from any other computer that has an internet connection. All you have to do is log in to your Office account to access your OneDrive storage.

 To save to OneDrive, just click the OneDrive icon (shown in the margin) on the Save As page. You can then browse the folders in your OneDrive storage, as shown in Figure 2-9. When you find the right folder, click Save to save your presentation.

CHAPTER 2 Taking the Backstage Tour   39

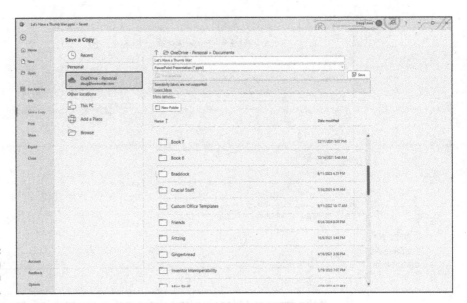

FIGURE 2-9: Saving a presentation to OneDrive.

Here are some of the benefits of saving files to OneDrive instead of your local computer:

- » **When you save a presentation to OneDrive, PowerPoint automatically enables AutoSave.** With AutoSave enabled, PowerPoint frequently saves your presentation so the file is always up-to-date with your most recent changes. (You can still manually activate AutoSave if you save your presentations to your local hard disk, but AutoSave is automatic for files stored on OneDrive.)

- » **Files stored on OneDrive can be shared with other users.** In fact, two or more people can actually edit a file on OneDrive simultaneously. This magic is one of the main benefits of using Microsoft 365. (You can find out more about this feature in Chapter 21.)

- » **Microsoft dutifully makes multiple backup copies of your OneDrive files.** Microsoft is so obsessive about these backups that you're far more likely to lose your files to a disk failure or a cyberattack when they're stored on your local computer's disk than when they're stored in OneDrive.

Still, security is a concern with OneDrive. If your Microsoft 365 login credentials fall into the hands of a bad actor, the files stored on your OneDrive may be stolen, so make sure that you keep your login credentials secure. (I recommend enabling two-factor authentication if you use OneDrive. For information on how to do that, search the web for "Microsoft 365 2FA.")

Saving a copy of a presentation

If you're working on a presentation and you decide you'd like to save a copy of it with a different filename or in a different folder (or both), select the File tab to open Backstage view and choose Save a Copy. The Save a Copy page appears; it's identical to the Save As page that appears when you save a presentation for the first time. You can navigate to the location where you want to save the file, change the filename if you want, and then click Save to create your copy.

Note that after you do this, you'll be working on the copy you created, not the original file you were working on.

Opening a Presentation

After you save your presentation to your hard drive, you can retrieve it later when you want to make additional changes or print it. As you may guess, PowerPoint gives you about 2,037 ways to accomplish the retrieval. Here are two of the most common:

» Select the File tab to switch to Backstage view, and then choose Open.

» Press Ctrl+O.

Both options take you to the Open screen in Backstage view (see Figure 2-10). From here, you can select a file from a list of recently opened presentations or you can open a file that you've saved to your OneDrive account.

To browse your computer for a file, click the Browse icon (shown in the margin). This brings up the Open dialog box, as shown in Figure 2-11. The Open dialog box has controls that enable you to rummage through the various folders on your hard drive in search of your files. If you know how to open a file in any Windows application, you know how to do it in PowerPoint (because the Open dialog box is pretty much the same in any Windows application).

If you seem to have lost a file, rummage around in different folders to see whether you can find it. Perhaps you saved a file in the wrong folder by accident. Also, check the spelling of the filename. Maybe your fingers weren't on the home row when you typed the filename, so instead of `Thumb War.pptx`, you saved the file as `Yji,b Est.pptx`. I hate it when that happens.

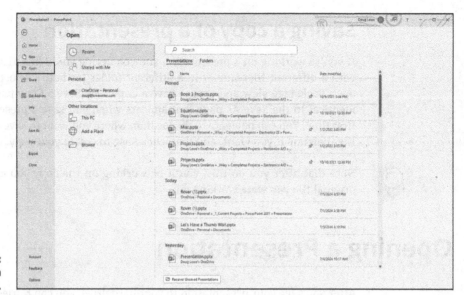

FIGURE 2-10:
Opening a file in Backstage view.

FIGURE 2-11:
The Open dialog box.

TIP

The fastest way to open a file from the Open dialog box is to double-click the file. This spares you from having to click the file once and then click OK. Double-clicking also exercises the fast-twitch muscles in your index finger.

PowerPoint keeps track of the files you've recently opened and displays them in the File menu. To open a file that you recently opened, select the File tab to open the Home page in Backstage view, and then inspect the files in the Recent list. If the file that you want is in the list, click it to open it.

Pinning a Presentation for Easy Access

In addition to a list of recently opened presentations, the Home page in Backstage view lets you view a list of your pinned presentations. To view your list of pinned presentations, select the File tab to open Backstage view, and then click Pinned (located beneath the search bar) on the Home page. This reveals the list of pinned presentations (see Figure 2-12). You can then click any of the presentations in this list to open the presentation.

FIGURE 2-12: Your pinned presentations.

 The easiest way to pin a presentation is to open it, select the File tab to return to Backstage view, click the file you just opened at the top of the Recent list, and then click the Pin icon (shown in the margin).

IN THIS CHAPTER

» Moving around in a presentation

» Working with objects and editing text

» Undoing a mistake and deleting slides

» Finding and replacing text

» Rearranging slides

Chapter **3**

Editing Slides

If you're like Mary Poppins ("practically perfect in every way"), you can skip this chapter. Perfect people never make mistakes, so everything that they type in PowerPoint comes out right the first time. They never have to press Backspace to erase something they typed incorrectly, or go back and insert a line to make a point they left out, or rearrange their slides because they didn't add them in the right order to begin with.

If you're more like Jane ("rather inclined to giggle; doesn't put things away") or Michael ("extremely stubborn and suspicious"), you probably make mistakes along the way. This chapter shows you how to go back and correct those mistakes.

Reviewing your work and correcting it if necessary is called *editing*. It's not a fun job, but it has to be done. A spoonful of sugar usually helps.

This chapter focuses mostly on editing text objects. Many of these techniques also apply to editing other types of objects, such as clip art or drawn shapes. For more information about editing other types of objects, see Part 4.

Moving from Slide to Slide

On a computer with a keyboard, the easiest way to move in a PowerPoint presentation is to press the Page Down and Page Up keys:

» **Page Down:** Press Page Down to move forward to the next slide in your presentation.

» **Page Up:** Press Page Up to move backward to the preceding slide in your presentation.

You can also use the vertical scroll bar on the right side of the window to navigate through your presentation:

» **Double-headed arrows:** You can move forward or backward through your presentation one slide at a time by clicking the double-headed arrows at the bottom of the vertical scroll bar.

» **Single-headed arrows:** You can also scroll forward or backward through your presentation by clicking and holding the single-headed arrows at the top and/or bottom of the vertical scroll bar. (Note that if the zoom factor is set so that a single slide is visible in the presentation window, clicking the single-headed arrows moves to the next or preceding slide.)

» **Scroll box:** Another way to move quickly from slide to slide is by dragging the scroll bar up or down. When you drag the scroll bar, a little tooltip pops up next to it, telling you which slide will be displayed if you stop dragging at that point.

If you have a touchscreen, you can use a flick of your finger to move from slide to slide.

Working with Objects

In the beginning, the User created a slide. And the slide was formless and void, without meaning or content. And the User said, "Let there be a text object." And there was a text object. And there was evening and there was morning, one day. Then the User said, "Let there be a picture object." And there was a picture object. And there was evening and there was morning, a second day. This continued for 40 days and 40 nights, until there were 40 objects on the slide, each after its own kind. And the User was laughed out of the auditorium by the audience who could not read the slide, for the slide was great with clutter.

I present this charming little parable solely to make the point that PowerPoint slides are nothing without objects. *Objects* are items (such as text, pictures, and charts) that give meaning and content to otherwise formless and empty slides. When it comes to objects, however, sometimes less is more. Don't overdo it by cluttering your slides with so many objects that the main point of the slide is obscured.

Most of the objects on your slides are text objects, which let you type text on your slides. (For more information about working with text objects, see Chapter 11.)

Every slide has a *slide layout* that consists of one or more placeholders. A *placeholder* is simply an area on a slide that's reserved for text, clip art, a graph, or some other type of object. For example, a slide that uses the Title Slide has two placeholders for text objects — one for the title and the other for the subtitle. You use the Slide Layout task pane to select the layout when you create new slides. You can change the layout later, as well as add more objects to the slide. You can also delete, move, or resize objects if you want. You'll find more information about slide layouts later in this chapter, in the section "Working with Slide Layouts."

You can add many different types of objects, such as clip art, charts, graphs, shapes, and so on. You can add more objects to your slide with one of the tools that appears on the Drawing toolbar at the bottom of the screen or by using the icons that appear in the center of slides created using any of the layouts with Content placeholders such as Title and Content or Two Content. (For more information about adding objects to your slides, see Part 4.)

Each object occupies a rectangular region on the slide. The contents of the object may or may not visually fill the rectangular region, but you can see the outline of the object when you select it (see the next section, "Selecting objects").

Objects can overlap. Usually, you don't want them to, but sometimes doing so creates a jazzy effect. You may want to lay some text on top of some clip art, for example.

Selecting objects

Before you can edit anything on a slide, you have to select the object that contains whatever it is that you want to edit. For example, you can't start typing away to edit text on-screen. Instead, you first have to select the text object that contains the text you want to edit. Likewise, you must select other types of objects before you can edit their contents.

Note that you must be in Normal view to select individual objects on the slide. In Slide Sorter view, you can select whole slides but not the individual elements on them.

TIP

Here are some guidelines to keep in mind when selecting objects:

- **Text objects:** To select a text object so that you can edit its text, move the insertion point over the text that you want to edit and then click. (On a touchpad, double-tap the text.) A rectangular box appears around the object, and a text insertion point appears so you can start typing.

- **Nontext objects:** Other types of objects work a little differently. Click an object, and the object is selected. The rectangular box appears around the object to let you know that you've hooked it. After you've hooked the object, you can drag it around the screen or change its size, but you can't edit its contents.

- **The Ctrl key:** You can select more than one object by selecting the first object and then holding down the Ctrl key while clicking to select additional objects.

- **Click and drag:** Another way to select an object — or more than one object — is to use the insertion point to drag a rectangle around the object(s) that you want to select. Point to a location above and to the left of the object(s) that you want to select, and then click and drag the mouse down and to the right until the rectangle surrounds the object(s). When you release the button, all the objects within the rectangle are selected.

- **The Tab key:** You can press the Tab key to select objects. Press Tab once to select the first object on the slide. Press Tab again to select the next object. Keep pressing Tab until the object that you want is selected.

  Pressing Tab to select objects is handy when you can't easily point to the object that you want to select. This problem can happen if the object that you want is buried underneath another object or if the object is empty or otherwise invisible and you're not sure where it is.

Resizing or moving an object

When you select an object, an outline box appears around it, as shown in Figure 3-1. In this slide, a picture of William Shakespeare is selected. If you look closely at the picture, you can see that it has a little circle on each corner and in the middle of each edge. I like to calls these little circles *love handles*. You can use the love handles to adjust the size of an object. You can also grab the box edge between the love handles to move the object on the slide. (Technically, the love handles are called *sizing handles*.)

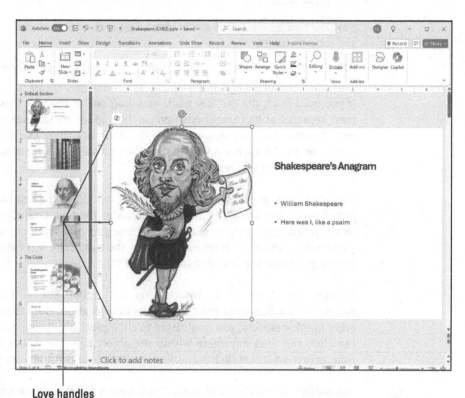

FIGURE 3-1: You can resize this object by taking hold of its love handles.

Love handles

When you move or resize an object, the object will have a tendency to align itself with nearby objects. You'll see alignment lines pop up when you move the object into alignment with other objects on the slide. If you release the mouse button when the alignment marks appear, the object will snap to the alignment indicated.

In addition to the love handles, many types of objects — including images — feature a circular arrow called the *rotate handle*. You can rotate the object by grabbing this handle and dragging it around in a circle. (Not all types of objects can be rotated, however. For example, you can't rotate charts.)

To change the size of an object, click the object to select it and then grab one of the love handles by clicking. Hold down the mouse button and then move the mouse to change the object's size.

CHAPTER 3 **Editing Slides** 49

The various handles on an object give you different ways to change the object's size:

- The handles at the corners enable you to change both the height and the width of the object.
- The handles on the top and bottom edges enable you to change just the object's height.
- The handles on the right and left edges change just the width of the object.

If you hold down the Ctrl key while you drag one of the love handles, the object stays centered at its current position on the slide as its size adjusts. Try it to see what I mean. Also, try holding down the Shift key while you drag an object by using one of the corner love handles. This combination maintains the object's proportions when you resize it.

Changing a text object's size doesn't change the size of the text in the object — it just changes the size of the *frame* that contains the text. Changing the width of a text object is equivalent to changing the margins of a Word document: It makes the text lines wider or narrower. To change the size of the text within a text object, you must change the font size (see Chapter 11).

To move an object, click anywhere on the outline box — except on a love handle — and then drag the object to its new location. Note that for shapes and other graphic objects, you don't have to click precisely on the outline box — you can click and drag anywhere within the object to move it. But for objects that contain text, you must click the outline box itself to drag the object to a new location.

The outline box can be hard to see if you have a fancy background on your slides. If you select an object and have trouble seeing the outline box, try squinting or cleaning your monitor screen. Or, in severe weather, try selecting the View tab on the Ribbon and then choosing one of the Color/Grayscale options:

- **Color:** Displays slides in full color
- **Grayscale:** Displays colors as shades of gray
- **Pure Black and White:** Displays the slides in black and white

Viewing the slide in Grayscale or Pure Black and White might make the love handles easier to spot. To switch back to full-color view, click Back to Color View.

COPILOT EXPLAINS THE KING JAMES SHAKESPEARE THEORY

The PowerPoint slides in this chapter relate to a weird theory that William Shakespeare — who was alive when the King James Bible was translated — somehow managed to get his name squeezed into the biblical text. So, I decided to ask Copilot about it, by asking it the question: "Is there a thing about William Shakespeare's name and one of the psalms in the King James Bible?"

Sure enough, Copilot found what I was asking about and explained "the thing":

> *There is a popular theory that suggests William Shakespeare might have had a hand in translating the King James Bible. Specifically, it is believed that he worked on Psalm 46. The theory points out that if you count 46 words from the beginning of Psalm 46, you find the word "shake," and if you count 46 words from the end (excluding the word "Selah"), you find the word "spear." Since Shakespeare was 46 years old in 1611, the year the King James Bible was published, some people see this as a hidden signature. However, this is just a theory and has not been proven. It's an interesting piece of trivia that has captured the imagination of many.*

You can find more information about using Copilot to help generate ideas for your PowerPoint presentations in Chapter 8.

Editing a Text Object

When you select a text object for editing, PowerPoint transforms into a baby word processor so you can edit the text. Note that PowerPoint automatically wraps text, so you don't have to press Enter at the end of every line. Press Enter only when you want to begin a new paragraph.

Text in a PowerPoint presentation is usually formatted with a bullet character at the beginning of each paragraph. The default bullet character depends on the theme you've applied to the slide. But if you don't like the bullet provided by the theme, you can change it to just about any shape that you can imagine. The point to remember here is that the bullet character is a part of the paragraph format and not a character that you have to type in your text.

You can move around within a text object by pressing the arrow keys or by using the mouse. You can also use the End and Home keys to take the insertion point to the start or end of the line that you're on. Additionally, you can use the arrow keys in combination with the Ctrl key to move around even faster. For example, press the Ctrl key and the left- or right-arrow key to move left or right an entire word at a time.

You can delete text by pressing the Delete or Backspace key. To delete from the insertion point to the start or end of a word, use the Ctrl key along with the Delete or Backspace key. If you first select a block of text, the Delete and Backspace keys delete the entire selection. (The next section has some tips for selecting text.)

Selecting Text

Some text-editing operations — such as amputations and transplants — require that you first select the text on which you want to operate. Here's how to select blocks of text:

» **When using the keyboard,** hold down the Shift key while you press any of the arrow keys to move the insertion point.

» **When using the mouse,** point to the beginning of the text that you want to mark and then click and drag over the text. Release the mouse button when you reach the end of the text that you want to select.

PowerPoint has an automatic word-selection option that tries to guess when you intend to select an entire word. If you use the mouse to select a block of text that spans the space between two words, the selected text jumps to include entire words while you move the mouse. If you don't like this feature, you can disable it by selecting the File tab and then clicking the Options button in Backstage view. Then deselect the When Selecting, Automatically Select Entire Word check box.

TIP

You can use the following tricks to select different amounts of text:

» **A single word:** To select a single word, point the insertion point anywhere in the word and double-click.

» **An entire paragraph:** To select an entire paragraph, point the insertion point anywhere in the paragraph and triple-click. (Although this works with a mouse, you can't select an entire paragraph by triple-tapping on a touchscreen.)

After you've selected text, you can edit it in the following ways:

» **Delete:** To delete the entire block of text that you've selected, press Delete or Backspace.

» **Replace:** To replace an entire block of text, select it and then begin typing. The selected block vanishes and is replaced by the text that you're typing.

>> **Cut, Copy, and Paste:** You can use the Cut, Copy, and Paste commands from the Clipboard group with selected text blocks. The following section describes these commands.

Using Cut, Copy, and Paste

Like any good Windows program, PowerPoint uses the standard Cut, Copy, and Paste commands. These commands work on text that you've selected, or if you've selected an entire object, the commands work on the object itself. In other words, you can use the Cut, Copy, and Paste commands with bits of text or with entire objects.

Cut, Copy, and Paste all work with one of the greatest mysteries of Windows — the *Clipboard.* The Clipboard is where Windows stashes stuff so that you can get to it later. The Cut and Copy commands add stuff to the Clipboard, and the Paste command copies stuff from the Clipboard to your presentation.

For basic cutting, copying, and pasting, you can use the standard Windows keyboard shortcuts: Ctrl+X for Cut, Ctrl+C for Copy, and Ctrl+V for Paste. Because these three keyboard shortcuts work in virtually all Windows programs, memorizing them pays off.

The Ribbon buttons for working with the Clipboard are found in the Clipboard group of the Home tab. Three of the four buttons in this section are for working with the Clipboard:

Button	Function
Paste	Paste
Cut	Cut
Copy	Copy

Notice that the Copy button includes a drop-down arrow. If you click the center of the Copy button, the selected object is copied to the Clipboard. But if you click the drop-down arrow instead, a small menu with two icons is displayed. Clicking the first icon copies the selection; clicking the second icon makes a duplicate. For more information about creating duplicates, see the next section, "Duplicating an Object."

Here's a cool feature: PowerPoint lets you preview how the contents of the Clipboard will appear before you actually paste it into your slide. To use this feature, copy or cut something to the Clipboard. Then click the down arrow beneath the Paste button. This reveals a menu with several buttons representing different ways to paste the selection. Hover the mouse over each icon to see a preview of how the item will appear when pasted. When you find a button whose paste preview you approve of, click the button to paste the item.

If you want to blow away an entire object permanently, select it and then press Delete or Backspace. This step removes the object from the slide but doesn't copy it to the Clipboard. It's gone forever. Well, sort of — you can still get it back by using the Undo command but only if you act fast. See the later section "Oops! I Didn't Mean It (The Marvelous Undo Command)" for more information.

Note that PowerPoint lets you paste text that you copied from somewhere else, such as Word or Excel. If you use the Paste button or the keyboard shortcut Ctrl+V, the pasted text will assume the formatting of the PowerPoint text you paste the text into. If you'd prefer to retain the formatting of the original text as it appeared in the Word or Excel document, you can right-click where you want to insert the text, and then choose Paste Options. Then you can choose to use the destination formatting or keep the source formatting. You can also choose to insert the copied text as a picture, which means that the text will appear exactly as it did in the source you copied it from, but you won't be able to edit it.

To include the same object on each of your slides, you can use a better method than copying and pasting: Add the object to the *slide master*, which governs the format of all the slides in a presentation (see Chapter 14).

Duplicating an Object

PowerPoint has a Duplicate command you can use to quickly create copies of objects. Select the object you want to duplicate; then press Ctrl+D to create a duplicate of the object. You probably need to move the duplicate object to its correct location.

An even easier way to duplicate an object is to select the object, hold down the Ctrl key, press and hold the left mouse button, and drag the object to a new location on the slide. After you release the mouse button, a duplicate copy of the object is created.

Using the Clipboard Task Pane

The Clipboard task pane lets you gather up to 24 items of text or graphics from any Microsoft 365 program and then selectively paste them into your presentation. To summon the Clipboard task pane, click the dialog box launcher from the Home tab on the Ribbon at the lower right of the Clipboard group. The Clipboard task pane appears. In Figure 3-2, you can see the Clipboard task pane at the left side of the PowerPoint window, with several objects held in the Clipboard.

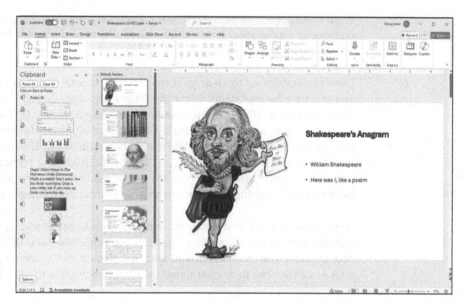

FIGURE 3-2: The Clipboard task pane.

To paste an item from the Clipboard task pane, simply click the item you want to insert.

Oops! I Didn't Mean It (The Marvelous Undo Command)

Made a mistake? Don't panic. Use the Undo command. Undo is your safety net. If you mess up, Undo can save the day.

You have two ways to undo a mistake:

» Click the Undo button on the Quick Access Toolbar (QAT).

» Press Ctrl+Z.

Undo reverses whatever you did last. If you deleted text, Undo adds it back. If you typed text, Undo deletes it. If you moved an object, Undo puts it back where it was. You get the idea.

Undo is such a useful command that committing the Ctrl+Z keyboard shortcut to memory is a good idea. If you want, think of the word *zip* to help you remember how to zip away your mistakes.

Undo remembers up to 20 of your most recent actions. You can undo each action one at a time by repeatedly using the Undo command. Or you can click the down arrow next to the Undo button (shown in the margin) on the QAT and then choose the actions you want to undo from the list that appears. However, as a general rule, you should correct your mistakes as soon as possible. If you make a mistake, feel free to curse, kick something, or fall on the floor in a screaming tantrum if you must, *but don't do anything else on your computer!* If you use the Undo command before you do anything else, you can reverse your mistake and get on with your life.

PowerPoint also offers a Redo command (shown in the margin), which is sort of like an Undo for Undo. In other words, if you undo what you thought was a mistake by using the Undo command and then decide that it wasn't a mistake after all, you can use the Redo command. Here are two ways to use the Redo command:

» Click the Redo button on the QAT.

» Press Ctrl+Y.

Note that if the last action you performed wasn't an Undo command, the Redo button is replaced by a Repeat button (shown in the margin). You can click the Repeat button to repeat the last command.

Working with Slide Layouts

A *slide layout* is an arrangement of various object placeholders. Up to this point, the presentations shown in this book have used just two of the many types of slide layouts that are available in PowerPoint: the Title Slide layout and the Title and Content layout. The full list of slide layouts that are available in PowerPoint is shown in Table 3-1.

TABLE 3-1 PowerPoint's Slide Layouts

What It Looks Like	What It's Called	What It Includes
	Title Slide	Text placeholders for a presentation title and a subtitle
	Title and Content	A text placeholder for a slide title and a content placeholder for content
	Section Header	Text placeholders for a section title and a section introduction
	Two Content	A text placeholder for a slide title and two content placeholders
	Comparison	A text placeholder for a slide title, two text placeholders for column headers, and two content placeholders
	Title Only	A single placeholder for a title
	Blank	No placeholders
	Content with Caption	A text placeholder for a slide title, an additional text placeholder for a caption immediately beneath the slide title, and a content placeholder
	Picture with Caption	A text placeholder for a slide title, an additional text placeholder for a caption immediately beneath the slide title, and a picture placeholder

By default, when you insert a slide, the new slide's layout is Title with Content. However, you can insert a slide with a different layout by clicking the down arrow next to the New Slide icon (shown in the margin). This reveals a drop-down gallery that lists the slide layouts that are available (see Figure 3-3). Click the layout you want to use for the new slide.

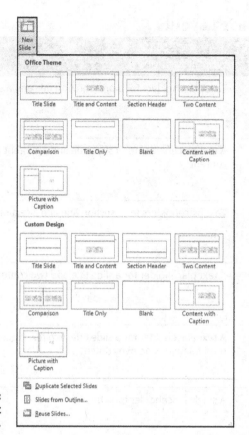

FIGURE 3-3:
Picking the layout for a new slide.

Note that Figure 3-3 shows the layout gallery for a presentation with no theme applied. When you apply a theme to your presentation, the gallery will reflect the theme you've chosen.

Layout ⌄ You can easily change the layout of an existing file by using the Layout button (shown in the margin) in the Slides section of the Home tab. Just navigate to the slide whose layout you want to change, click the Layout button, and then choose the layout you want to use from the gallery that appears.

Deleting a Slide

Want to delete an entire slide? No problem. Simply move to the slide that you want to delete and click the Delete button in the Slides group of the Home tab on the Ribbon. Zowie! The slide is history.

Another way to delete a slide is to click the miniature of the slide in the Slide Preview pane (on the left side of the screen) and then press the Delete key or the Backspace key.

Deleted the wrong slide, eh? No problem. Just press Ctrl+Z or click the Undo button to restore the slide.

Duplicating a Slide

PowerPoint sports a Duplicate Slide command that lets you duplicate an entire slide — text, formatting, and everything else included. That way, after you toil over a slide for hours to get its formatting just right, you can create a duplicate to use as the basis for another slide.

To duplicate a slide — or slides — select the slide(s) you want to duplicate. Then select the Home tab on the Ribbon, click the arrow at the bottom of the Add Slide button in the Slides group, and click the Duplicate Selected Slides button. A duplicate of the slide is inserted in your presentation.

If you're a keyboard shortcut fanatic, all you have to do is select the slide that you want to duplicate in the Slides pane (located on the left side of the screen) and then press Ctrl+D.

Finding Text

You know that buried somewhere in that 60-slide presentation about configurable snarfblatts is a slide that lists the options available on the vertical snarfblatt, but where is it? This sounds like a job for the PowerPoint Find command!

The Find command can find text buried in any text object on any slide. These steps show you the procedure for using the Find command:

1. **Think of what you want to find.**

   Snarfblatt will suffice for this example.

2. **Click the Find button (shown in the margin) in the Editing group of the Home tab or use the keyboard shortcut Ctrl+F.**

   The Find dialog box appears (see Figure 3-4). It contains the secrets of the Find command.

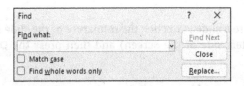

FIGURE 3-4:
The Find
dialog box.

3. **Type the text that you want to find.**

   The text you typed displays in the Find What box.

4. **Press Enter.**

   Or click the Find Next button. Either way, the search begins.

If the text that you type is located anywhere in the presentation, the Find command takes you to the slide that contains the text and highlights the text. You can then edit the text object or search for the next occurrence of the text within your presentation. If you edit the text, the Find dialog box stays on-screen to make it easy to continue your quest.

Here are some additional capabilities of the Find command:

» **Finding the next occurrence:** To find the next occurrence of the same text, press Enter or click the Find Next button again.

» **Editing the text:** To edit the text you found, click the text object. The Find dialog box remains on-screen. To continue searching, click the Find Next button again.

» **Starting anywhere:** You don't have to be at the beginning of your presentation to search the entire presentation. When PowerPoint reaches the end of the presentation, it automatically picks up the search at the beginning and continues to the point at which you started the search.

» **Giving up:** You may receive the following message:

   ```
   We couldn't find what you were looking for.
   ```

   This message means that PowerPoint has given up. The text that you're looking for just isn't anywhere in the presentation. Maybe you spelled it wrong, or maybe you didn't have a slide about snarfblatts after all.

» **Matching case:** If the right mix of uppercase and lowercase letters is important to you, select the Match Case check box before beginning the search. This option is handy when you have, for example, a presentation about Mr. Smith the Blacksmith.

» **Finding whole words:** Use the Find Whole Words Only check box to find your text only when it appears as a whole word. If you want to find the slide on

60 PART 1 **Getting Started with PowerPoint**

which you discuss Smitty the Blacksmith's mitt, for example, type **mitt** for the Find What text and select the Find Whole Words Only check box. That way, the Find command looks for *mitt* as a separate word. It doesn't stop to show you the *mitt* in *Smitty*.

» **Replacing text:** If you find the text that you're looking for and decide that you want to replace it with something else, click the Replace button. This step changes the Find dialog box to the Replace dialog box, which is explained in the following section.

» **Closing the Find dialog box:** To make the Find dialog box go away, click the Close button or press Esc.

Replacing Text

Suppose that the Rent-a-Nerd company decides to switch to athletic consulting, so it wants to change the name of its company to Rent-a-Jock. Easy. Just use the handy Replace command to change all occurrences of the word *Nerd* to the word *Jock*. The following steps show you how:

1. **Click the Replace button (shown in the margin) in the Editing group on the Home tab on the Ribbon, or use the keyboard shortcut Ctrl+H.**

   The Replace dialog box appears (see Figure 3-5).

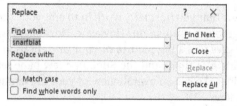

FIGURE 3-5: The Replace dialog box.

2. **In the Find What box, type the text that you want to find.**

   Enter the text that you want to replace with something else (**Nerd**, in this example).

3. **Type the replacement text in the Replace With box.**

   Enter the text you want to use to replace the text that you typed in the Find What box (**Jock**, in this example).

4. **Click the Find Next button.**

   PowerPoint finds the first occurrence of the text.

5. **Click the Replace button to replace the text.**

   Read the text first to make sure that it found what you're looking for.

6. **Repeat the Find Next and Replace sequence until you're finished.**

   Click Find Next to find the next occurrence, click Replace to replace it, and so on. Keep going until you finish.

If you're absolutely positive that you want to replace all occurrences of your Find What text with the Replace With text, click the Replace All button. This step dispenses with the Find Next and Replace cycle. The only problem is that you're bound to find at least one spot where you didn't want the replacement to occur. Replacing the word *mitt* with *glove*, for example, results in *Sglovey* rather than *Smitty*. Don't forget that you can also use the Find Whole Words Only option to find and replace text only if it appears as an entire word.

REMEMBER

If you totally mess up your presentation by clicking Replace All, you can use the Undo command to restore sanity to your presentation.

Rearranging Your Slides in Slide Sorter View

Normal view is the view that you normally work in to edit your slides, move things around, add text or graphics, and so on. However, Normal view has one serious limitation: It doesn't give you a big picture of your presentation. You can see the details of only one slide at a time, and the Slide Preview pane lets you see snapshots of only a few slides. To see an overall view of your presentation, you need to work in Slide Sorter view.

You can switch to Slide Sorter view (see Figure 3-6) in two easy ways:

- » Click the Slide Sorter button (shown in the margin) at the right side of the status bar.
- » Select the View tab on the Ribbon, and then click the Slide Sorter button in the Presentation Views group.

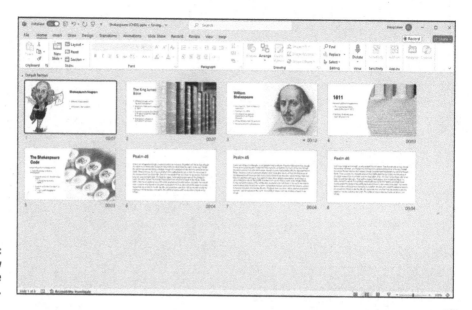

FIGURE 3-6:
Slide Sorter view lets you see the big picture.

The following list tells you how to rearrange, add, or delete slides from Slide Sorter view:

- » **Moving a slide:** To move a slide, click and drag it to a new location. Point to the slide and then hold down the mouse button. Drag the slide to its new location and release the button. PowerPoint adjusts the display to show the new arrangement of slides.

- » **Deleting a slide:** To delete a slide, click the slide to select it and then press Delete or Backspace. This works only in Slide Sorter view.

- » **Adding a new slide:** To add a new slide, click the slide that you want the new slide to follow and then click the New Slide button. The Slide Layout task pane appears, allowing you to select the layout for the new slide. To edit the contents of the slide, return to Normal view via the view buttons in the Status bar or in the View tab on the Ribbon or by double-clicking the new slide.

TIP

If your presentation contains more slides than can fit on-screen at one time, you can use the scroll bars to scroll through the display. Or you can use the zoom slider at the lower-right corner of the screen to make the slides smaller.

Slide Sorter view may seem kind of dull and boring, but it's also the place where you can add jazzy transitions, build effects, or add cool animation effects to your slides. For example, you can make your bullets fall from the top of the screen like bombs and switch from slide to slide by using strips, wipes, or blinds.

CHAPTER 3 **Editing Slides** 63

IN THIS CHAPTER

» Understanding the outline

» Focusing on substance instead of form

» Promoting and demoting, and the lateral arabesque

» Adding a slide with the Outline tab

» Collapsing and expanding the outline

Chapter 4
Working in Outline View

Many presentations consist of slide after slide of bulleted lists. You may see a chart here or there and an occasional bit of clip art thrown in for comic effect, but the bread and butter of the presentation is the bulleted list. It sounds boring — and it often is. But in some cases, an endless stream of bullet points turns out to be the best way to get your point across.

Such presentations lend themselves especially well to outlining. PowerPoint's Outline view lets you focus on your presentation's main points and subpoints. In other words, it enables you to focus on content without worrying about appearance.

Calling Up the Outline

In Normal view, the left side of the PowerPoint window is devoted to showing thumbnail images of your slides. But you can easily switch your presentation into Outline view by clicking the Outline View button (shown in the margin) on the Ribbon's View tab. Then your presentation appears as an outline, with the title of each slide as a separate heading at the highest level of the outline, and the text on each slide appears as lower-level headings subordinate to the slide headings (see Figure 4-1). Note that if a slide doesn't have a title, the slide still appears in the outline, but the top-level heading for the slide is blank.

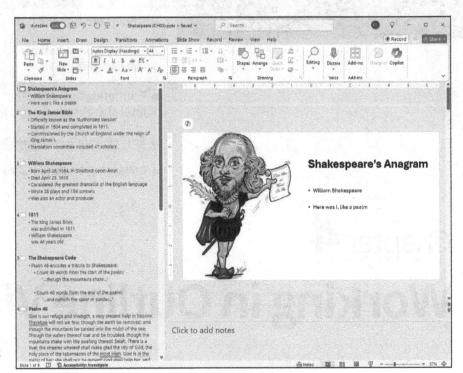

FIGURE 4-1:
Viewing the outline.

TIP

You can expand the area devoted to the outline by clicking and dragging the border of the Outline pane.

The following list highlights a few important things to notice about the outline:

» **The outline is composed of the titles and body text of each slide.** Any other objects that you add to a slide — such as pictures, charts, and so on — are not included in the outline. Also, if you add any text objects to the slide in addition to the basic title and body text placeholders in the slide layout, the additional text objects are not included in the outline.

» **Each slide is represented by a high-level heading in the outline.** The text of this heading is taken from the slide's title, and an icon that represents the entire slide appears next to the heading. Also, the slide number appears to the left of the Slide icon.

» **Each text line from a slide's body text appears as an indented heading.** This heading is subordinate to the slide's main title heading.

>> **An outline can contain subpoints that are subordinate to the main points on each slide.** PowerPoint enables you to create as many as nine heading levels on each slide, but your slides will probably get too complicated if you go beyond two heading levels. You can find more about working with heading levels in the section "Promoting and Demoting Paragraphs," later in this chapter.

Selecting and Editing an Entire Slide

When you work with the Outline tab, you often have to select an entire slide. You can do that by clicking the icon for the slide. This selects the slide title and all its body text. In addition, any extra objects such as graphics that are on the slide are also selected, even though those objects don't appear in the outline.

You can delete, cut, copy, paste, or duplicate an entire slide:

>> **Delete:** To delete an entire slide, select it and then press Delete.

>> **Cut, copy, or paste:** To cut or copy an entire slide to the Clipboard, select the slide and then press Ctrl+X (Cut) or Ctrl+C (Copy), or use the Cut or Copy button on the Home tab on the Ribbon. You can then move the cursor to any location in the outline and press Ctrl+V or use the Paste button to paste the slide from the Clipboard. (You can also cut or copy a slide by right-clicking the slide and choosing Cut or Copy from the menu that appears.)

>> **Duplicate:** To duplicate a slide, select it and then press Ctrl+D. This step places a copy of the selected slide immediately after it. (Actually, you don't have to select the entire slide to duplicate it. Just click anywhere in the slide's title or body text.)

Selecting and Editing One Paragraph

You can select and edit an entire paragraph along with all its subordinate paragraphs. To do so, just click the bullet next to the paragraph that you want to select. To delete an entire paragraph along with its subordinate paragraphs, select it and then press Delete.

To cut or copy an entire paragraph to the Clipboard along with its subordinates, select it and then press Ctrl+X (Cut) or Ctrl+C (Copy). You can then press Ctrl+V to paste the paragraph anywhere in the presentation.

Promoting and Demoting Paragraphs

To *promote* a paragraph is to move it up one level in the outline — that is, to move the indentation of the paragraph to the left. If you promote the "Was also an actor and a producer" paragraph in Figure 4-1, for example, that paragraph becomes a separate slide rather than a bullet under "William Shakespeare."

To promote a paragraph, place the cursor anywhere in the paragraph and then press Shift+Tab or click the Decrease List Level button (shown in the margin) in the Paragraph group on the Home tab on the Ribbon. (Note that you can't promote a paragraph that is already at the highest outline level.)

To *demote* a paragraph is to move it down one level in the outline — that is, to move the indentation of the paragraph to the right. If you demote the "Died April 23, 1616" paragraph in Figure 4-1, it becomes a subpoint under "Born April 26, 1564 in Stratford-upon-Avon" rather than a separate main point. Then the outline for that slide will look like this:

William Shakespeare
- Born April 26, 1564, in Stratford-upon-Avon
  - Died April 23, 1616
- Considered the greatest dramatist of the English language
- Wrote 38 plays and 154 sonnets
- Was also an actor and producer

To demote a paragraph, place the cursor anywhere in the paragraph and then either press the Tab key or click the Increase List Level button (shown in the margin) in the Paragraph group on the Home tab on the Ribbon.

Note that you can't promote a slide title. Slide title is the highest rank in the outline hierarchy. If you demote a slide title, the entire slide is *subsumed* into the preceding slide. In other words, the slide title becomes a main point in the preceding slide.

You can promote or demote paragraphs by using the mouse, but the technique is a little tricky. When you move the cursor over a bullet (or the Slide button), the pointer changes from a single arrow to a four-cornered arrow. This arrow is your signal that you can click to select the entire paragraph (and any subordinate paragraphs). Then you can use the mouse to promote or demote a paragraph along with all its subordinates by dragging the selected paragraph left or right.

Be gentle when you demote paragraphs. Being demoted can be an emotionally devastating experience.

Adding a New Paragraph

To add a new paragraph to a slide with the outline that appears on the Outline tab, move the insertion point to the end of the paragraph that you want the new paragraph to follow and then press Enter. PowerPoint creates a new paragraph at the same outline level as the preceding paragraph.

If you move the insertion point to the end of the title line and press Enter, PowerPoint creates a new slide. You can then press the Tab key to change the new slide to a paragraph on the preceding slide.

If you position the insertion point at the beginning of a paragraph and press Enter, the new paragraph is inserted above the cursor position. If you position the cursor in the middle of a paragraph and press Enter, the paragraph is split in two.

After you add a new paragraph, you may want to change its level in the outline. To do that, you must promote or demote the new paragraph (as described in the preceding section). To create a subpoint for a main point, for example, position the cursor at the end of the main point and press Enter. Then demote the new paragraph by pressing the Tab key.

Adding a New Slide

You can add a new slide in many ways when you're working with the outline. Here are the most popular methods:

- **Promote existing text.** Promote an existing paragraph to the highest level. This method splits a slide into two slides.
- **Promote new text.** Add a new paragraph and then promote it to the highest level.
- **Press Enter.** Place the cursor in a slide's title text and press Enter. This method creates a new slide before the current slide. Whether the title text

stays with the current slide, goes with the new slide, or is split between the slides depends on the location of the cursor within the title when you press Enter.

- » **Press Ctrl+Enter.** Place the cursor anywhere in a slide's body text and press Ctrl+Enter. This method creates a new slide immediately following the current slide. The position of the cursor within the existing slide doesn't matter; the new slide is always created after the current slide. (The cursor must be in the slide's body text, however, in order for this method to work. If you put the cursor in a slide title and press Ctrl+Enter, the cursor jumps to the slide's body text without creating a new slide.)
- » **Insert a new slide.** Place the cursor anywhere in the slide and use the keyboard shortcut Ctrl+M or click the Add Slide button in the Slides group of the Home tab on the Ribbon.
- » **Duplicate an existing slide.** Select an existing slide by clicking the slide's icon or triple-clicking the title, and then press Ctrl+D to duplicate it.

Because the outline focuses on slide content rather than on layout, new slides receive the basic Title and Content layout, which includes title text and body text formatted with bullets.

Moving Text Up and Down

The outline is a handy way to rearrange your presentation. You can easily change the order of individual points on a slide, or you can rearrange the order of the slides.

You can rearrange your presentation by right-clicking the paragraphs that you want to move and then clicking the Move Up or Move Down button in the menu that appears. Or you can point to the bullet next to the paragraph that you want to move. Then, when the cursor changes to the four-cornered arrow, click and drag the paragraph up or down. A horizontal line appears, showing the horizontal position of the selection. Release the mouse button when the horizontal line is positioned where you want the text.

Be careful when you're moving text in a slide that has more than one level of body text paragraphs. Notice the position of the horizontal line when you drag the selection; the entire selection is inserted at that location, which may split up sub-points. If you don't like the result of a move, you can always undo it by pressing Ctrl+Z or clicking the Undo button.

Collapsing and Expanding the Outline

If your presentation has many slides, you may find that grasping its overall structure is difficult, even when looking at the outline. Fortunately, PowerPoint enables you to *collapse* the outline so that only the slide titles are shown. Collapsing an outline doesn't delete the body text; it merely hides the body text so you can focus on the order of the slides in your presentation.

Expanding a presentation restores the collapsed body text to the outline so that you can, once again, focus on details. You can collapse and expand an entire presentation, or you can collapse and expand one slide at a time.

To collapse the entire presentation, right-click anywhere in the outline and then choose Collapse ⇨ Collapse All or use the keyboard shortcut Alt+Shift+1. To expand the presentation, right-click and choose Expand ⇨ Expand All or press Alt+Shift+9.

To collapse a single slide, right-click anywhere in the slide and then choose Collapse ⇨ Collapse from the menu that appears. To expand a single slide, right-click the collapsed slide and choose Expand ⇨ Expand.

> **IN THIS CHAPTER**
>
> » Checking your spelling
>
> » Using the thesaurus
>
> » Capitalizing and punctuating the right way
>
> » Using the AutoCorrect feature

Chapter **5**

Proofing Your Presentations

I was voted Worst Speller in the sixth grade. Not that being Worst Speller qualifies me to run for president or anything, but it shows how much I appreciate computer spellcheckers. Spelling makes no sense to me. I felt a little better after watching *The Story of English* on public television. Now at least I know who to blame for all the peculiarities of English spelling — the Anglos, the Norms (including the guy from *Cheers*), and the Saxophones.

Fortunately, PowerPoint has a pretty decent spellchecker. In fact, the spellchecker in PowerPoint is so smart that it knows that you've made a spelling mistake almost before you make it. The spellchecker watches over your shoulder as you type and helps you to correct your spelling errors as you work.

Besides the spellchecker, PowerPoint has a plethora of features for proofing, reviewing, and otherwise improving your presentations, including a thesaurus (which helped me find the word *plethora*), features to help you get your capitalization and punctuation right, and features to automatically correct common mistakes.

Checking Spelling as You Go

Spelling errors in a Word document are bad, but at least they're small. In a PowerPoint presentation, spelling errors are small only until you use a projector to throw your presentation onto a 30-foot screen. Then they get all blown out of proportion. Nothing is more embarrassing than a 3-foot-tall spelling error. And if you're like me, you probably try to look for mistakes in other people's presentations just for kicks. Thank goodness for PowerPoint's on-the-fly spellchecker.

The PowerPoint spellchecker doesn't make you wait until you finish your presentation and run a special command to point out your spelling errors. It boldly points out your mistakes right when you make them by underlining any word it doesn't recognize with a wavy red line, as shown on several of the badly misspelled words in Figure 5-1.

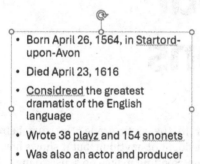

FIGURE 5-1: Look at all the spelling mistakes PowerPoint found in this text box!

When you see the telltale wavy red line, you have several options:

>> **Make the correction.** You can retype the word using the correct spelling.

>> **Let PowerPoint help.** You can right-click the word to call up a menu that lists suggested spellings for the word. In most cases, PowerPoint can figure out what you meant to type and suggests the correct spelling. (In fact, PowerPoint was able to suggest the correct spelling in each of the four misspelled words in Figure 5-1.) To replace the misspelled word with the correct spelling, just click the correctly spelled word in the menu.

>> **Ignore the misspelling.** Sometimes, you want to misspell a word on purpose (for example, if you run a restaurant named "The Koffee Kup"). More likely, the word is correctly spelled, but PowerPoint just doesn't know about the word. The right-click menu will help in either case: You can right-click the word in question and then choose either Ignore All to ignore the misspelling or Add to Dictionary to add it to PowerPoint's spelling dictionary so it doesn't flag the word again.

Spell-Checking After the Fact

If you prefer to ignore the constant nagging by PowerPoint about your spelling, you can always check your spelling the old-fashioned way: by running the spell-checker after you finish your document. The spellchecker works its way through your entire presentation, looking up every word in its massive list of correctly spelled words and bringing any misspelled words to your attention. It performs this task without giggling or snickering. As an added bonus, the spellchecker even gives you the opportunity to tell it that you're right and it's wrong and that it should know how to spell words the way you do.

The following steps show you how to check the spelling for an entire presentation:

1. **If the presentation that you want to spell-check is not already open, open it.**

Spelling

2. **Select the Review tab on the Ribbon and then click the Spelling button (shown in the margin), which is found in the Proofing group.**

3. **Tap your fingers on your desk.**

   PowerPoint is searching your presentation for embarrassing spelling errors. Be patient.

4. **Don't be startled if PowerPoint finds a spelling error.**

   If PowerPoint finds a spelling error in your presentation, it switches to the slide that contains the error, highlights the offensive word, and displays the misspelled word along with a suggested correction, as shown in Figure 5-2.

5. **Choose the correct spelling and click the Change button; alternatively, click Ignore and laugh in PowerPoint's face.**

   If you agree that the word is misspelled, scan the list of corrections that PowerPoint offers and select the one that you like. Then click the Change button.

   If you like the way that you spelled the word in the first place (maybe it's an unusual word that isn't in the PowerPoint spelling dictionary, or maybe you like to spell the way Chaucer did), click the Ignore button. Watch as PowerPoint turns red in the face.

   If you want PowerPoint to ignore all occurrences of a particular misspelling in the current presentation, click the Ignore All button. Likewise, if you want PowerPoint to correct all occurrences of a particular misspelling, click the Change All button.

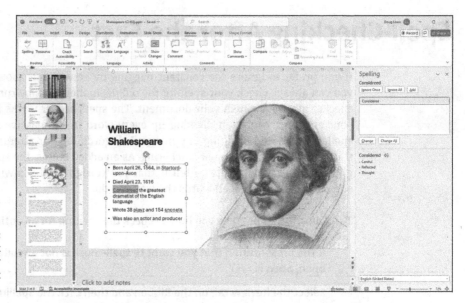

FIGURE 5-2:
The PowerPoint spellchecker points out a boo-boo.

6. **Repeat Step 5 until PowerPoint gives up.**

   When you see the following message, you're finished:

   ```
   Spell check complete.
   ```

   PowerPoint always checks spelling in the entire presentation, beginning with the first slide — unless you specify a single word or group of words by highlighting them first. PowerPoint checks the spelling of titles, body text, notes, and text objects added to slides. It doesn't check the spelling in embedded objects, however, such as charts or graphs.

TIP

If you get tired of PowerPoint always complaining about a word that's not in its standard dictionary, click Add to add the word to the custom dictionary. If you can't sleep at night until you know more about the custom dictionary, read the nearby sidebar, "Don't make me tell you about the custom dictionary."

TIP

The PowerPoint spellchecker is good, but it isn't perfect. It does a reasonably good job of catching *your* when you meant *you're* or *its* when you meant *it's*. But it can't catch an error such as "In a few ours we can go home." For this reason, spell-checking is no substitute for good, old-fashioned proofreading. Print your presentation, sit down with a cup of cappuccino, and *read* it.

76 PART 1 **Getting Started with PowerPoint**

> ## DON'T MAKE ME TELL YOU ABOUT THE CUSTOM DICTIONARY
>
> The PowerPoint spellchecker can use more than one spelling dictionary. Besides the standard dictionary, which contains untold thousands of words that were all reviewed for correctness by Noah Webster himself (just kidding), you can have one or more custom dictionaries, which contain words that you've added by clicking the Add button when the spellchecker found a spelling error.
>
> Custom dictionaries are shared by other Microsoft programs that use spellcheckers — most notably, Word. So, if you add a word to a custom dictionary in Word, the PowerPoint spellchecker knows about the word, too.
>
> What if you accidentally add a word to the dictionary? Then you have a serious problem. You have two alternatives. You can petition Noah Webster to have your variant spelling officially added to the English language, or you can edit the Custom.dic file. The easiest way to edit the Custom.dic file is to select the File tab and then, in Backstage view, click Options, click Proofing, and click the Custom Dictionaries button. Then select the Custom.dic file and click Edit Word List to edit its contents. Search through the file until you find the bogus word; then delete it.

Using the Thesaurus

PowerPoint includes a built-in thesaurus that can quickly show you synonyms for a word that you've typed. Using it is easy:

1. **Right-click a word that you've typed and choose Synonyms from the menu that appears.**

   A menu listing synonyms for the word appears. (Sometimes PowerPoint throws an antonym into the list just to be contrary.)

2. **Select the word that you want to use to replace your word.**

   PowerPoint replaces the original word with your selection.

Thesaurus

If you choose Thesaurus from the Synonyms menu or click the Thesaurus button (shown in the margin) on the Review tab on the Ribbon, the Thesaurus section of the Research task pane appears with the synonyms listed, as well as antonyms, as shown in Figure 5-3. The Thesaurus lets you look up words to find even more synonyms. For example, if you select *falloff* from the list of synonyms, you get another set of words. You can keep clicking words to find other synonyms as long as you'd like, until you're ready to get back to real work.

FIGURE 5-3: The thesaurus appears in the Research task pane.

Capitalizing Correctly

The PowerPoint Change Case command enables you to capitalize the text in your slides properly. These steps show you how to use it:

1. **Select the text that you want to capitalize.**

2. **Choose the Home tab on the Ribbon and then click the Change Case button (shown in the margin) in the Font section.**

   Doing so reveals a menu of Change Case choices.

3. **Study the options for a moment, and then click the one that you want.**

   Here are the case options:

   - *Sentence case:* The first letter of the first word in each sentence is capitalized. Everything else is changed to lowercase.
   - *lowercase:* Everything is changed to lowercase.
   - *UPPERCASE:* Everything is changed to capital letters.
   - *Capitalize Each Word:* The first letter of each word is capitalized.
   - *tOGGLE cASE:* This option turns uppercase into lowercase and turns lowercase into uppercase, for a ransom-note look.

4. **Check the results.**

TIP

Always double-check your text after using the Change Case command to make sure that the result is what you intended. This is especially true when you select Capitalize Each Word. In most cases, you should *not* capitalize articles (like *a* and *the*) and prepositions (like *of* and *from*). The Capitalize Each Word option capitalizes every word in the title, so you'll have to manually change articles and prepositions back to lowercase.

Slide titles should almost always use *title case* (where all words except articles like *a* or *the* and prepositions like *for* and *to* are capitalized). The first level of bullets on a slide can use title case or *sentence case* (where only the first word of each title is capitalized). Lower levels usually should use sentence case.

WARNING

Avoid uppercase if you can. IT'S HARD TO READ — AND IT LOOKS LIKE YOU'RE SHOUTING.

Using the AutoCorrect Feature

PowerPoint includes an AutoCorrect feature that can automatically correct spelling errors and style errors as you type them. For example, if you accidentally type *teh*, PowerPoint automatically changes your text to *the*. And if you forget to capitalize the first word of a sentence, PowerPoint automatically capitalizes it for you. AutoCorrect can even catch certain multiword mistakes. For example, if you type *their are*, AutoCorrect will substitute *there are*.

TIP

Any time PowerPoint makes a correction that you don't like, just press Ctrl+Z to undo the correction. For example, if you really intended to type *teh*, press Ctrl+Z immediately after PowerPoint corrects it to *the*.

If you move the insertion pointer back to a word that has been corrected (or if you click the word), a small blue line appears beneath the first letter of the word. Point your mouse at this blue line, and the button with a lightning bolt in it appears. Click this button to bring up a menu that enables you to undo the correction that was made, tell PowerPoint to stop making that type of correction, or summon the AutoCorrect dialog box to adjust your AutoCorrect settings.

To control PowerPoint's AutoCorrect feature, select the File tab to switch to Backstage view and then click Options. The PowerPoint Options dialog box appears. Next, select the Proofing tab on the left side of the PowerPoint Options dialog box, and click the AutoCorrect Options button to display the AutoCorrect dialog box (see Figure 5-4).

As you can see, the AutoCorrect dialog box contains check boxes for a variety of options that govern how AutoCorrect works:

>> **Show AutoCorrect Options Buttons:** This option displays the AutoCorrect button beneath words that were changed by the AutoCorrect feature, which allows you to undo the change or tell PowerPoint to stop making that particular type of correction.

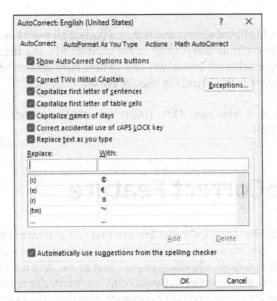

FIGURE 5-4: The AutoCorrect dialog box.

» **Correct TWo INitial CApitals:** Looks for words with two initial capitals and changes the second one to lowercase. For example, if you type *BOther*, PowerPoint changes it to *Bother*. However, if you type three or more capitals in a row, PowerPoint assumes that you did it on purpose, so no correction is made.

» **Capitalize First Letter of Sentences:** Automatically capitalizes the first word of a new sentence if you forget.

» **Capitalize First Letter of Table Cells:** Automatically capitalizes the first word of table cells. (For more information about tables in PowerPoint, turn to Chapter 20.)

» **Capitalize Names of Days:** You know, Monday, Tuesday, Wednesday, and so forth.

» **Correct Accidental Use of cAPS LOCK Key:** This feature is especially cool. If PowerPoint notices that you're capitalizing everything backward, it assumes that you accidentally pressed the Caps Lock key, so it turns off Caps Lock and corrects the words that you capitalized the wrong way.

» **Replace Text as You Type:** This option is the heart of the AutoCorrect feature. It consists of a list of words that are frequently typed incorrectly, along with the replacement word. For example, *teh* is replaced by *the,* and *adn* is replaced by *and.* The AutoCorrect list also contains some shortcuts for special symbols. For example, *(c)* is replaced by the copyright symbol (©), and *(tm)* is replaced by the trademark symbol (™).

TIP

You can add your own words to this list. In the Replace text box, type the word that you want PowerPoint to watch for. In the With text box, type the word that you want PowerPoint to substitute for the first word. Then click Add.

The AutoCorrect feature also includes several formatting options that can automatically apply formats as you type. To set these options, select the AutoFormat As You Type tab. The options shown in Figure 5-5 appear. These options let you control formatting features, such as automatically converting straight quotes to curly quotes, changing fractions such as 1/2 to fraction symbols such as ½, and so on.

FIGURE 5-5: The AutoFormat As You Type options.

IN THIS CHAPTER

» Creating speaker notes to get you through your presentation

» Adjusting the notes page to make long notes fit

» Adding a new slide from Notes Page view

» Printing your notes pages

» Displaying your notes on a separate monitor

Chapter **6**

Don't Forget Your Notes!

Ever had the fear — or maybe the actual experience — of showing a beautiful slide, complete with snappy text and perhaps an exquisite chart, and suddenly forgetting why you included the slide in the first place? You stumble for words. "Well, as you can see, this is a beautiful chart, and, uh, this slide makes the irrefutable point that, uh, well, I'm not sure. . . . Are there any questions?"

Fear not! One of the slickest features in PowerPoint is its capability to create speaker notes to help you get through your presentation. You can make these notes as complete or as sketchy as you want or need. You can write a complete script for your presentation or just jot down a few key points to refresh your memory.

The best part about speaker notes is that you're the only one who sees them. They don't actually show up on your slides for all the world to see. Instead, notes pages are displayed separately on your computer's monitor but not displayed by the projector. Or, if you have two monitors, you can display the presentation on one and the notes on the other. And you can print your notes pages so you have them available as a handy reference during your presentation.

Understanding Notes

Notes are like an adjunct attachment to your slides. They don't appear on the slides themselves but are displayed separately. Each slide in your presentation has its own page of notes.

When you work in Normal view, the notes are shown in a tiny Notes pane below the main slide image. The Notes pane is just large enough to display a line or two of text. You can recognize the Notes pane because it initially contains the words `Click to add notes`. To work with notes, first enlarge the Notes pane to give yourself some room to work (see the section "Adding Notes to a Slide," later in this chapter).

 PowerPoint also has a separate view designed for working with notes pages, called — you guessed it — Notes Page view. To call up Notes Page view, select the View tab on the Ribbon and then click the Notes Page button (shown in the margin), found in the Presentation Views group. Each notes page consists of a reduced version of the slide and an area for notes, as shown in Figure 6-1.

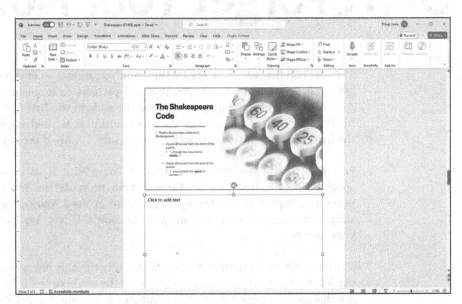

FIGURE 6-1: Notes Page view lets you see your notes.

Depending on the size of your monitor, these notes are too small to see or work with in Notes Page view unless you increase the zoom setting. But on smaller monitors, you can zoom in to see your work.

Unfortunately, no keyboard shortcut is available to switch directly to Notes Page view. Earlier versions of PowerPoint included a button for this alongside the other view buttons in the lower-right corner of the screen. But for some mysterious reason, Microsoft decided to omit this button in recent versions of PowerPoint. So, the only way to get to Notes Page view now is to use the Ribbon's Notes Page button.

Adding Notes to a Slide

To add notes to a slide while working in Normal view, as shown in Figure 6-2, follow this procedure:

1. **Switch to Notes view by clicking Notes Page on the View tab of the Ribbon.**
2. **Move to the slide to which you want to add notes.**
3. **Click and drag the Notes pane border, if necessary, to bring the notes text into view.**
4. **Click the notes text object, where it reads** `Click to add text`.
5. **Type away.**

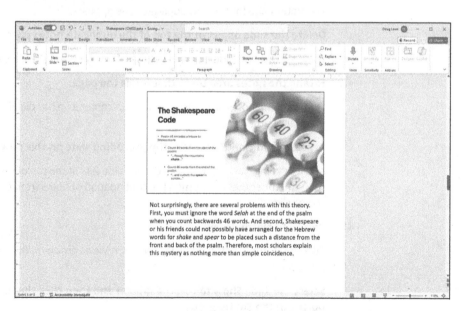

FIGURE 6-2: A slide with notes.

The text that you type appears in the notes area. As you create your notes, you can use any of the PowerPoint standard word-processing features, such as Cut, Copy, and Paste. Press Enter to create new paragraphs.

Note that there is also a Notes button in the status bar at the bottom of the PowerPoint screen. You can click this button to hide or reveal notes.

Adding an Extra Notes Page for a Slide

PowerPoint doesn't provide a way to add more than one page of notes for each slide. However, these steps show you a trick that accomplishes essentially the same thing:

1. **Create a duplicate slide immediately following the slide that requires two pages of notes.**

   To duplicate the slide, move to the slide that you want to duplicate in Normal view and press Ctrl+D to duplicate the slide.

2. **Click the Notes Page button in the Presentation Views group on the View tab on the Ribbon.**

   The Notes Page for the new duplicate slide appears.

3. **Delete the slide object at the top of the duplicate notes page.**

   To do so, click the slide object at the top of the page and press Delete.

4. **Extend the notes area up so that it fills the page.**

   To extend the notes area, just drag the top-center love handle of the notes area up.

5. **Type the additional notes for the preceding slide on this new notes page.**

   Add a heading, such as "Continued from slide 23," at the top of the text to help you remember that this portion is a continuation of notes from the preceding slide.

6. **Return to Normal view.**

   Click the Normal button in the Presentation Views group on the View tab on the Ribbon.

7. **Select the Slide Show tab on the Ribbon and then click the Hide Slide button in the Set Up group.**

   The Hide Slide button hides the slide, which means that it isn't included in an on-screen slide show.

The result of this trick is that you now have two pages of notes for a single slide, and the second notes page doesn't have an image of the slide on it and is not included in your slide show. (If your slides use animations or slide transitions, as I describe in Chapter 13, you may need to fiddle a bit to prevent the animations or transitions from running on your notes-only slide.)

If you're printing overhead transparencies, you may want to deselect the Print Hidden Slides check box in the Print dialog box. This way, the hidden slide isn't printed. Be sure to select the check box when you print the notes pages, though. Otherwise, the notes page for the hidden slide isn't printed either — and the reason you created the hidden slide in the first place was to print a notes page for it!

Think twice before creating a second page of notes for a slide. Do you really have that much to say about a single slide? Maybe the slide contains too much to begin with and should be split into two slides.

Adding a New Slide from Notes Page View

If you're working in Notes Page view and you realize that you want to create a new slide, you don't have to return to Normal view. Just click the Add Slide button in the Slides group on the Home tab on the Ribbon to add the new slide. Or press Ctrl+M.

If you want to work on the slide's appearance or contents, however, you have to switch back to Normal view. You can't modify a slide's appearance or contents from Notes Page view.

Printing Notes Pages

If you don't have a computer that can show your slides on a projector and your notes on a separate monitor, you can always print your notes on paper and then use the printed notes while you give your presentation. These steps show you how to print your notes:

1. **Choose the Print command from the File tab on the Ribbon.**

   The Print page appears in Backstage view.

2. **Under Settings, choose Notes Pages.**
3. **Make sure that the Print Hidden Slides check box is selected if you want to print notes pages for hidden slides.**

   The Print Hidden Slides check box is located under Settings. This check box is dimmed if the presentation doesn't have any hidden slides.

4. **Click OK or press Enter.**

   You can find more information about printing in Chapter 7.

Displaying Notes on a Separate Monitor

As you discover in Chapter 7, PowerPoint can display your presentation in a special mode called Presenter view, which displays the slides on a projector or second monitor and helpful information, including your notes, on your computer's main monitor. As shown in Figure 6-3, Presenter view shows the main slide on the left and a thumbnail of the next slide on the right, with your notes immediately below the next slide preview. To activate this view, simply select the Use Presenter View option in the Monitors group on the Slide Show tab on the Ribbon.

FIGURE 6-3: Presenter view shows you your notes during a slide show.

Note that Presenter view is especially helpful if you're presenting remotely (for example, in a Zoom or Microsoft Teams meeting). In that case, you can share the screen that has the main presentation but have Presenter view visible on a monitor that isn't shared. That way, only you will be able to see your notes. Everyone else in the meeting will be blown away by your brilliance!

You can find more information about Presenter view in Chapter 7.

IN THIS CHAPTER

» Printing slides

» Printing handouts, notes, and outlines

» Setting up and starting a slide show

» Getting acquainted with Presenter view

» Using your keyboard and mouse during your presentation

» Using the tools of the presentation trade

» Getting your slide timings just right

» Creating and showing a custom show

Chapter 7
Show Time!

Overture, curtains, lights. This is it — the night of nights.

No more rehearsing and nursing a part,

We know every part by heart.

Overture, curtains, lights. This is it, you'll hit the heights.

And oh, what heights we'll hit,

On with the show, this is it.

The old *Bugs Bunny* theme song (written by Mack David and Jerry Livingston) strikes a chord when your presentation is all finished and all that remains is to present it to your audience.

This chapter shows you how to finish the final preparations by printing copies of your slides, notes, and handouts. Then the chapter delves into the task of setting up a projector and actually presenting your show.

This is it!

The Quick Way to Print

The Print command. The Printmeister. Big presentation comin' up. Printin' some slides. The Printorama. The Mentor of de Printor. Captain Toner of the Good Ship Laseroo.

Don't worry — when you print a PowerPoint presentation, no one's waiting to ambush you with annoying one-liners like that guy who used to be on *Saturday Night Live*. All that awaits you is a handful of boring dialog boxes with boring check boxes. Point-point, click-click, print-print.

The fastest way to print your presentation is to click the Quick Print button, which appears on the Quick Access Toolbar (QAT). This button does not appear on the QAT by default, though. To add it, click the down arrow to the right of the QAT and click the Quick Print button.

Clicking the Quick Print button prints your presentation without further ado, using the current printer settings, which I explain in the remaining sections of this chapter. Usually, this action results in printing a single copy of all the slides in your presentation. But if you've altered the settings on the Print screen in Backstage view during the current PowerPoint session, clicking the Print button uses the altered settings automatically.

You can find more information about printing from Backstage view in the next section.

Printing from Backstage View

For precise control over how you want your presentation to be printed, you have to switch to Backstage view and conjure up the Print screen, as shown in Figure 7-1. To summon this screen, choose Office ⇨ Print or press Ctrl+P.

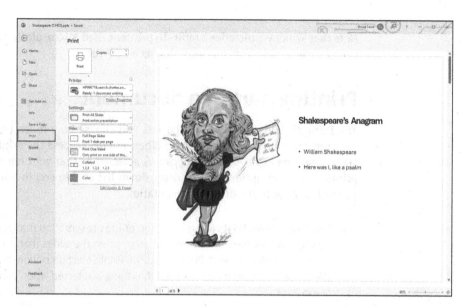

FIGURE 7-1: Behold the Print screen.

After you call up the Print screen, click the big Print button (shown in the margin) or press Enter to print all the slides in your presentation. Fiddle around with the settings to print a select group of slides; more than one copy; or handouts, speaker notes, or an outline. The following sections show you the treasures that lie hidden in this screen.

TIP

Printing can be es-el-oh-double-ewe, so don't panic if your presentation doesn't start printing right away. PowerPoint printouts tend to demand a great deal from the printer, so sometimes the printer has to work for a while before it can produce a finished page. Be patient. The Great and Powerful Wizard of Printing has every intention of granting your request.

Printing more than one copy

The Copies field lets you print more than one copy of your presentation. Click one of the arrows next to this field to increase or decrease the number of copies, or type directly in the field to set the number of copies.

Changing printers

If you're lucky enough to have two or more printers at your disposal, you can use the Printer list to pick the printer you want to use. Each printer must first be successfully installed in Windows — a topic that's beyond the reach of this humble book. However, you can find plenty of information about installing printers in the appropriate version of *Windows For Dummies* (Wiley).

Note that Windows includes a built-in printer called Microsoft Print to PDF, which you can use to save your presentation as a PDF file.

Printing part of a document

The Print All Slides drop-down list lets you choose how much (or what part) of your presentation you want to print. When you first access the Print page in Backstage view, the Print All Slides option is selected so that your entire presentation prints. The other options in this drop-down list enable you to tell PowerPoint to print distinct portions of your presentation:

» **Print Selection:** Prints just the portion of the presentation that you selected before invoking the Print command. First, select the slides that you want to print. Then choose File ⇨ Print, select the Print Selection option, and click OK. (Note that this option is grayed-out if nothing is selected when you choose File ⇨ Print.)

» **Print Current Slide:** Prints just the current slide. Before you choose File ⇨ Print, you should move to the slide that you want to print. Then select this option in the Print dialog box and click OK. This option is handy when you make a change to one slide and don't want to reprint the entire presentation.

» **Custom Range:** Lets you type specific slide numbers you want to print.

» **Custom Shows:** If you set up one or more custom slide shows, you can use this option to select the show that you want to print (see "Using Custom Shows," later in this chapter).

But wait, there's more! Beneath the Print All Slides drop-down list are several other controls:

» **Full Page Slides:** Lets you indicate how many slides per page you want to print. You can also use this same drop-down list to print notes pages or the outline rather than slides.

» **Collated:** This option tells PowerPoint to print each copy of your presentation one at a time. In other words, if your presentation consists of ten slides and you select three copies and select the Collate check box, PowerPoint first prints all ten slides of the first copy of the presentation, then all ten slides of the second copy, and then all ten slides of the third copy. If you don't select the Collate check box, PowerPoint prints three copies of the first slide, followed by three copies of the second slide, followed by three copies of the third slide, and so on.

» **Color:** This drop-down list lets you choose whether to print your slides in color, in black and white, or with shades of gray.

Using Print Preview

The Print screen of Backstage view includes a Print Preview feature that lets you see how your pages will appear before you actually print them.

From the Print screen, you can zoom in to examine the preview more closely by clicking anywhere in the preview area. You can also scroll through the pages by using the scroll bar or the navigation arrows beneath the preview area.

Setting Up a Slide Show

The PowerPoint printing features are useful, but PowerPoint is really designed to create slides that are presented directly on a screen rather than printed out. The screen can be your computer's own monitor, a projector, or an external monitor, such as a giant-screen TV. This section and the sections that follow show you how to set up and show a presentation.

Set Up Slide Show

In most cases, the default settings for showing a presentation are adequate. However, in some cases, you may need to change the default settings. To do so, open the presentation that you want to set up, select the Slide Show tab on the Ribbon, and click the Set Up Slide Show button (shown in the margin), found in the Set Up group. This action summons the Set Up Show dialog box, as shown in Figure 7-2. In this dialog box, you can fiddle with the various options that are available for presenting slide shows.

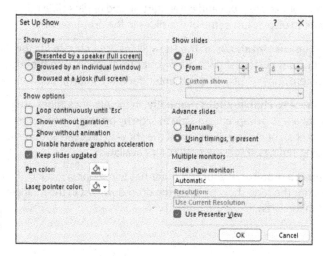

FIGURE 7-2:
The Set Up Show dialog box.

With the options in the Set Up Show dialog box, you can do the following:

- **Configure the presentation.** You can configure the presentation for one of three basic slide show types: Presented by a Speaker (Full Screen), Browsed by an Individual (Window), or Browsed at a Kiosk (Full Screen).

- **Loop through slides.** Select the Loop Continuously until 'Esc' check box if you want the show to run indefinitely. If you enable this setting, the show jumps back to the first slide after the last slide is shown, and the show continues to repeat until you press Esc.

- **Simplify the presentation.** Deselect the Show without Narration and Show without Animation options if you want to simplify the presentation by not playing narrations that you've recorded or animations that you've created.

- **Disable hardware graphics acceleration.** Select this option only if your computer is having trouble properly displaying the graphics, media, or animations in your presentation.

- **Keep slides updated.** If you select this option, any changes made by someone else to any of the slides will be reflected immediately in your presentation. Uncheck this box to ensure that changes made by other people don't show up while you're in the middle of presenting.

- **Select pen and laser pointer color.** Select the color to use for the pen or laser pointer. (See the sections "Scribbling on your slides" and "Using the Laser Pointer feature," later in this chapter, for more information about using the pen and the laser pointer.)

- **Select slides.** In the Show Slides area, select All to include all slides in the slide show or choose From and enter starting and ending slide numbers if you want to display just some of the slides in the presentation.

- **Set up custom shows.** In the Show Slides area, choose Custom Show if you've set up any custom shows within your presentation. (See the section "Using Custom Shows," later in this chapter, for more information.)

- **Choose to change slides manually.** In the Advance Slides area, choose Manually to advance from slide to slide by pressing Enter, pressing the spacebar, or clicking. If you want the show to proceed automatically, select the Using Timings, If Present option if it's available.

- **Select a monitor.** If your computer has two monitors, select the monitor to use for the slide show by using the drop-down list in the Multiple Monitors area.

Starting a Slide Show

When you want to run a slide show in a one-on-one or small group setting without a projector, beginning the show is just a click away. To start a slide show immediately, click the Slide Show button (shown in the margin), which is located, along with the other View buttons, in the lower-right corner of the screen. PowerPoint fills the entire screen with the first slide of the slide show. To advance to the next slide, click the mouse button or press Enter, the down arrow, Page Down, or the spacebar.

TIP

If you're in a hurry and you have a good memory for keyboard shortcuts, just press F5.

You can also start a slide show by selecting the Slide Show tab on the Ribbon and clicking one of the following buttons:

From Beginning

>> **From Beginning:** Starts the slide show from the first slide. Clicking this button is the same as clicking the Slide Show button in the lower-right corner of the screen or pressing F5.

From Current Slide

>> **From Current Slide:** Starts the slide show from the currently selected slide.

Working in Presenter View

If you have a projector or second monitor connected to your computer, PowerPoint will show the presentation's slides on the projector or second monitor and switch the primary monitor to Presenter view. Figure 7-3 shows Presenter view in action.

Here are the various features that are available in Presenter view:

>> **Current slide:** The current slide is displayed in the center-left portion of the screen.

>> **Next slide or animation:** The next slide or animation to be displayed is shown at the upper right of the screen.

>> **Notes:** Any notes you've created for the current slide are shown at the lower right of the screen.

>> **Timer:** A timer appears above the current slide to help you keep track of how long your presentation has dragged on.

FIGURE 7-3:
Presenter view.

» **Tools:** Beneath the current slide are icons representing various tools that let you draw on your slides, magnify the slide to draw the audience's attention to a particular point, hide the current slide so you can draw the audience's attention away from the screen and to you, and perform a few other interesting on-screen tricks. These tools are described in the section "Using Presentation Tools," later in this chapter.

» **Slide Navigator:** These controls let you advance forward or backward through your slide show.

SETTING UP A PROJECTOR OR TV

If you're going to present your show by connecting your laptop to a projector or large-screen TV, you need to know how to connect the TV or projector to your laptop, as well as how to set up the TV or projector, turn it on, focus it, and so on. Most of these details vary from one TV or projector to the next, so you may have to consult the manual that came with the TV or projector or bribe someone to set everything up for you. Here are a few general tips that may help:

- **Connecting the TV or projector:** Most laptops have an external video port on the back or side, and most TVs or projectors have a video input connection. Newer TVs, projectors, and laptops use HDMI or USB-C connectors, but older devices may use other types of connectors, such as DVI or VGA. Note that depending on the type of connectors on your laptop and projector, you may need a special adapter to match the laptop's connector to the projector's connector. At any rate, make sure you have the correct cable and adapter to connect the TV or projector to your laptop.

- **Activating the external video port:** On some laptops, you need to activate the external video port to use a projector. Some laptops automatically detect a projector when it's connected. If yours doesn't, you have to press a key or combination of keys to activate the external port.

- **Selecting the TV or projector video input:** Most TVs and projectors can accept input from more than one source. The TV or projector should have some buttons or perhaps a menu setting that lets you select the input used to display the correct input source. If everything seems connected properly but you still don't get a picture, make sure that the correct input source is selected.

- **Using sound:** If your presentation has sound, you need to connect your computer's sound outputs to a set of amplified speakers or, if you're showing the presentation in a large auditorium, a public address (PA) system. The correct cable to connect to a PA system depends on the PA system, but a cable with a mini stereo plug on one end and a ¼-inch plug on the other will probably do the trick. Or you may be able to connect via Bluetooth instead. Note that if you're using an HDMI connection, the sound output will be supplied to the projector or TV via the HDMI output.

Controlling Your Presentation with the Keyboard and Mouse

During an on-screen slide show, you can use the keyboard and mouse to control your presentation. Tables 7-1 and 7-2 list the keys and clicks that you can use.

TABLE 7-1   Keyboard Tricks for Your Slide Show

To Do This	Press Any of These Keys
Display the next slide	Enter, spacebar, Page Down, or N
Display the preceding slide	Backspace, Page Up, or P
Display the first slide	1+Enter
Display a specific slide	Slide number+Enter
Toggle the screen black	B or . (period)
Toggle the screen white	W or , (comma)

(continued)

TABLE 7-1 *(continued)*

To Do This	Press Any of These Keys
Show or hide the pointer	A or = (equal sign)
Erase screen doodles	E
Stop or restart an automatic show	S or + (plus sign)
Display the next slide even if hidden	H
Display a specific hidden slide	Slide number of hidden slide+Enter
Change the pen to an arrow	Ctrl+A
Change an arrow to a pen	Ctrl+P
End the slide show	Esc, Ctrl+Break (the Break key doubles as the Pause key), or - (hyphen)

TABLE 7-2 **Mouse Tricks for Your Slide Show**

To Do This	Do This
Display the next slide	Click.
Move through slides	Roll the wheel on your mouse (if your mouse has a wheel).
Call up a menu of actions	Right-click.
Display the first slide	Hold down both mouse buttons for 2 seconds.
Use the laser pointer	Hold down the Ctrl key and then hold the left mouse button and move the mouse.
Doodle	Press Ctrl+P to change the mouse arrow to a pen and then draw on-screen like an NFL color commentator.

TIP

If the cursor is hidden, you can summon it by jiggling the mouse. Then, when the cursor is visible, a faint menu appears in the lower-left corner of the slide. You can use this menu to activate various slide show features.

Using Presentation Tools

Presentation view has several icons that are useful during your presentation, as described in the following sections.

Using the Laser Pointer feature

The Laser Pointer feature displays a bright red dot on the screen, which you can move around by moving the mouse. It's not quite as good as using a real laser pointer, but if you don't happen to have one, the PowerPoint laser pointer will do. Figure 7-4 shows the laser pointer in action. If you look closely at this figure, you can see that the laser pointer is pointing at the number 46 in the first bullet item.

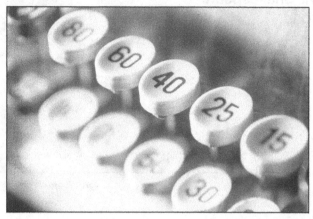

FIGURE 7-4:
Using the laser pointer.

Ingram Publishing/Alamy Stock Photo

You can activate the laser pointer in three ways:

- >> In Presenter view, click or tap the Pen and Laser Pointer button (shown in the margin) and then choose Laser Pointer. Then use your mouse to move the laser pointer around on the slide.

- >> Hold down the Ctrl key, and then click and hold the left mouse button and move the mouse. The laser pointer will appear on the screen and move as you move the mouse.

- >> If you're using a tablet or a computer with a touchscreen monitor, just press down firmly on the slide; the laser pointer will appear. You can then drag it around with your finger. Lift your finger off the screen to hide the pointer.

When you release the left mouse button, the laser pointer disappears.

Scribbling on your slides

You can doodle on your slides to draw your audience's attention to a particular part of the slide. For example, Figure 7-5 shows a slide on which I've drawn a circle around the three occurrences of the number 46 in the slide.

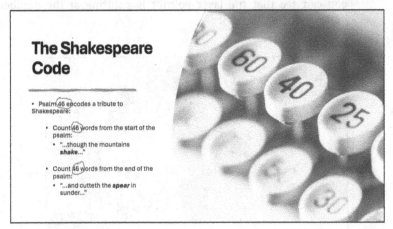

FIGURE 7-5:
Using
the Pen tool.

Ingram Publishing/Alamy Stock Photo

 To use the Pen tool to draw on a slide, click the Pen and Laser Pointer button (shown in the margin) in Presenter view and select the Pen tool. Then use your mouse to draw on the slide, holding down the left button and dragging the mouse around as best you can to leave your mark.

Here are some additional thoughts worth mentioning:

» Instead of a solid pen, you can also use a transparent highlighter. Just choose the Highlighter tool instead of the Pen tool, and then use the mouse to mark on the slide. The Highlighter tool works best on slides that have a light background.

» You can change the color of the marks left by the Pen tool. Click the Pen and Laser Pointer button, and then choose Ink Color and select the color you'd like to use.

» When you finish your presentation, you're given the option to keep your doodles as annotations in your presentation. Then you won't have to redraw the doodles next time.

» On a touchscreen device, you'll find additional buttons in the bottom-left corner of the presentation to call up the Laser Pointer tool, Pen tool, Highlighter tool, and so on.

Rehearsing Your Slide Timings

You can use the PowerPoint Rehearsal feature to rehearse your presentation. The Rehearsal feature lets you know how long your presentation takes, and it can even set slide timings so that slides automatically advance based on the timings you set during the rehearsal.

Rehearse Timings

To rehearse a slide show, click the Rehearse Timings button (shown in the margin) in the Set Up section of the Slide Show tab on the Ribbon. This starts the slide show with a special Recording dialog box visible, as shown in Figure 7-6.

FIGURE 7-6: The rehearsal timer.

Now rehearse your presentation. Click or use keyboard shortcuts to advance slides. As you rehearse, the Rehearse dialog box keeps track of how long you display each slide and the total length of your presentation.

When you end the presentation, PowerPoint displays a dialog box that gives you the option of applying or ignoring the timings recorded during the rehearsal to the slides in the presentation. If you were satisfied with the slide timings during the rehearsal, click Yes.

If you mess up during a rehearsal, click the Repeat button. Clicking this button restarts the rehearsal from the beginning.

You can also rehearse your presentation using a feature called the Presenter Coach. This feature uses speech recognition and artificial intelligence (AI) to evaluate your performance. To use it, you must have a microphone connected to your computer.

Rehearse with Coach

Click the Rehearse with Coach button (shown in the margin). Then rehearse your presentation. When you finish, the coach displays a summary of its findings, along with recommendations for how you may be able to improve your presentation, as shown in Figure 7-7. Keep in mind that the coach is just a computer, so take its recommendations with a grain of salt. It's not smart enough to tell you if your jokes are funny, but it may let you know that you rambled a bit too much or that you just read your slides verbatim.

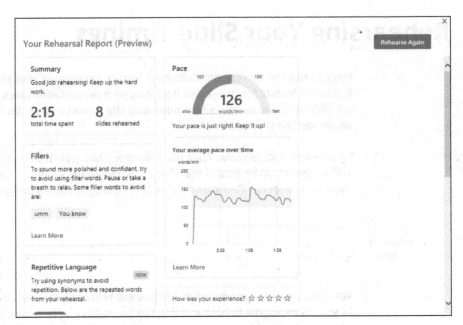

FIGURE 7-7:
The Presentation Coach critiques your performance.

Using Custom Shows

The Custom Shows feature in PowerPoint lets you create several similar slide shows stored in a single presentation file. For example, suppose you're asked to give presentations about company benefits to management and nonmanagement staff. You can create a presentation containing slides for all the company benefits and then create a custom show containing only those slides describing benefits that are available to nonmanagement staff. (This custom slide show can leave out slides such as "Executive Washrooms," "Golf Days," and "Boondoggles.") You may then show the complete presentation to management but show the custom show to nonmanagement staff.

A presentation can contain as many custom shows as you want. Each custom show is simply a subset of the complete presentation — comprised of selected slides from the complete presentation.

Creating a custom show

To create a custom show, follow these steps:

Custom Slide Show

1. **On the Slide Show tab on the Ribbon, click the Custom Slide Show button (shown in the margin) in the Start Slide Show group, and then choose Custom Shows from the menu that appears.**

   The Custom Shows dialog box appears.

2. **Click the New button.**

   The Define Custom Show dialog box appears (see Figure 7-8).

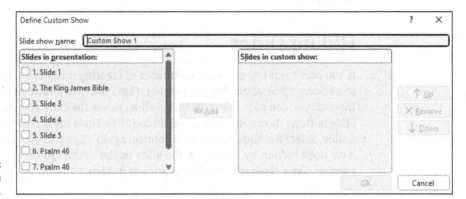

FIGURE 7-8:
Defining a custom show.

3. **Type a name for the custom show in the Slide Show Name field.**

4. **Add the slides that you want to appear in the custom slide show.**

   All the slides available in the presentation are listed in the list box on the left side of the Define Custom Show dialog box. To add a slide to the custom show, select the slide that you want to add and then click Add. The slide appears in the list box on the right side of the dialog box.

TIP

   You don't have to add slides to the custom show in the same order that the slides appear in the original presentation. Slides for a custom show can appear in any order you want. You can also include a slide from the original presentation more than once in a custom show.

   To remove a slide that you've added by mistake, deselect the slide that you want to remove in the list box on the right side of the Define Custom Show dialog box, and then click Remove.

   You can use the up and down arrows near the right edge of the Define Custom Show dialog box to change the order of the slides in the custom show.

5. **Click OK.**

   You return to the Custom Shows dialog box.

6. **Click Close to dismiss the Custom Shows dialog box.**

Showing a custom show

To show a custom show, first open the presentation that contains the custom show. Then select the Slide Show tab on the Ribbon, click the Custom Slide Show button, and choose Custom Shows from the menu that appears. This displays the Custom Shows dialog box, which lists any custom shows in the presentation. You can then select the custom show you want and start the show by clicking the Show button.

Hiding slides

Hide Slide

If you don't want to go to all the trouble of creating a custom show, but you want to exclude a few slides from a presentation, you don't have to delete the slides. Instead, you can hide them. To hide a slide, select the slide and then click the Hide Slide button (shown in the margin) on the Slide Show tab on the Ribbon. To unhide a slide, select the slide and click the button again. (You can determine which slides have been hidden by looking at the slide in the Slides tab on the left. If the slide number has a slash through it, the slide is hidden.)

Creating with Copilot

IN THIS PART . . .

Gain experience with Copilot, the Microsoft 365 assistant powered by artificial intelligence (AI).

Use the free version of Copilot.

Create entire presentations based on a few descriptive sentences.

Create high-quality pictures to perfectly suit your slides.

Use Copilot to write your narration.

Improve your experience with Copilot by perfecting your prompts.

IN THIS CHAPTER

» Understanding what Copilot is and what it can do

» Choosing between the free and paid versions of Copilot

» Creating PowerPoint slides using the free version of Copilot

Chapter **8**

Getting Started with Copilot

The newest and most interesting new feature of PowerPoint is Copilot, Microsoft's version of chat-based artificial intelligence (AI) that has taken the computing world by storm over the past few years. Copilot, which was introduced in 2023, is Microsoft's response to the sudden popularity of ChatGPT and other similar AI platforms. Copilot is fully integrated into the core Microsoft 365 applications, including Word, Excel, Outlook, Teams, and — most important for this book — PowerPoint.

As you'll see in this chapter and the subsequent chapters in this part, Copilot can help you craft your PowerPoint presentations. It can help you with research, create draft versions of your slides, create visuals, and even help you craft your speaker notes.

So, let's get into Copilot! In this chapter, I explain what Copilot is, how to get it, and how to use the free version to help you create PowerPoint presentations.

What Is Microsoft Copilot?

You've probably heard of the generative AI tool known as ChatGPT. It's a chatbot that generates uncannily human responses to questions. You can ask ChatGPT almost anything, and it will generate a surprisingly well-written answer. You can then ask it to refine its answer. For example, you can ask for more — or less — detail or a different style or tone. You can ask it to dive deeper into a certain point or to de-emphasize a part of its response.

ChatGPT was introduced in late 2022 and within two months had more than 100 million users. It remains the fastest-growing software product of all time. If you haven't seen it, you can browse to https://chatgpt.com to get a taste of how it works.

For example, I posed the following question to ChatGPT (knowing it to be a trick question): "Who won the World Cup in 1980?" Here is ChatGPT's reply:

> There was no FIFA World Cup in 1980. The FIFA World Cup is held every four years, and the tournaments closest to 1980 were:
>
> **1978:** The World Cup was held in Argentina, and **Argentina** won, defeating the Netherlands 3-1 after extra time in the final.
>
> **1982:** The World Cup was held in Spain, and **Italy** won, defeating West Germany 3-1 in the final.
>
> However, there was the **1980 Cricket World Cup,** which was the first-ever Cricket World Cup. It was held in **England,** and **West Indies** won the tournament, defeating Australia in the final.
>
> Would you like more details on either of these events?

Notice that ChatGPT assumed that I meant soccer (well, here in the United States anyway — football everywhere else), and it didn't give up just because there was no World Cup in 1980. It inferred that I may want to know about the 1978 or 1982 World Cup tournaments and gave me those results. It also considered whether I meant a different sport — cricket — which also has a World Cup and did have one in 1980. Finally, it asked if I wanted additional details about any of those events.

ChatGPT's English is pretty darn good — although it did misuse the word *either* in its final question. *Either* always implies a choice between two and only two alternatives. *Any of these events* would've been better. That's pretty nitpicky, though!

ChatGPT relies on a technology called *generative AI*, which means that it uses AI to generate written language. The specific generative AI technology it uses is called a *generative pre-trained transformer*, from which it gets the *GPT* part of its name. In essence, ChatGPT uses a GPT engine to chat with humans.

Microsoft Copilot also uses GPT — in fact, it uses the same GPT technology that ChatGPT uses. I posed the exact same question about the 1980 World Cup to Copilot and got nearly the same answer:

> There was no FIFA World Cup held in 1980. The FIFA World Cup is held every four years, and the tournaments around that time were in 1978 and 1982. The 1978 World Cup was won by Argentina, and the 1982 World Cup was won by Italy.

This answer was followed by links I could click to find out more about the 1978 or 1982 World Cups or to find out about other major sporting events that happened in 1980.

But Copilot went a step beyond what ChatGPT did: It provided two footnotes as a part of its response. I could click either of those footnotes to go to websites that confirmed Copilot's answer. In other words, Copilot provided evidence to back up its claims. These footnotes are an incredibly helpful feature of Copilot, because generative AI technology is known to occasionally create unreliable answers.

REMEMBER

There is a very close relationship between ChatGPT and Copilot. Both share the same GPT technologies, which are developed by an independent research organization known as OpenAI. Not coincidentally, Microsoft owns 49 percent of OpenAI. Although ChatGPT and Copilot are not identical, they have many similarities.

IS COPILOT JUST A NEW VERSION OF CLIPPY?

The idea of an intelligent digital assistant to help people use Microsoft Office applications dates back to the late 1990s, when Bill Clinton was president and Al Gore was still busy inventing the internet. In 1997, Microsoft introduced a feature called the *Office Assistant*. Colloquially known as "Clippy," the Office Assistant was an animated character (specifically, a paper clip) that would sometimes pop up within an Office application to offer help. For example, if you tried to create a mail merge in Word, Clippy would appear and say something like, "It looks like you're trying to create a mail merge. Would you like me to help?"

(continued)

(continued)

The Office Assistant was a bit of a disaster for Microsoft. Clippy proved to be more annoying than helpful. It lasted just a few years before being sent to the oblivion of deprecated software.

In 2015, Microsoft tried again, this time by stealing a character from its wildly popular video game series *Halo*, an AI named *Cortana*. Unlike Clippy, Cortana actually talked. If you ever purchased a computer with Windows 10, you've probably met Cortana. The first time you turned on a Windows 10 computer, Cortana came to life, saying, "Hi, there! I'm Cortana, and I'm here to help. A little sign-in here, a touch of Wi-Fi there, and we'll have your PC ready for all you plan to do."

Cortana used a combination of computer-generated speech and prerecorded responses. Fun fact: The prerecorded responses were voiced by the actress Jen Taylor, who had voiced the character in the games and in one season of the Paramount+ streaming series based on the games. But Cortana never really caught on. It's now hanging out with Clippy in the junkyard of obsolete software.

It isn't surprising that people may wonder whether Copilot is just another half-hearted attempt to capitalize on the hype of AI by tricking you into thinking Microsoft 365 is smarter than it actually is. Is Copilot genuinely helpful? Only time will tell, but I think that Copilot is here to stay.

Choosing Between the Free and Paid Versions of Copilot

There are actually three distinct versions of Copilot: a free version, which anyone can use, and two paid versions, which require a monthly subscription. The free version has fewer features than the paid versions and is not integrated with Microsoft 365 programs. And, it has a few limitations when compared with the paid versions. In particular, the free version has the following limitations:

» You can access it only from a browser or from the Copilot app in Windows 11.

» It isn't integrated with Microsoft 365 apps such as Outlook, Word, Excel, and PowerPoint.

» You're limited to just 300 separate chats per day.

- Each chat session is limited to just 30 separate interactions.
- Response time during peak hours may be slower.

Unfortunately, the paid versions of Copilot aren't cheap. The Copilot Pro version adds integration with certain Microsoft 365 apps, including Outlook, Word, Excel, OneNote, and PowerPoint. For $30 per month, you can upgrade to Copilot for Microsoft 365, which adds integration with Teams and a host of other features.

TIP I recommend starting out with the free version to get a taste of what Copilot can do. You may discover that the free version meets your needs. Or you may decide to purchase a subscription so you can use Copilot directly in PowerPoint and other Microsoft 365 applications.

The rest of this chapter is devoted to showing you how to use the free version of Copilot to help you craft a PowerPoint presentation. In Chapter 9, I explain how to use Copilot in PowerPoint using either of the subscription versions.

Using the Free Version of Copilot

You can easily use the free version of Copilot to help you create a PowerPoint presentation. Here are some ideas for how Copilot can help you work in PowerPoint:

- **Researching:** You can use Copilot to help you research your topic. If you ask the right questions, Copilot can help you gather all the information you need for your presentation, regardless of the topic.
- **Outlining:** Copilot can help you craft an outline for your presentation. Just ask it to help you set up a PowerPoint presentation about any topic, and it will suggest which slides the presentation should include.
- **Fleshing out individual slides:** Ask Copilot to help you flesh out a single slide on a particular topic. It can suggest the slide title and several bullet points to include on the slide.
- **Creating illustrations:** You can ask Copilot to create images that you can incorporate into your presentation. Just describe what you'd like the image to contain, and Copilot will try to generate the image for you.
- **Creating speaker notes:** You can ask Copilot to create a draft of your speaker notes, either in outline form or as a full narrative that you can simply read aloud as you make your presentation.

Accessing the Free Version of Copilot

You can access the free version of Copilot in three different ways, as I describe in the following sections.

Using the Copilot app

The Copilot app, shown in Figure 8-1, is a self-contained app that is included as part of Windows 11. To launch it, click the Start button and search for Copilot. If you use this app frequently, you may want to pin it to the Start menu or to the taskbar.

FIGURE 8-1: The Copilot app in Windows 11.

To get started with the Copilot app, type your first message into the text box at the bottom of the screen. For example, type **Please create a PowerPoint slide that explains the rules of pickleball** and press the Enter key. Copilot will think for a moment and then display its response, as shown in Figure 8-2.

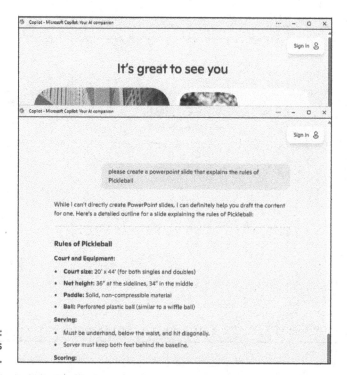

FIGURE 8-2: Copilot responds to a prompt.

TECHNICAL STUFF

In the lingo of AI, the text that you send to a generative AI tool such as Copilot is called the *prompt*, because it's how you prompt the AI to generate a response. When dealing with computers, people typically use the term *prompt* to mean a question that the computer is asking you, not a question that you're asking the computer.

REMEMBER

Whenever you see the word *prompt* in the context of Copilot, it's a question that you're formulating for the computer to respond to with an AI-generated answer.

Using Copilot in Bing

A second way to use Copilot is to browse to Bing in your web browser. Just point your browser to www.bing.com to summon the Bing home page. At the top, you'll see the Copilot icon (shown in the margin). Click it to summon the Copilot page, as shown in Figure 8-3.

Just as with the Copilot app, you can initiate a conversation with Copilot in Bing by typing a prompt in the Message Copilot box at the bottom of the screen. Figure 8-4 shows how Copilot responds to the prompt "Please create a PowerPoint slide that explains the rules of pickleball."

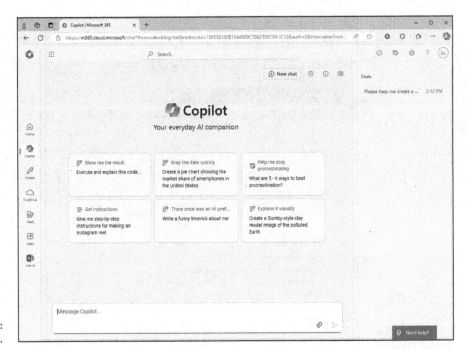

FIGURE 8-3:
Copilot in Bing.

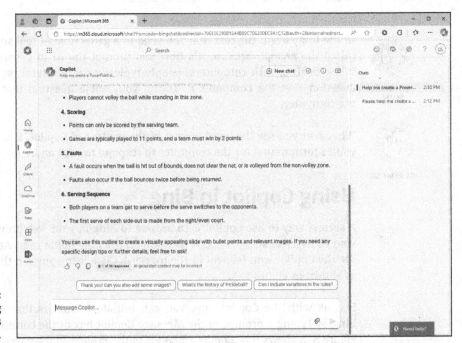

FIGURE 8-4:
Copilot in Bing responds to a prompt.

116 PART 2 Creating with Copilot

Using the Edge sidebar

The third way to use the free version of Copilot is to open the sidebar in Edge, the web browser that is included with Microsoft Windows. You can get there by clicking the Copilot icon (shown in the margin) at the upper right of the Edge window. If you don't see this icon, open the Edge settings page (click the three-dots at the upper right of the browser window and choose Settings), search for "Copilot," and ensure that the Edge sidebar is enabled.

Like the Copilot app and Copilot in Bing, the Edge sidebar includes a text box at the bottom in which you can type your request. Figure 8-5 shows the answer to the same prompt ("Please create a PowerPoint slide that explains the rules of pickleball"), which you can see in the sidebar.

FIGURE 8-5: A response shown in the Edge sidebar.

Refining Copilot's Response

Sometimes the response you get from Copilot isn't exactly what you want. In that case, you can ask Copilot to refine its response. Copilot keeps track of your conversation as you continue to send it additional prompts, and its responses will always be in the context of the entire conversation. So, you don't have to repeat the original prompt every time.

For example, suppose you find that its response to "Please create a PowerPoint slide that explains the rules of pickleball" is too detailed. Maybe it gave you six bullet points, each with a number of subpoints, and that's just too much information for a single slide.

You could ask Copilot to shorten its response by prompting it like this: "Please be a little less detailed, and limit the slide to no more than four bullet points." Here's the response I got from this prompt:

> Got it! Here's a more concise version for your pickleball rules slide:
>
> Title: Rules of Pickleball
>
> Slide Content:
>
> 1. **Serve:** Serve diagonally, underhand, and below the waist.
> 2. **Double Bounce Rule:** Ball must bounce once on each side before volleys.
> 3. **Non-Volley Zone (Kitchen):** No volleys allowed in the non-volley zone.
> 4. **Scoring:** Only the serving team can score; games are played to 11 points, win by 2.

Notice that Copilot understood the new prompt in the context of the entire conversation and, thus, provided a shorter answer. This shorter version provides the same information but in a form that's more appropriate for a single slide.

Getting Copilot's Content into PowerPoint

When you've used Copilot to create some content for you, getting that content into PowerPoint is simple: Just copy and paste. You can select the text you want to copy and then press Ctrl+C, or you can click the handy Copy button (shown in the margin) that appears beneath the response. You can then switch to PowerPoint, create a new slide, and paste the Copilot text into the slide. Figure 8-6 shows a PowerPoint slide created from Copilot's suggestion for a slide that explains the rules of pickleball.

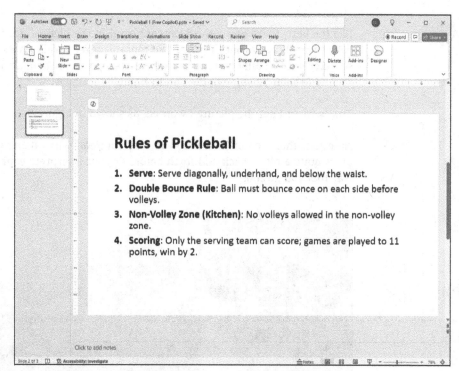

FIGURE 8-6:
A PowerPoint slide created from a Copilot response.

Creating a Picture with Copilot

Besides creating text, Copilot is adept at creating images that you can use in your presentations. All you have to do is ask!

For example, I'll ask Copilot to create a picture to accompany the slide that explains the rules of pickleball. I think the picture should be lighthearted, and nothing is more lighthearted than the Queen's favorite pooches, corgis. So I put the following prompt to Copilot: "Create an image of two cute corgis playing pickleball."

In its first attempt, the corgis were playing pickleball but not on an outdoor court. Instead, they were in what looked like someone's living room. So, I added the clarification, "Please make sure they are playing on a pickleball court outdoors."

The result was closer, but still not right. Each of the corgis had a racket, but the rackets were on the ground. No balls were visible, and in the picture that I actually like the best, there was a third random corgi in the picture. So, I clarified again: "That's really close, but the one I like contains three corgis. Can you redo that one so that there are only two corgis in the picture, both of them actually holding the rackets in their paws, with the ball in flight?"

That's when I got the picture I wanted, as shown in Figure 8-7.

Note that this type of interaction is very common when using Copilot. It often takes quite a bit of back and forth before Copilot interprets your prompts in the way that you intend.

FIGURE 8-7: Using Copilot to create an image.

When I got the image I wanted, I downloaded it by clicking the Download button (shown in the margin) and then pasted the image into the slide in PowerPoint. PowerPoint immediately summoned the Designer to help me incorporate the image into the slide, offering several alternatives to choose from. Figure 8-8 shows the result I ended up using.

TIP

The paid versions of Copilot eliminate all the copying and pasting by allowing you to access Copilot directly from within PowerPoint. (Chapter 9 walks you through that process.)

FIGURE 8-8:
A finished slide explaining the rules of pickleball, all generated by Copilot.

> **IN THIS CHAPTER**
> » Creating a new presentation using a Copilot prompt
> » Using Copilot to create detailed speaker notes
> » Using Copilot to tweak your presentation

Chapter 9

Using Copilot in PowerPoint

In Chapter 8, I show you how the free version of Microsoft Copilot can help you create PowerPoint presentations. Using the free version involves a lot of cutting and pasting between Copilot and PowerPoint. Wouldn't it be better if you could just use Copilot inside of PowerPoint?

The good news is that you can. And when you do, you'll find that Copilot actually knows that it lives inside of PowerPoint, understands what PowerPoint can do, and knows how to do it. In other words, when you use Copilot inside of PowerPoint, you can actually ask it to create a new presentation, create a slide, or even generate and insert a picture onto a slide.

There are two types of paid subscriptions for Copilot. The least expensive, Copilot Pro, costs $20 per month (as of this writing). The more expensive option, Copilot for Microsoft 365, costs $30 per month (as of this writing) and offers more features. Both versions work within Outlook, Word, Excel, and PowerPoint. So, if the only place you want to use Copilot is in those four programs, Copilot Pro is the right subscription for you. If you want to use Copilot in Microsoft Teams or need the more advanced features of Copilot, Copilot for Microsoft 365 may be the better choice.

You don't have to use any of Copilot's proposed prompts. Instead, you can start from scratch by composing a fresh prompt in the text box.

In this chapter, I show you how to use Copilot directly from within PowerPoint. I cover everything from how to create an entire presentation from just a brief description to how to finish off your speaker notes.

REMEMBER

You need a subscription to either Copilot Pro or Microsoft 365 Copilot to use these features.

Creating a Presentation with Copilot

After you've activated a paid Copilot subscription, you'll see a Copilot icon (shown in the margin) appear at the right side of the Home tab on the Ribbon. You can click this icon to summon a Copilot sidebar that lets you enter prompts to be processed by Copilot. For more information about the Copilot sidebar, see the section "Using the Copilot Sidebar" later in this chapter.

For now, we'll forgo the Copilot sidebar and use an easier method to get started with Copilot in PowerPoint. Start by choosing File ⇨ New to create a new presentation. You can select a template if you want, but I'll just create a blank presentation without a template so that I can focus on creating content slides.

After your new presentation opens up, you'll notice a Copilot icon (shown in the margin) at the upper left of the title slide of your empty presentation. Click this icon, and then choose Create a Presentation About from the menu that appears. Copilot appears in a separate dialog box, as shown in Figure 9-1.

In the Copilot dialog box, you can type a prompt that describes your presentation in as much or as little detail as possible. The prompt will automatically start with "Create a presentation about," so you don't have to retype that part. Instead, just describe the presentation you want to create.

TIP

The more detail you include, the better Copilot will do. I recommend identifying not only the topic of your presentation but how you'll be using the presentation and who you plan on showing it to. For example, suppose you want to create a presentation that you'll present to your local school board to convince them that they should install two pickleball courts at your child's elementary school, which is named Thornton Wilder Elementary School in the fictional town of Grover's Corners, New Hampshire.

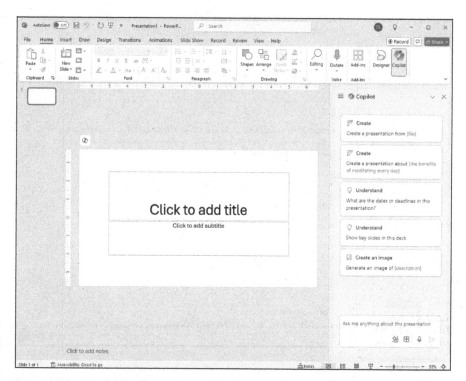

FIGURE 9-1: Creating a presentation with Copilot.

You can add the following to complete the prompt for the new presentation:

Create a presentation about a request to build two pickleball courts at our local elementary school, Thornton Wilder Elementary School. The presentation will be shown to the school board of Grover's Corners, New Hampshire. The tone should be persuasive, emphasizing the benefits that the pickleball courts will have for both the students and the community.

When you submit the prompt, Copilot thinks for a moment, and then responds with an outline for its proposed presentation, as shown in Figure 9-2.

If you want, you can refine your prompt and submit it again. When you're happy with the outline, click Generate Slides. Copilot builds a presentation using the outline, as shown in Figure 9-3.

Although it isn't evident from the figure, Copilot generated a total of 23 slides for this presentation. It selected graphics to supplement the content and chose an attractive layout for the slides. In short, Copilot provided an excellent starting point for the presentation. It's hard to estimate how much time Copilot saved on this task or how much additional time you would need to perfect the presentation. But using Copilot to create a first draft of a presentation like this is definitely a time-saver.

CHAPTER 9 **Using Copilot in PowerPoint** 125

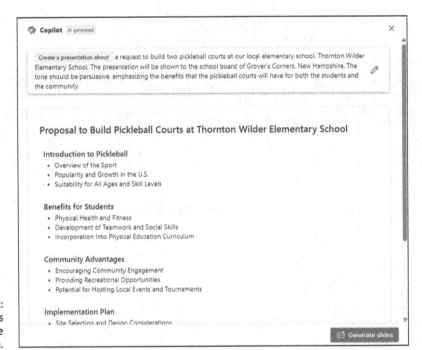

FIGURE 9-2: Copilot proposes an outline for the presentation.

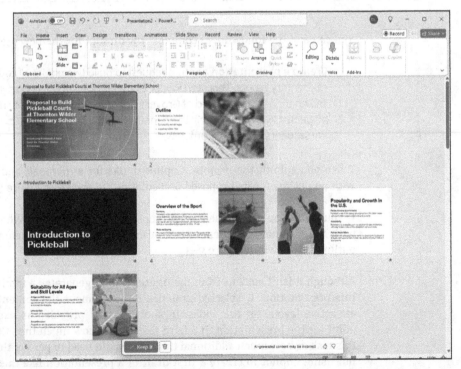

FIGURE 9-3: Copilot creates a presentation from the proposed outline.

Using the Copilot Sidebar

 You can summon the Copilot sidebar any time you want to interact with Copilot while working on a presentation. Just click the Copilot icon (shown in the margin) on the Home tab of the Ribbon to summon the sidebar, as shown in Figure 9-4.

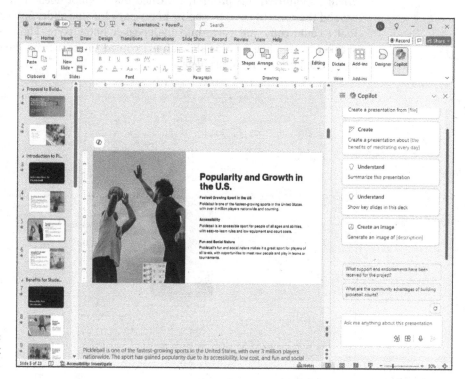

FIGURE 9-4: The Copilot sidebar.

As you can see, Copilot provides several suggested prompts to help you create new content or understand the existing content in a presentation. At the bottom of the Copilot sidebar is the prompt text box where you can compose any prompt and send it to Copilot. If you click on any of the suggested prompts, some starter text for a prompt is pasted into the text box. You can then customize the prompt however you want.

In Figure 9-4, you may notice that when Copilot generated the slides for this presentation, it also created speaker notes. In this case, those notes aren't very detailed. Suppose you'd like to expand the notes for this particular slide, possible adding an example of the way a pickleball court can help foster a sense of community among its users?

CHAPTER 9 **Using Copilot in PowerPoint** 127

Here's a prompt you could send:

> Can you expand the speaker notes for this slide, perhaps providing additional details about the popularity of pickleball in the U.S., and more details about the accessibility, fun, and social opportunities that pickleball can provide?

When I submitted this prompt, I learned that Copilot doesn't have the ability to expand the contents of the speaker notes page for this slide. But it *did* provide text that I could copy and paste into the speaker notes page. Figure 9-5 shows the speaker notes page for this slide after I copied the text from the Copilot sidebar and pasted it into the notes page.

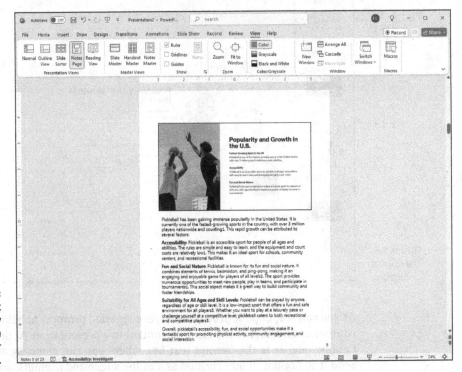

FIGURE 9-5: Using text generated by Copilot on a slide's speaker notes page.

Using the Copilot Sidebar to Change a Picture

You may have noticed that the image on the slide in Figure 9-4 showed people playing basketball, not pickleball. You can use Copilot to help you find more appropriate images for your presentations. To find a better picture for this slide, I entered the following prompt in the Copilot sidebar:

128 PART 2 **Creating with Copilot**

Can you help me find a better picture for this page? The picture you selected shows people playing basketball, not pickleball. I'd rather use a picture of people playing pickleball.

Figure 9-6 shows Copilot's response. As you can see, Copilot found four alternative photographs for me to choose from. The first one (upper right) is perfect: It shows an older gentleman playing pickleball. Unfortunately, the other three completely miss the mark. The photo at the upper right is a track and field athlete throwing the discus. The one at the lower left is an adult and a child practicing volleyball. And the one on the lower right appears to be an adult retrieving a tennis ball on a tennis court.

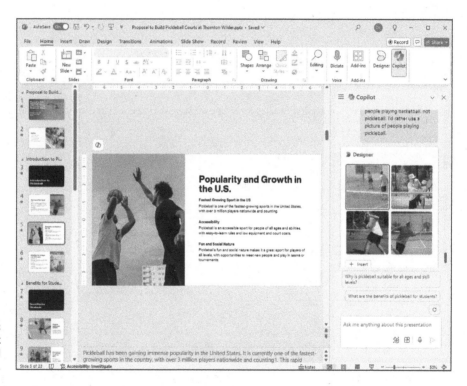

FIGURE 9-6: Using the Copilot sidebar to find alternate images.

REMEMBER

It's not uncommon for Copilot to misinterpret your prompts and return incorrect results. You can always try running the same prompt again. Or you can refine your prompt in the hopes of getting more accurate results.

In any event, when you find the photo you'd rather use, delete the original image from the slide. Then double-click the image Copilot found. Copilot will insert it onto the slide, but you may have to resize, move, or crop it to improve its appearance.

> **IN THIS CHAPTER**
> » Creating successful prompts
> » Adding clarifying details and setting expectations
> » Helping Copilot give you the best responses it can

Chapter 10
Perfecting Your Prompts

According to my copy of the Oxford English Dictionary, the word *prompt* has 23 distinct definitions. As a verb, the most common meaning is to make something happen. For example, "The rain will surely prompt the deployment of an umbrella." As an adjective, it most often means to do something in a timely manner. For example, "The festivities begin at 8:00. Please be prompt."

Some of those 23 definitions are obsolete. For example, in Shakespeare's play *The Tempest*, the main character, Prospero, says, "It goes on, I see, as my soul prompts it." The meaning here is obsolete. What the line means is "I see that everything is happening just as my soul *hoped* it would."

The one definition that my dictionary does *not* list is this: "To give an instruction to an artificial intelligence model such as Microsoft Copilot." I guess my dictionary is a tad out of date. That's probably because the 20-volume set that occupies an entire shelf in my library is the 1989 version. I'm sure, by now, the current version has been updated to include this meaning.

When it comes to using Copilot effectively, prompting is everything. There's an old saying about computers: "Garbage in, garbage out." Where Copilot is concerned, that translates to "Bad prompts lead to bad results."

In this chapter, I present some of the basic techniques you can use to improve your prompts when using Copilot. A good prompt can give you a good result. And who knows? A great prompt just might get you the result your soul hopes for.

Stating the Goal

Copilot is goal-oriented. In other words, it tries to figure out what you're looking for and does its best to deliver. So, you should be as obvious as possible about what you want Copilot to do. If you want it to create an entire presentation about astronomy, say so:

> Create a new presentation about astronomy.

If you need help researching a topic, such the history of telescopes, say so:

> Help me research the history of telescopes.

If you want it to add a photograph of an observatory, say so:

> Add a picture of an observatory.

In other words, be as clear as possible about what your desired result is.

TIP

Being Specific

If you ask Copilot to add a picture of person riding a bicycle, the pictures you get may not be what you had in mind. You can be more specific by adding the type of bicycle:

> Add a picture of a person riding a mountain bike.

Even better, add a description of where you'd like them to be riding the mountain bike:

> Add a picture of a person riding a mountain bike on a dirt road.

Better yet, add some additional detail about anything else you'd like to see in the picture:

> Add a picture of a person riding a mountain bike on a dirt road with a sunset in the background.

The more specific your prompt, the more likely you are to get you the results you want.

REMEMBER

Providing Context

Providing context can go a long way toward steering Copilot to the kind of help you're looking for. If you're asking Copilot to create an entire presentation, let it know the purpose of the presentation, such as who you'll be showing it to and what you hope to accomplish. For example:

> Create a presentation about the need for a tiny library in our neighborhood. For context, I live in a gated community and would like to design and build the library myself, at my own expense. The purpose of the presentation is to secure the HOA board's approval of my idea. To help persuade them, include a few slides about what a tiny library is, how it works, what its benefits are to the neighborhood, and so on. Make sure they understand that I will build the library with my own funds, that I will submit the design to the board for approval before I build it, and that I am committed to maintaining the library, repainting it as needed, and keeping it clean and organized.

This kind of prompt should get you well on your way toward a solid presentation.

Laying Out Your Expectations

Another way to improve your prompt is to tell Copilot what you expect the resulting presentation to look and feel like. Here are some examples of expectations you may want to set for a request to create a new presentation from scratch:

- » **The tone you'd like the presentation to have:** Do you want it to feel professional? Somber? Lighthearted? Whimsical?
- » **How detailed the presentation should be:** Should it just be a few summary slides, or should it dive deep into the weeds?
- » **Whether you want the presentation to include illustrations:** If you do, what kind of illustrations do you want? Graphs? Photographs? Cartoonish pictures? You can always work on the illustrations later, on a slide-by-slide basis.
- » **Any specific topics you want to make sure are covered.**
- » **Whether you want Copilot to add detailed speaker notes, or just short summary notes:** You can work on this detail later, one slide at a time.
- » **Whether Copilot should lean more toward absolute accuracy or precision in its results or can employ some degree of creativity.**

Here's an example of a prompt that clearly sets expectations:

> Create a presentation that persuasively argues that the Earth is, indeed, not flat. Make sure you include slides that specifically refute the arguments commonly advanced by those who believe the Earth is flat. Provide at least one slide on the history of humankind's knowledge that the Earth is actually spherical. The tone of the presentation should be lighthearted, and any illustrations included should be cartoonish and fun.

When I ran this prompt, Copilot created a presentation with 23 slides. It included a slide that showed how the Ancient Greek mathematician calculated the diameter of the Earth to a remarkable degree of accuracy, explained how Magellan circumnavigated the Earth in 1521, refuted bogus arguments about the horizon, and included some fun thought experiments about what would happen if the Earth actually were flat. Finally, it concluded with an interesting section on curiosity, skepticism, and the beauty of science. Overall, the presentation generated from this prompt met my expectations and generated an excellent starting point for a full presentation on the subject.

Keeping Copilot Honest

Copilot, like all generative artificial intelligence (AI) tools, has an unfortunate habit of making up answers when it can't find what it thinks you're looking for. In AI circles, this phenomenon is known as *hallucinating*. As a user of Copilot, it's up to you to verify the accuracy of any information you get from Copilot.

One helpful feature of Copilot is that it provides footnotes to document the factual sources of its answers. Always click on each of these footnotes to confirm the sources. If something seems fishy about the source, do some additional research.

You can also include an expectation about accuracy in your prompt. I often say something like the following in my prompts:

> If you aren't sure, please do not fabricate an answer or hallucinate. I would rather you just tell me you don't know than make up an answer.

I often find that this technique works: Copilot will simply tell me that it couldn't find the answer.

Structuring Your Prompts

Believe it or not, the order in which you provide the details of your prompts can affect the results you get. In general, I suggest you structure your prompts like this:

1. **Start with the basic goal (that is, what you're asking Copilot to do).**

   For example, start by asking Copilot to generate a presentation, research a topic, create an image, or rewrite the notes for a specific slide.

2. **Provide context by adding specifics.**

   Tell Copilot who the audience is; what the purpose of the presentation, slide, or illustration is; and how you'll use the presentation.

3. **Add your expectations for style, tone, accuracy, specific elements you want to ensure are included, and so on.**

That being said, I recommend spending some time experimenting with similar prompts but expressed in a different order. The order can sometimes make a significant difference, especially if you're asking Copilot to do something creative such as write a story. For example, you'll get two very different stories in response to the following two prompts:

First prompt: Write a short story about a monkey that escapes from a zoo and wreaks havoc at a nearby elementary school, focusing on the way the kids respond to the crazy things the monkey does.

Second prompt: Focusing on the way the kids respond to the crazy things the monkey does, write a short story about a monkey who wreaks havoc at a nearby elementary school after escaping from a zoo.

When I submitted these two prompts to Copilot, I got two versions of a similar story about a monkey named Max. The first version focused more on Max and how clever he was to find his way to the school. The second version also named the monkey Max, but it spotlighted two of the children, named Emily and Mia, as they reacted to Max's exploits.

Prompting Etiquette

Copilot doesn't have feelings. It doesn't help to use polite words such as *Please* or *Thank you*. It also doesn't help to express anger or frustration to Copilot when it makes a mistake. You can't convince Copilot to give you better results by lathering it with praise or by hurling insults at it.

On the other hand, a little politeness doesn't hurt. And it can help you focus on improving your prompts if you try to stay polite. I recommend maintaining a level tone when crafting your prompts. And if it helps you stay focused, by all means say "Please" when asking Copilot for help!

Keep Trying!

One final point, and perhaps the most important one: Keep trying! Getting the results you want from Copilot will almost always involve writing multiple iterations of your prompt. Fortunately, Copilot keeps track of your entire conversation and stays aware of what you've asked for. If the result isn't quite what you need, offer a clarification. Tell it where it missed, and give it hints on how it can improve its response.

Feel free to laugh when Copilot completely misunderstands what you're asking of it, and be amazed when it surprises you with surprisingly good answers. And, most of all, keep learning!

3 Creating Great-Looking Slides

IN THIS PART . . .

Stun your audience and receive *ooohs* and *aaahs* from the crowd by formatting text and giving your slides a spectacular appearance.

Create good-looking slides in minutes with PowerPoint themes.

Use slide transitions and animations to make even the dullest content look amazing.

Use slide masters to add something to every slide.

> **IN THIS CHAPTER**
>
> » Changing the way your text looks
>
> » Formatting your text
>
> » Making fanciful text with the WordArt feature

Chapter 11
All about Fonts and Text Formatting

A good presentation is like a fireworks show: At every new slide, the audience gasps, "*Oooh... aaah.*" The audience is so stunned by the spectacular appearance of your slides that no one really bothers to read them!

Well, not really. Substance is much more important than style. But your substance can be lost if your presentation's style is dull. So a few *ooohs* and *aaahs*, in moderation, are important.

This chapter gets you on the road toward fantastic design by showing you how to take charge of the formatting of your text. If you use PowerPoint templates as the basis for your presentations, your text formats are already controlled by the template. But to put the right amount of polish on your presentation, you need to know a few basic formatting tricks.

TIP

Many PowerPoint text-formatting capabilities work the same as in Word. If you want to format text a certain way and you know how to do it in Word, try formatting it the same way in PowerPoint. Odds are, it'll work.

Changing the Look of Your Text

The theme that's applied to your presentation determines the basic look of the presentation's text. However, you'll often want to change that look, sometimes subtly and sometimes dramatically.

You can control the most commonly used font settings by using the Font group on the Home tab on the Ribbon, as shown in Figure 11-1.

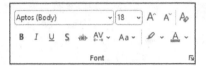

FIGURE 11-1: The Font group on the Home tab on the Ribbon.

If the Font group on the Home tab doesn't provide enough options for formatting your text, you can call up the Font dialog box (shown in Figure 11-2) for additional options. To summon this dialog box, just select the dialog launcher for the Font group. (The dialog launcher is the cursor at the lower-right corner of the group.)

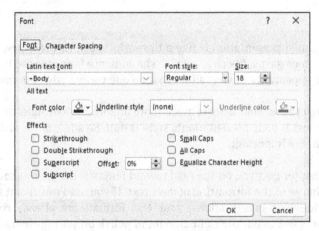

FIGURE 11-2: The Font dialog box.

Many font formatting options also have handy keyboard shortcuts. Table 11-1 lists the formatting commands along with their Ribbon buttons and equivalent keyboard shortcuts.

TABLE 11-1 Character-Formatting Commands

Button	Keyboard Shortcut	Formatting Command
Aptos (Body)	None	Font
18	None	Size
A˄	Ctrl+Shift+>	Increase font size
A˅	Ctrl+Shift+<	Decrease font size
A⌂	Ctrl+spacebar	Clear all formatting
B	Ctrl+B	Bold
I	Ctrl+I	Italic
U	Ctrl+U	Underline
S	None	Text shadow
ab	None	Strikethrough
AV	None	Character spacing
Aa	Shift+F3	Change case
✏	None	Text highlight color
A	None	Font color

It's true: PowerPoint has many keyboard shortcuts for character formatting. You don't have to know them all, though. The only ones I know and use routinely are the shortcuts for bold, italic, underline, and clear all formatting. Study these, and you'll be in good shape. You get the added bonus that these keyboard shortcuts are the same as the shortcuts that many other Microsoft 365 programs use. If you're mouse-happy and keyboard-annoyed, click away for goodness' sake. What matters most is that you can easily find and use what you need.

You can format text in two basic ways:

» **To format existing text,** highlight the text that you want to format. Then click the toolbar button or use the keyboard shortcut for the format that you want. For example, to make existing text bold, highlight it and then click the Bold button or press Ctrl+B.

» **To type new text using a fancy format,** click the toolbar button or use the keyboard shortcut for the format. Then type away. The text that you type is given the format you selected. To return to normal formatting, click the button or use the keyboard shortcut again. Or press Ctrl+spacebar.

Changing the size of characters

Whether text is difficult to read or you simply want to draw attention to it, you can make part of the text bigger than the surrounding text. The easiest way to change the size of your text is to use the Font Size drop-down list that appears next to the font name in the Font group on the Home tab on the Ribbon. Just choose among the sizes that appear in the Font Size drop-down list or click in the Font Size box and type whatever size you want to use.

You can also change the size of your text by using the Increase Font Size or Decrease Font Size buttons, or by using the Ctrl+Shift+> or Ctrl+Shift+< keyboard shortcuts. These commands increase or decrease the font size in steps, respectively.

If you type more text than will fit in a text placeholder, PowerPoint automatically makes your text smaller so the text will fit within the placeholder.

Be careful about using text that's too small to read. Just how small is too small depends on the size at which the image will be projected and the size of the room. A good rule of thumb is to stand 10 feet or so away from your monitor and make sure you can still read your slides. If you can't, you've made the fonts too small.

Choosing text fonts

If you don't like the looks of a text font, you can easily switch to a different font. To change the font for existing text, select the text. Then click the arrow next to the Font control (found in the Font group on the Home tab on the Ribbon) and choose the font that you want to use. If you're allergic to the mouse, you can get to the font list by pressing Ctrl+Shift+F. Then you can use the up- or down-arrow keys to choose the font you want to use.

Here are additional points to ponder concerning fonts:

- Although you can change the font from the Font dialog box, the Font control on the Ribbon has one major advantage over the Font dialog box: It displays each of your fonts by using the font itself, so you can see what each font looks like before you apply it to your text. In contrast, the Font dialog box displays the name of each font by using the standard Windows system font.
- If you want to change the font for all the slides in your presentation, switch to Slide Master view and then change the font (see Chapter 14).
- PowerPoint automatically moves the fonts that you use the most to the head of the font list. This feature makes picking your favorite font even easier.
- Don't overdo it with fonts! Just because you have many different font choices doesn't mean you should try to use them all on the same slide. Don't mix more than two or three typefaces on a slide; use fonts consistently throughout the presentation.
- If you want to set a font that is used consistently throughout a presentation, the best way to do so is to set the font for the presentation's theme (see Chapter 12).

Adding color to your text

Color is an excellent way to draw attention to text in a slide. To change text color, first select the text whose color you want to change. Then click the Font Color button (shown in the margin) and choose the color that you want to use from the color menu that appears.

TIP

If you don't like any color that the Font Color button offers, click More Colors. A bigger dialog box with more color choices appears. If you still can't find the right shade of teal, select the Custom tab and have at it. (Check out Chapters 12 and 15 if you need more help with colors.)

If you want to change the text color for your entire presentation, do so in Slide Master view (see Chapter 14). And see the same chapter for information about changing font colors by using the theme.

Yet another way to change the color of your text is to use the Eyedropper tool (shown in the margin). The Eyedropper lets you match the color of your text with a color that appears in an image. To use it, first select the text you want to color. Then click the drop-down arrow on the Font Color tool and select the Eyedropper tool. Point the Eyedropper at the part of the image whose color you want to match and click. *Voilà!* The text color changes to match the color in the image.

Another way to use color to draw attention to your text is to highlight it. You can use the Text Highlight Color button (shown in the margin) to add one of 15 highlight colors to text. Just select the color you want to use, and then drag over the text you want to highlight.

TIP

Avoid using odd combinations of colors that may make your text difficult to read, especially for those in your audience with less-than-perfect vision. For example, about 8 percent of all males have difficulty distinguishing red from green.

Adding shadows

Adding a shadow behind your text can make the text stand out against its background, which makes the entire slide easier to read. For that reason, many of the templates supplied with PowerPoint use shadows.

You can apply a shadow to any text by first selecting the text and then clicking the Text Shadow button (shown in the margin) in the Font section of the Home tab on the Ribbon. If you want all the text on a slide to be shadowed, however, you should use Slide Master view to create the shadow format (see Chapter 14).

Big Picture Text Formatting

The Paragraph group on the Home tab on the Ribbon, shown in Figure 11-3, has several buttons that apply formats to entire paragraphs. The following sections describe the most common uses for the buttons in this group.

FIGURE 11-3: The Paragraph group on the Home tab on the Ribbon.

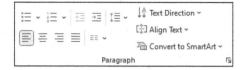

Biting the bulleted list

Most presentations have at least some slides that include a bulleted list, which is a series of paragraphs accented by special characters lovingly known as *bullets*. In the old days, you had to add bullets one at a time. Nowadays, PowerPoint comes with a semiautomatic bullet shooter that is illegal in 27 states.

TIP

PowerPoint lets you create fancy bullets that are based on bitmap pictures rather than simple dots and check marks. Before you go crazy with picture bullets, take a look at the basic way to bite the bullet.

To add bullets to a paragraph or series of paragraphs, take aim and fire, like so:

1. **Highlight the paragraphs to which you want to add bullets.**

   To add a bullet to just one paragraph, you don't have to highlight the entire paragraph. Just place the cursor anywhere in the paragraph.

2. **Click the Bullets button (shown in the margin) found in the Paragraph group on the Home tab on the Ribbon.**

   PowerPoint adds a bullet to each paragraph that you select.

The Bullets button works like a toggle: Press it once to add bullets; press it again to remove bullets. To remove bullets from previously bulleted text, select the text and click the Bullets button.

If you don't like the appearance of the bullets that PowerPoint uses, you can select a different bullet character, a picture, or even a motion clip by clicking the down arrow at the right side of the Bullets button. This action reveals a list of choices for various types of bullets.

If none of the bullets in this list is acceptable, you can bring up the Bullets and Numbering dialog box (see Figure 11-4) by clicking the arrow at the right of the Bullets button and then choosing Bullets and Numbers. From this dialog box, you can choose a different bullet character, change the bullet's color, or change its size relative to the text size.

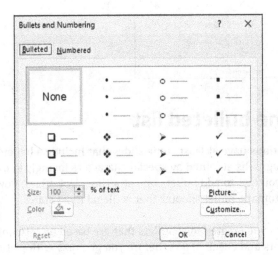

FIGURE 11-4:
The Bullets and Numbering dialog box.

Here are some important tidbits to keep in mind when you use bullets:

>> **Customizing bullet characters:** You can choose from among several collections of bullet characters that are available. If you don't like any of the bullet characters displayed for you, click Customize in the lower-right corner of the dialog box. This brings up another dialog box that lists a variety of useful alternative bullet characters, such as pointing fingers, a skull and crossbones, and a time bomb. Pick the bullet that you want to use and then click OK. If you can't find a bullet that suits your fancy, choose a different font in the Font drop-down list.

TIP

>> **Changing the size of bullet characters:** If the bullet characters don't seem large enough, increase the size in the Bullets and Numbering dialog box. The size is specified as a percentage of the text size.

>> **Changing the color of bullet characters:** To change the bullet color, use the Color drop-down list to choose the color that you want to use. Colors from the current color scheme appear in the drop-down list. For additional color choices, choose More Colors to call up a dialog box that offers a complete range of color choices. (For more information about using colors, see Chapter 12.)

>> **Using images for your bullet characters:** To use a picture bullet, click the Picture button located in the lower right of the Bullets and Numbering dialog box. This brings up the dialog box shown in Figure 11-5, which lets you choose from several sources for a picture to use as a bullet.

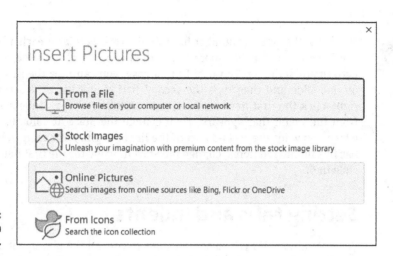

FIGURE 11-5:
Using a picture bullet.

Creating numbered lists

If you want your slide to include a numbered list, use the Numbering button (shown in the margin), which appears next to the Bullets button on the Home tab on the Ribbon. When you click the Numbering button, PowerPoint adds simple numbers to the selected paragraphs.

If you want to change the numbering format, click the arrow next to the Numbering button to display a list of number style choices. Then you can select the style that suits your fancy.

If none of the styles in the list is right, choose Bullets and Numbering to reveal the numbering options on the Numbered tab of the Bullets and Numbering dialog box (see Figure 11-6).

FIGURE 11-6:
More ways to format numbers.

CHAPTER 11 All about Fonts and Text Formatting   **147**

TIP Normally, the starting number for each list reverts to 1 for each new slide. What if you have a list that has more items than can fit on one slide, such as a David Letterman–style Top Ten list? In that case, you can type the first half of the list on one slide and then type the second half of the list on a second slide. Next, right-click the first item on the second slide and choose Bullets and Numbering from the menu that appears. Then change the Start At value to the number at which you want the second part of the list to begin. For example, if the first slide has five numbered items, change the Start At value for the first item on the second slide to 6.

Setting tabs and indents

PowerPoint enables you to set tab stops to control the placement of text within a text object. For most presentations, you don't have to fuss with tabs. Each paragraph is indented according to its level in the outline, and the template that you use to create the presentation presets the amount of indentation for each outline level.

If you're stubborn about tabs, you can mess with the indent settings and tab stops — that is, if you're adventurous and you have no real work to do today. Here's how you do it:

1. **If the rulers aren't visible, summon them by selecting the View tab on the Ribbon and then selecting the Ruler check box in the Show/Hide group.**

   Rulers appear above and to the left of the presentation window and show the current tab and indentation settings.

2. **Select the text object whose tabs or indents you want to change.**

   Each text object has its own tabs and indents settings. After you click a text object, the ruler shows that object's tabs and indents.

3. **Move the cursor to the ruler location where you want to add a tab stop and then click.**

   A tab stop appears.

4. **Grab the indentation doohickey (shown in the margin) and then drag it to change the indentation.**

   The indentation doohickey (that's not its official name) is the control that looks like an hourglass sitting on a little box, normally positioned at the left side of the ruler. It actually consists of three parts:

   - The top upside-down triangle sets the indentation for the first line of the paragraph.

- The middle triangle sets the indentation for the remaining lines of the paragraph.
- The box at the bottom sets the indentation for the paragraph.

Try dragging the different parts of the indentation doohickey to see what happens. Have fun!

Each text object is initially set up with default tab stops set at every inch. When you add a tab stop, any default tab stops located to the left of the new tab stop disappear.

TIP To remove a tab stop, use the mouse to drag the tab stop off the ruler. (For instance, click the tab stop, drag it off the ruler, and then release the mouse button.)

Spacing out

Feeling a little spaced out? Try tightening the space between text lines. Feeling cramped? Space out the lines a little. These steps show you how to do it all:

1. **Highlight the paragraph(s) whose line spacing you want to change.**

2. **Click the Line Spacing button (shown in the margin) and then select the amount of line spacing you want.**

   The Line Spacing button displays the most common line spacing options: 1.0, 1.5, 2.0, 2.5, and 3.0. If you want to set the line spacing to a value that isn't shown on the Line Spacing button, select Line Spacing Options to display the Paragraph dialog box (see Figure 11-7).

FUN WITH TAB TYPES

PowerPoint isn't limited to just boring left-aligned tabs. In all, it has four distinct types of tabs: left, right, center, and decimal. The square button that appears at the far-left side of the ruler when you select text tells you which type of tab is added when you click the ruler. Click this button to cycle through the four types of tabs:

- **Standard left-aligned tab:** Press Tab to advance the text to the tab stop.
- **Right-aligned tab:** Text is aligned flush right with the tab stop.
- **Centered tab:** Text lines up centered over the tab stop.
- **Decimal tab:** Numbers line up with the decimal point centered over the tab stop.

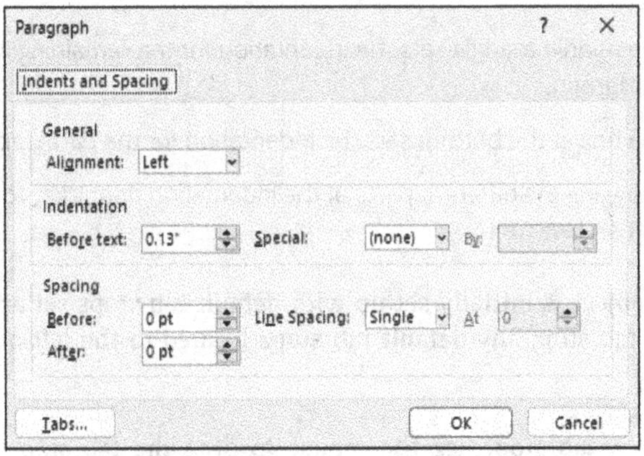

FIGURE 11-7: Change the line spacing.

Lining things up

PowerPoint enables you to control the way your text lines up on the slide. You can center text, line it up flush left or flush right, or *justify* it (that is, line up the text on both the left and right sides). You can change these alignments by using the alignment buttons in the Paragraph group on the Home tab on the Ribbon. You can also use the keyboard shortcuts described in Table 11-2.

TABLE 11-2 Paragraph Alignment Commands

Button	Keyboard Shortcut	Alignment
	Ctrl+L	Align Left
	Ctrl+E	Center
	Ctrl+R	Align Right
	Ctrl+J	Justify

Here are some semirandom thoughts on aligning paragraphs:

» **Centered text lines up right down the middle of the slide.** Actually, text lines up down the middle of the text object that contains the text; a text line appears centered on the slide only if the text object is centered on the slide.

» **Bulleted lists look best when they're left aligned.** Otherwise, the bullets don't line up.

Making columns

Most slides place all their text in a single column. However, you can easily create multiple columns by using the Columns button (shown in the margin) in the Paragraph section on the Home tab on the Ribbon. To create a one-, two-, or three-column layout, just click the Columns button and then choose one, two, or three columns from the menu that appears. If you want more than three columns, select the More Columns command and then choose the number of columns you want to use.

Creating Fancy Text with WordArt

WordArt is a fun feature that lets you create fancy text effects, like gradient fills or curved paths. WordArt is integrated into PowerPoint, so you can apply WordArt formatting to any bit of text in your presentation just by highlighting the text and applying the WordArt formats. Figure 11-8 is an example of what you can do with WordArt in just a couple of minutes.

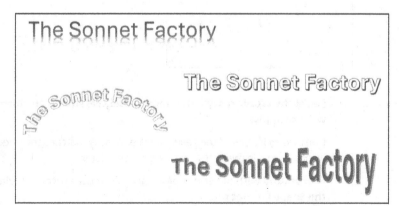

FIGURE 11-8: You, too, can create fancy text effects like this using WordArt.

Follow these steps to transform mundane text into something worth looking at:

1. **Select the text you want to apply WordArt formatting to.**

   The text can be anywhere in your presentation. For example, you can apply WordArt formatting to a slide title or body text.

2. **Select the Shape Format tab on the Ribbon.**

   The Shape Format tab includes a WordArt Styles group, as shown in Figure 11-9. As you can see, this Ribbon group includes several preconfigured WordArt styles, as well as buttons that let you control the text fill, outline style, and text effects, such as shadows and glowing.

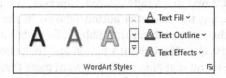

FIGURE 11-9:
The WordArt Styles group on the Shape Format tab.

3. **Click the More button at the bottom of the scroll bar to the right of the predefined WordArt styles.**

   The WordArt Quick Styles gallery appears (see Figure 11-10).

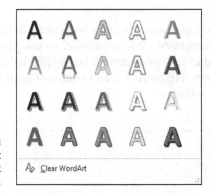

FIGURE 11-10:
The WordArt Quick Styles gallery.

4. **Select the WordArt style that most closely resembles the formatting you want to apply.**

   Don't worry if none of the gallery choices exactly matches the effect you want — you can tweak the text's appearance later.

5. **Fool around with other WordArt controls in the WordArt Styles group of the Shape Format tab.**

   Table 11-3 describes the other controls in the WordArt Styles group. Experiment with these controls as much as you want until you get the text to look just right.

TABLE 11-3 Buttons on the WordArt Shape Format Tab

Control	What It's Called	What It Does
A Text Fill ˅	Text Fill	Sets the fill color. The fill can be a simple color, a *gradient* (which gradually blends two or more colors), a picture, a pattern, or a texture.
A Text Outline ˅	Text Outline	Sets the properties of the text outline. You can select a color, a pattern, and a thickness.
A Text Effects ˅	Text Effects	Lets you apply fancy text effects such as shadows, reflections, glowing text, beveled text, 3-D rotations, and transforms.

TIP The Text Effects button is the key to creating fancy logos, such as text that wraps around circles or text that has a three-dimensional look. When you click this button, a menu with various text-formatting options appears. Table 11-4 lists the formatting options available on this menu.

TIP Be judicious when using these text effects. A subtle text effect used occasionally can draw attention to specific text, but overusing these effects will just make your presentations hard to read.

TABLE 11-4 Formatting Options on the Text Effects Menu

Control	What It's Called	What It Does
A	Shadow	Adds a shadow to the text. The shadow can be directly behind the text, or it can appear beneath the text, which creates the impression that the text is floating above an invisible surface.
A	Reflection	Creates a faint reflection on an invisible surface beneath the text.
A	Glow	Adds a glowing effect to the text.
A	Bevel	Adds a beveled effect to the text, which creates the impression that the text has been chiseled from a solid object.
A	3-D Rotation	Rotates the text around three dimensions.
abc	Transform	Transforms the overall shape of the text.

IN THIS CHAPTER

» Getting acquainted with the Design tab

» Understanding how to use themes

» Changing the size of your slides

» Playing with the background

» Using the Designer to quickly improve your design

Chapter **12**

Designing Your Slides

One of the most important tasks of putting together a good PowerPoint presentation is making the presentation look good. Always wanting to be helpful in such matters, Microsoft has endowed PowerPoint with a feature called *themes* that lets you create good-looking slides in minutes. One of the best features of themes is that they work not only in PowerPoint but also in Word and Excel. Thus, you can use themes to create PowerPoint presentations, Word documents, and Excel spreadsheets that have a consistent appearance.

The main way to access PowerPoint themes is from the Design tab on the Ribbon. This entire chapter is devoted to this Design tab. To keep things simple, I approach this most useful tab from left to right, even though that's not always the order in which you use the controls it contains.

Looking at the Design Tab

To get things started, Figure 12-1 shows the Design tab on the Ribbon. As you can see, the Design tab contains several groups of controls that let you set various aspects of the slide design used within your presentation. You can access the Design tab by clicking it on the Ribbon or by using the handy keyboard shortcut Alt+G.

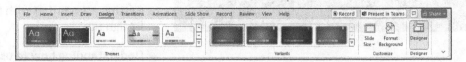

FIGURE 12-1:
The Design tab.

Here's the general purpose of each group of controls on the Design tab:

» **Themes:** Lets you apply a theme to the presentation. This is the group you work with most while you play with the design of your slides.

» **Variants:** Lets you choose from several minor variants of a given theme.

» **Customize:** Lets you change the slide size and background appearance.

» **Designer:** Lets you use the intelligent Designer, which uses the content of your slides to suggest appropriate designs.

Working with Themes

The Themes group of the Design tab lets you select a theme to apply to your slides. PowerPoint comes with a ton of carefully crafted themes that give a professional look to your presentations. If you're somewhat artsy, you can design your own themes as well.

A *theme* is a set of design elements that are applied to one or more slides in a presentation. Each theme includes several basic components:

» **A set of colors that work well together:** Each theme has four colors that can be used for text or backgrounds and six colors that can be used for accents.

» **A set of fonts that look good when used together:** Each theme has a font used for headings and a font used for regular text.

» **A set of background styles:** These are a combination of background colors and effects, such as patterns or gradient fills.

» **A set of design effects:** These include line and fill styles.

Microsoft 365 includes about 40 predefined themes, but the exact count changes from time to time as Microsoft's designers come up with new ideas and retire old ones. Each theme is available in four color variations, so you can choose from more than 100 predefined theme variants to apply to your slides.

Applying themes

To apply a theme to an entire presentation, simply click the theme you want to apply in the Themes group on the Design tab. If the theme you want to apply isn't visible, use the scroll buttons on the right side of the Themes group to display additional themes.

After you've selected a theme in the Themes group, variations on the theme will appear in the Variants group. You can then click the variant you want to use.

TIP

To see a preview of how your presentation will appear with a particular theme, hover the mouse over that theme in the gallery. After a moment, the current slide momentarily appears formatted with the theme. If you move the mouse off the theme without actually clicking the theme, the current slide reverts to its previous formatting.

TIP

You can click the down arrow in the scroll bar in the Theme gallery, which displays an expanded list of themes, as shown in Figure 12-2. As you can see, this window displays PowerPoint's built-in themes and also includes links that let you browse for additional themes. A link even lets you save the current combination of theme elements as a new theme.

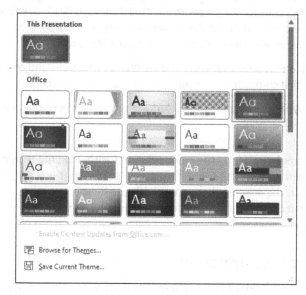

FIGURE 12-2:
The Theme gallery.

TIP Not all the slides in a presentation have to follow the same theme. To apply a theme to a single slide, or a set of slides, select the slide(s). Then right-click the theme you want to apply and choose Apply to Selected Slides.

Using theme colors

Each PowerPoint theme includes a built-in *color scheme*, which consists of sets of colors chosen by color professionals. Microsoft paid these people enormous sums of money to debate the merits of using mauve text on a teal background. You can use these professionally designed color schemes, or you can create your own if you think you have a better eye than the Microsoft-hired color guns.

As far as I'm concerned, the color schemes in PowerPoint themes are the best things to come along since peanut M&M's. Without color schemes, people like me are free to pick and choose from among the 16 million or so colors that PowerPoint lets you incorporate into your slides. The resulting slides can easily appear next to the worst-dressed celebrities at next year's Golden Globe Awards.

Each color scheme has 12 colors, with each color designated for a particular use:

» **Four Text/Background colors:** These four colors are designed to be the primary colors for the presentation. One from each pair is used for the text and the other is used for the background. (You can use the same color for both, but that would make the slides impossible to read!)

» **Six accent colors:** These colors are used for various bits and pieces of your slides that complement the basic text and background colors.

» **Two hyperlink colors:** These colors are used only when your presentation includes hyperlinks.

When you apply a theme, the color scheme for that theme is applied along with the other elements of the theme. However, PowerPoint lets you change the color scheme from the scheme that comes with the theme. For example, you can apply a theme such as Opulent but then change the color scheme to the scheme from the Verve theme.

Applying a color variant

To change the standard color scheme used for your slides, select a theme. Then click the More button at the lower-right corner of the Variants gallery on the Design tab and click Colors. This exposes the available color variants, as shown in Figure 12-3.

158 PART 3 Creating Great-Looking Slides

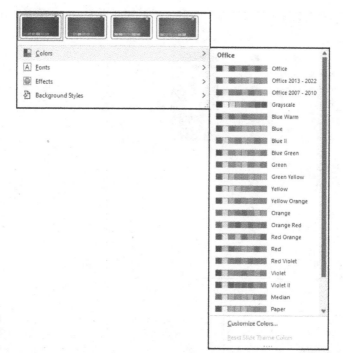

FIGURE 12-3:
Choosing a color variant.

Creating your own color scheme

If you don't like any color schemes that come with the built-in themes, you can create your own color scheme. Here's how:

1. **Select a color scheme that's close to the one you want to use.**

   WARNING

   If you're going to deviate from the preselected color scheme combinations, you'd better have some color sense. If you can't tell chartreuse from lime, you should leave this stuff to the pros.

2. **Select Customize Colors from the bottom of the color variants list.**

   The Create New Theme Colors dialog box appears, as shown in Figure 12-4.

3. **Click the button for the color you want to change.**

   For example, to change the first accent color, click the Accent 1 button. You then see a gallery of color choices, as shown in Figure 12-5.

4. **Pick a color you like.**

   As you can see, you have a plethora of color choices. This gallery reminds me of the shelf of color chips in the paint section of a hardware store.

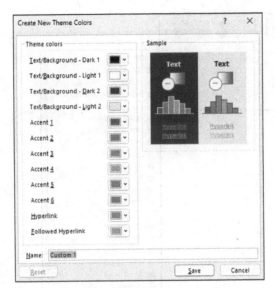

FIGURE 12-4: Creating new theme colors.

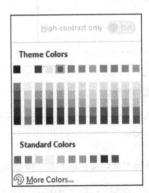

FIGURE 12-5: Changing a color.

5. **If you don't like any of the choices, click the More Colors button.**

   The Colors dialog box appears (see Figure 12-6). As you can see, PowerPoint displays a honeycomb-like arrangement of colors. (Note that this dialog box comes up with the Standard tab selected. If you used the Custom tab the last time you used this dialog box, the Custom tab is selected instead.)

6. **Click the color that you want and then click OK.**

   You're whisked back to the Create New Theme Colors dialog box.

7. **(Optional) Repeat Steps 3 through 6 for any other colors you want to change.**

8. **Click Save.**

   The new color scheme is saved.

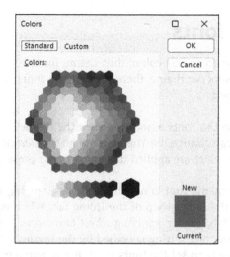

FIGURE 12-6:
A wonderful world of color.

TECHNICAL STUFF

The Standard tab of the Colors dialog box (refer to Figure 12-6) shows 127 popular colors, plus white, black, and shades of gray. If you want to use a color that doesn't appear in the dialog box, click the Custom tab (see Figure 12-7). From the Custom tab, you can construct any of the 16 million colors that are theoretically possible with PowerPoint. You need a PhD in physics to figure out how to adjust the Red, Green, and Blue controls, though. Mess around with this stuff if you want, but you're on your own.

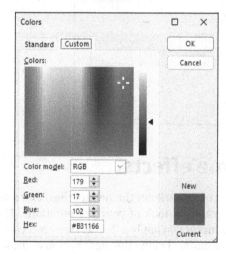

FIGURE 12-7:
PowerPoint offers 16 million colors from which you can choose.

CHAPTER 12 **Designing Your Slides** 161

Using theme fonts

Theme fonts are similar to theme colors, but theme fonts have fewer choices. Although there are 12 colors per theme, there are only two fonts: one for headings, and the other for body text.

If you don't want to use the fonts associated with the theme you've chosen for your presentation, you can change the Theme fonts on the Design tab on the Ribbon. Then the fonts you select are applied throughout your presentation.

TECHNICAL STUFF

Note that changing the theme font is not the same as changing the font via the Font controls found in the Font group of the Home tab. When you use the Font controls on the Home tab, you're applying *direct formatting*. Direct formatting temporarily overrides the font setting specified by the theme. As a general rule, you should use theme fonts to set the fonts used throughout a presentation. Use direct formatting sparingly — when you want to create a word or two in a font that differs from the rest of the presentation.

You can change the font used in a theme by clicking the More button at the lower right of the Variants gallery, choosing Fonts, and then choosing Customize Fonts. The Create New Theme Fonts dialog box appears (see Figure 12-8). Here you can change the font used for headings and body text.

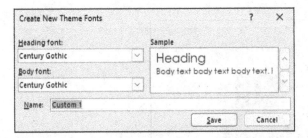

FIGURE 12-8: Changing theme fonts.

Applying theme effects

Another major component of PowerPoint themes are the *theme effects*, which apply subtle variations to the graphical look of your presentations. Theme effects are applied automatically whenever you apply a theme. However, you can apply theme effects from a different theme by clicking the More button at the lower right of the Variants gallery and choosing Theme. This brings up the Theme Effects gallery (see Figure 12-9). You can choose any of the theme effects listed.

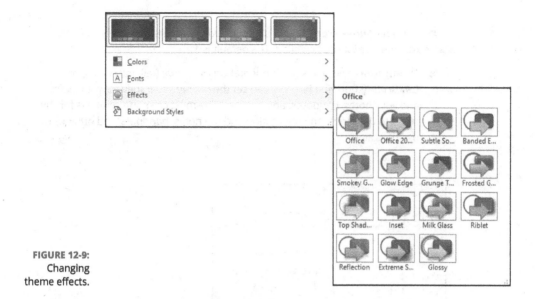

FIGURE 12-9: Changing theme effects.

Changing the Slide Size

The Customize group of the Design tab on the Ribbon includes a Slide Size control that lets you change the size of the slide from standard to widescreen. You should use widescreen only if you plan on showing the presentation on a projector that displays in widescreen format.

Besides standard and widescreen formats, you can also click the Slide Size button and then choose Customize Slide Size. The Slide Size dialog box appears (see Figure 12-10). This dialog box gives you extra control over your presentation's page setup:

>> **Slides Sized For:** This drop-down list lets you set the size of your slides based on how you plan to present them. The most common approach is to present the slides on a standard computer screen, which has an aspect ratio of 4:3. (The *aspect ratio* is the ratio of the screen's width to its height. Although 4:3 is a common aspect ratio, many newer computers use widescreen displays, which usually have an aspect ratio of 16:9.) Other options on this drop-down list include different screen ratios (suitable for widescreen displays), standard-size paper, and even 35mm slides. A Custom option even lets you set whatever width and height you want for your slides.

>> **Width:** Lets you set a custom width for your slides.

>> **Height:** Lets you set a custom height for your slides.

- » **Number Slides From:** If your slides include numbers, this option lets you set the number for the first slide. The default is 1.

- » **Orientation:** Lets you set the orientation to *Portrait* (tall and skinny) or *Landscape* (short and fat). You can set the setting separately for your slides and your notes, handouts, and outlines. The most common setting is for the slides to use landscape orientation and the notes, handouts, and outlines to use portrait.

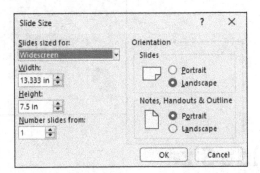

FIGURE 12-10: The Slide Size dialog box.

Applying Background Styles

A *background style* is a combination of a background color chosen from a theme color scheme and a background fill effect. The color scheme always includes four colors that can be used for the background — two light colors and two dark colors. In addition, you can choose from three background fill effects: Subtle, Moderate, and Intense. For example, the Subtle fill might be a solid color, the Moderate fill might be a gentle pattern applied to the color, and the Intense fill might be a bold gradient fill.

Each combination of the four background colors and three background fills is a *background style*. Thus, each theme provides a total of 12 background styles.

To apply one of the theme's background styles to your presentation, click the More button in the lower right of the Variants gallery, and then choose Background Styles. The Format Background pane appears (see Figure 12-11).

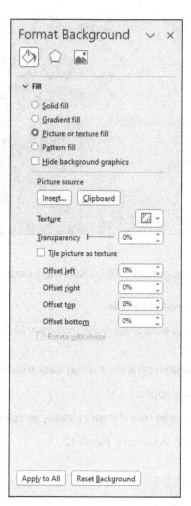

FIGURE 12-11:
Changing the background style.

Using a gradient fill

You may have noticed that the slide background used in many PowerPoint templates is not a solid color. Instead, the color is gradually shaded from top to bottom. This type of shading — called *gradient fill* — creates an interesting visual effect. For example, look at the slide shown in Figure 12-12. This slide was based on the standard Microsoft 365 theme that comes with PowerPoint. The background is light green in the center and fades to darker green on the edges.

FIGURE 12-12:
Using a gradient fill to create an interesting background.

You can create your own custom gradient fill by following these steps:

1. **Choose the slide that you want to shade.**

   This step isn't necessary if you want to apply the shading to all slides in the presentation.

2. **Select the Design tab, and then click the Format Background button.**

   The Format Background pane appears.

3. **Select the Gradient Fill radio button if it isn't already selected.**

   The gradient controls appear, as shown in Figure 12-13.

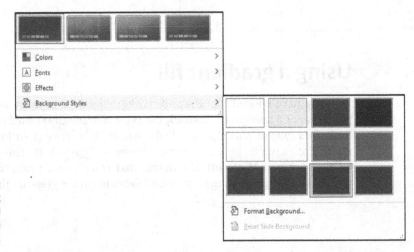

FIGURE 12-13:
The Format Background pane with gradient controls.

4. **Set the gradient fill options the way you want them.**

   You have to play with the controls until you get a feel for how they work. Start by selecting the present colors, which let you choose one of several predefined fill patterns. Then play with the controls until you get the fill to look the way you want. You can choose the colors to use for the fill, the transparency level, the direction, and several variants for each option.

5. **Click OK.**

Using other background effects

Besides gradient fills, you can use the Format Background pane to create several other interesting types of backgrounds (refer to Figure 12-11). For example, you can assign a picture of your choosing, or you can use one of several predefined patterns supplied with PowerPoint.

To use a texture, select the Picture or Texture Fill radio button. Then click the Texture button to reveal the Texture gallery, shown in Figure 12-14.

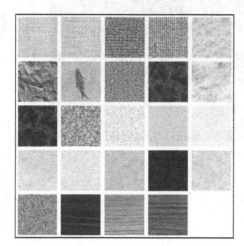

FIGURE 12-14: Applying a textured background.

You can also use the Picture or Texture Fill radio button to select an image file of your own — just click the File button and then select the file you want to use. Or you can import an image from the Clipboard or select a clip art image. The remaining controls in this dialog box let you further tweak the appearance of the picture or text you select.

Finally, you can use a Pattern Fill to create a background from one of several predefined patterns of hash lines.

Using the Designer to Improve Your Slides

The Designer is a feature powered by artificial intelligence (AI) that examines the content of a selected slide and offers you a variety of design choices based on what it finds. To use this feature, simply select a slide that you think needs some improvement and click the Designer button on the Design tab on the Ribbon (shown in the margin).

Figure 12-15 shows how the Design Ideas feature has suggested some design alternatives for a slide that contains a picture of William Shakespeare. To use one of the suggestions, simply double-click it in the Design Ideas pane.

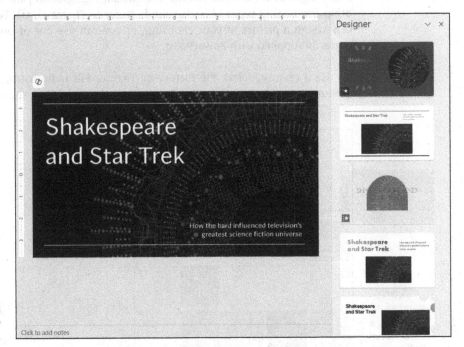

FIGURE 12-15: Using the Designer feature.

> **IN THIS CHAPTER**
> » **Creating slide transitions**
> » **Animating text**

Chapter 13
Animating Your Slides

If you plan to run your presentation on your computer's screen or on a computer projector, you can use (or abuse) a bagful of exciting on-screen PowerPoint animations. Your audience members probably won't be fooled into thinking that you hired Disney to create your slides, but they'll be impressed all the same. Animations are just one more example of how PowerPoint can make even the dullest content look spectacular.

This chapter begins with slide transitions, which aren't technically animations because they don't involve moving individual items on a slide. However, slide transitions are usually used in concert with animations to create presentations that are as much fun to watch as they are informative.

Using the Transitions Tab

A *transition* is how PowerPoint gets from one slide to the next during an on-screen slide show. The normal way to segue from slide to slide is simply cutting to the next slide — effective, yes, but also boring. PowerPoint enables you to assign any of the more than 50 different special effects to each slide transition. For example, you can have the next slide scoot over the top of the current slide from any direction, or you can have the current slide scoot off the screen in any direction to reveal the next slide. You can have slides fade out, dissolve into each other, open up like Venetian blinds, or spin in like spokes on a wheel.

You can control slide transitions using the Transitions tab of the Ribbon, as shown in Figure 13-1.

FIGURE 13-1:
The Transitions tab.

The Transitions tab consists of three groups of controls:

» **Preview:** This group includes a single control called Preview. Click it to display a preview of the transition effect you selected for the current slide.

TIP The transition is automatically previewed when you select a transition effect for a slide. As a result, you don't often need to click the Preview button.

» **Transition to This Slide:** This group lets you select the transition effect that will be used when the presentation moves from the previous slide to this slide. To apply a transition, just select it. In Figure 13-1, I applied the Fade transition, which causes the slide to fade in rather than just appear out of nowhere.

» **Timing:** This group lets you select options that affect how the transition effect is applied to the slide, such as how quickly the transition occurs and whether it's triggered by a mouse click or automatically after a time delay.

Creating a slide transition

To create a slide transition, follow these steps:

1. **Move to the slide to which you want to apply the transition.**

   Note that the transition applies when you come to the slide you apply the transition to, not when you go to the next slide. For example, if you apply a transition to slide 3, the transition is displayed when you move from slide 2 to slide 3, not when you move from slide 3 to slide 4.

   If you want to apply the animation scheme to *all* your slides, you can skip this step because it won't matter which slide you start from.

   TIP If you want to apply different transitions to different slides, you may prefer to work in Slide Sorter view (click the Slide Sorter View button near the lower-right corner of the screen), which allows you to see more slides at once. If you're going to use the same transition for all your slides, though, no benefit comes from switching to Slide Sorter view.

170 PART 3 Creating Great-Looking Slides

2. **Select the transition you want to apply from the Transition to This Slide section of the Transitions tab on the Ribbon.**

    If you want, you can display the complete gallery of transition effects by clicking the More button (shown in the margin) at the lower right of the mini-gallery of transition effects displayed on the Ribbon. Figure 13-2 shows the complete Transitions gallery.

   Note that when you select a transition, PowerPoint previews the transition by animating the current slide. If you want to see the preview again, just click the transition again.

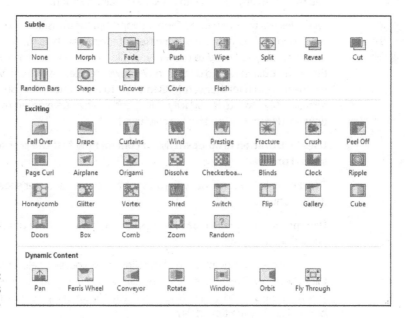

FIGURE 13-2: The Transitions gallery.

3. **Use the Effect Options drop-down list to select a variation of the transition effect you selected in Step 2.**

   The available variations depend on the transition you've chosen. For example, if you choose the Wipe transition, the following variations are available:

   - From Right
   - From Left
   - From Top
   - From Bottom
   - From Top-Right

- From Bottom-Right
- From Top-Left
- From Bottom-Left

4. **If you want, use the Sound drop-down list to apply a sound effect.**

   The Sound drop-down list includes a collection of standard transition sounds, such as applause, a cash register, and the standard *whoosh*. You'll need to click the Preview button to actually hear the sound effect you chose.

   You can also choose Other Sound to use your own .wav file. This option allows you to upload any .wav file to use as a transition sound.

TIP

.wav files are the only sound format supported for transition sound effects. If the sound you want to use is in a different format, such as the more popular .mp3 format, you'll need to convert your file to the .wav format. Unfortunately, there's no built-in way to do that in Windows. You can use your favorite search engine to search for "convert MP3 to WAV" to find options for converting sound formats. (My favorite is Audacity, a free and open-source program you can download from www.audacityteam.org.)

5. **Use the Duration drop-down list to control how fast the transition should proceed.**

   The default is 1 second, but you can specify a slower or faster speed if you want.

6. **Use the On Mouse Click or After options to indicate how the transition should be triggered.**

   If you want to control the pace of the slide show yourself, select the On Mouse Click check box. Then the slide will remain visible until you click the mouse. If you want the slide to advance automatically after a delay, select the After check box and specify the time delay.

TIP

To apply the animation to the entire presentation, click Apply to All. This applies the animation to all the slides in the presentation.

Here are some additional points to keep in mind when using slide transitions:

> » **Consider computer speed.** Transition effects look better on faster computers, which have more raw processing horsepower to implement the fancy pixel dexterity required to produce good-looking transitions. If your computer is a bit slow, change the speed setting to Fast so that the transition won't drag.

- » **Select sets of transitions.** Some of the transition effects come in matched sets that apply the same effect from different directions. You can create a cohesive set of transitions by alternating among these related effects from slide to slide. For example, set up the first slide with Wipe Right, the second slide with Wipe Left, the third slide with Wipe Down, and so on.

- » **Preview transitions.** When you work in Slide Sorter view, you can click the little star icon beneath each slide to preview the transition for that slide. Also, the automatic slide timing is shown beneath the slide if you set the slide to advance automatically.

- » **Don't overdo it.** PowerPoint offers you 49 different types of slide variations. Please don't use them all in a single presentation. You're much better off picking just one or two transition styles to use throughout your presentation. You want your audience to focus on the substance of your presentation, not the transitions.

Using the Morph transition effect

TIP

PowerPoint includes a special transition effect called *Morph*, which magically rearranges the elements from one slide to the next slide. For example, the Morph effect may start with a slide that features a large image, and then transition to a new slide that contains the same image at a smaller size, in a different location, with new text. When the transition triggers, the image simultaneously shrinks to the new size and moves to the new location, while the new text appears at the same time.

The Morph transition works best when the first and second slides in the transition contain one or more common elements, such as images or shapes. Elements that are not common to both slides will be faded in or out.

That's a bit difficult to explain, so ponder Figure 13-3, in which two slides are depicted. Slide 1 contains the title "William Shakespeare" and an image of Shakespeare's face. Slide 2 contains the same title and image but in different locations, and the image is smaller. In addition, Slide 2 contains a list of interesting tidbits about the Bard.

I set up these slides by first creating the second slide. Then I duplicated it to create two identical slides. Finally, I edited Slide 1 to remove the text and rearrange the title and image.

Slide 1:

Slide 2:

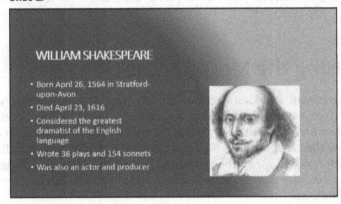

FIGURE 13-3:
Using the Morph transition effect.

If you apply the Morph transition to Slide 2, the transition will simultaneously do three things:

» Move the title from its location in Slide 1 down and to the left until it reaches its location in Slide 2. As the title moves, it reduces in size.

» Move the image from its location in Slide 1 down and to the right, while simultaneously decreasing its size until it lands at its location in Slide 2.

» Fade in the text box showing the interesting information about Shakespeare.

Using the Animations Tab

Besides slide transitions, the most common type of animation in PowerPoint is adding entrance and exit effects to the text that appears on the slide. This effect is especially useful for bulleted lists because it lets you display the list one item at a time. You can have each item appear out of nowhere, drop from the top of the screen, march in from the left or right, or do a back somersault followed by two cartwheels and a double-twist flip (talc, please!).

This type of animation is often called a *build effect* because it lets you build your points one by one. Applying this type of animation is easy using the Animations tab on the Ribbon (see Figure 13-4).

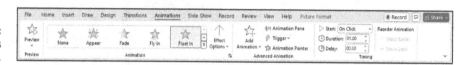

FIGURE 13-4: The Animations tab.

The Animations tab consists of four groups of controls:

» **Preview:** This group includes a single control — a Preview button — that displays a preview of the animation effects you selected for the current slide.

» **Animation:** This group lets you select one of several predefined animations for the selected object.

» **Advanced Animation:** The controls in this group let you customize your animations in advanced ways. For more information, see the section "Using advanced animations," later in this chapter.

» **Timing:** This group lets you set the timing of the animation. (For more information, see the section "Timing your animations," later in this chapter.)

To apply an animation effect, first select the text box that you want to animate. Then choose the animation style from the Animation gallery on the Animations tab.

Like other PowerPoint galleries, the Animation gallery includes a More button (shown in the margin) that summons the complete gallery, as shown in Figure 13-5.

After you apply a basic animation, you can use the Effect Options drop-down list to select one of several variations of the animation. For example, if you choose the Fly In animation, the Effect Options drop-down list lets you pick the direction from which the object will fly in to the slide.

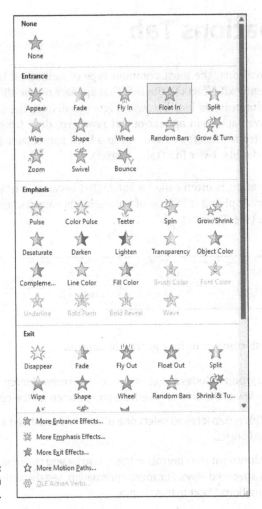

FIGURE 13-5:
The Animation gallery.

TIP

Notice that there are several More menu items at the bottom of the Animation gallery. You can click any of these buttons to reveal even more animation types.

For more complex animations, you need to use advanced animations, as I describe in the next section, "Using advanced animations."

Using advanced animations

Advanced animations are the nitty-gritty of PowerPoint animation. Advanced animations are the only way to apply text animation that's more complicated than the predefined Fade, Wipe, or Fly In styles of the Animation gallery. In addition to animating text, advanced animations let you animate other objects on your slides, such as pictures, shapes, and charts.

Understanding advanced animations

Before I get into the details of setting up advanced animations, you need to understand some basic concepts. Don't worry — this won't get too technical. But you need to know this stuff before you start creating advanced animations.

For starters, you can apply advanced animations to any object on a slide, whether it's a text placeholder, a drawing object such as an AutoShape or a text box, or a clip art picture. For text objects, you can apply the animation to the text object as a whole or to individual paragraphs within the object. You can also specify whether the effect goes all at once, word by word, or letter by letter. And you can indicate whether the effect happens automatically or whether PowerPoint waits for you to click the mouse or press Enter to initiate the animation.

You can create four basic types of animation effects for slide objects:

- » **Entrance effect:** This is how an object enters the slide. If you don't specify an entrance effect, the object starts in whatever position you placed it on the slide. If you want to be more creative, though, you can have objects appear by using any of the 40 different entrance effects, such as Appear, Blinds, Fade, Boomerang, Bounce, Swivel, and many others.

- » **Emphasis effect:** This effect lets you draw attention to an object that's already on the slide. PowerPoint offers 24 different emphasis effects, including Fill Color, Font Size, Grow/Shrink, Spin, Teeter, Flicker, Pulse, Blink, and many more.

- » **Exit effect:** This is how an object leaves the slide. Most objects don't have exit effects, but if you want an object to leave, you can apply one of the 40 different effects — which are similar to the entrance effects — including Disappear, Contract, Peek Out, Float Out, Spiral Out, and so on.

- » **Motion path:** Motion paths are the most interesting types of custom animation. A motion path lets you create a track along which the object travels when animated. PowerPoint provides you with 64 predefined motion paths, such as circles, stars, teardrops, spirals, springs, and so on. If that's not enough, you can draw your own custom path to make an object travel anywhere on the slide you want it to go.

    If the motion path begins off the slide and ends somewhere on the slide, the motion path effect is similar to an entrance effect. If the path begins on the slide but ends off the slide, the motion path effect is like an exit effect. And if the path begins and ends on the slide, it's similar to an emphasis effect; in that case, when the animation starts, the object appears, travels along its path, and then zips off the slide.

To draw a custom motion path, click the Add Effect button in the Advanced Animation group, choose Motion Paths Draw, and then choose Draw Custom Path and select one of the motion path drawing tools from the menu that appears. The tools include straight lines, curves, free-form shapes, and scribbles. You can then draw your motion path using the tool you selected.

You can create more than one animation for a given object. For example, you can give an object an entrance effect, an emphasis effect, and an exit effect. That lets you bring the object on-screen, draw attention to it, and then have it leave. If you want, you can have several emphasis or motion path effects for a single object. You can also have more than one entrance and exit effect, but in most cases, one will do.

Each effect that you apply has one or more property settings that you can tweak to customize the effect. All the effects have a Speed setting that lets you set the speed for the animation. Some effects have an additional property setting that lets you control the range of an object's movement. (For example, the Spin effect has an Amount setting that governs how far the object spins.)

TIP

If you want, you can create a *trigger* that causes an animation effect to operate when you click an object on the slide. For example, you might create a trigger so that all the text in a text placeholder pulsates when you click the slide title. To do so, first add the animation effect to the text. Then click Trigger in the Advanced Animation group and choose On Click Of. A list of all objects on the slide that can be clicked is displayed; select the Title placeholder. (You can also trigger an animation when a specific location is reached during playback of a video file. For more information, see Chapter 19.)

Using the Animation pane

The Animation pane is a task pane that appears to the right of the slide and displays important information about the animations you've added to your slides. The Animation pane is hidden by default, but I recommend you turn it on before you start adding advanced animations to your slides. To turn on the Animation pane, just click the Animation Pane button in the Advanced Animation group of the Animation tab on the Ribbon.

Figure 13-6 shows how the Animation pane appears for a slide that has not yet had any animations added to it.

In the sections that follow, you find out how to use the Animation pane as you create custom animations.

FIGURE 13-6:
The Animation pane.

Adding an effect

To animate an object on a slide, follow these steps:

1. **In Normal view, call up the slide that contains the object you want to animate and then click the object to select it.**

   For example, to animate text paragraphs, select the text placeholder that holds the text.

2. **Select the Animations tab on the Ribbon.**

3. **If you haven't already done so, click the Animation Pane button.**

   This step opens the Animation pane.

4. **Click the Add Animation button and then select the effect you want to create from the menu that appears.**

   Clicking the Add Animation button menu reveals a menu that lists the four types of effects: Entrance, Emphasis, Exit, and Motion Path. In this example, I chose the Fly In entrance effect.

   The entrance effect you selected is added to the Animation pane, as shown in Figure 13-7.

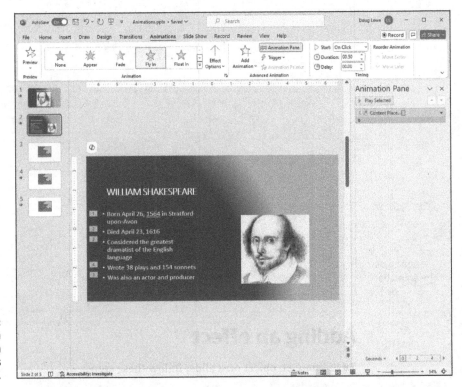

FIGURE 13-7: The Animation pane after an animation has been added.

Note that each of the paragraphs in the text placeholder has been assigned a number to indicate the sequence in which the paragraphs will be animated. In the Animation pane, the animation that was added in Step 4 is given the single number 1; numbers 2 through 5 don't appear in the pane. That's because although this animation is applied to five separate paragraphs, it's treated as a single animation in the Animation pane.

However, if you click the double down arrow beneath the animation, the individual animations will be listed separately, as shown in Figure 13-8.

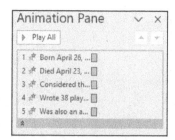

FIGURE 13-8:
Text paragraphs can be listed separately in the Animation pane.

5. **(Optional) Use the Effect Options control to select additional options for the effect.**

   To set the effect options, click the down arrow to the right of the animation for which you want to set effect options; then choose Effect Options from the drop-down menu (*not* the Effects Options button on the Ribbon). This brings up a dialog box that lets you choose options for the effect you've selected. For example, if you choose a Fly In effect, you can specify the direction from which you want the text to fly in.

6. **To preview the animation, click the Play button at the bottom of the Animation pane.**

   Or, if you prefer, just run the slide show to see how the animation looks. If nothing happens, click the mouse button to start the animation.

If you add more than one effect to a slide, the effects are initiated one at a time by mouse clicks, in the order in which you create them. You can drag effects up or down in the custom animation list to change the order of the effects. (For more information about changing the order or setting up automatic effects, see the "Timing your animations" section, later in this chapter.)

Effect Options

You can further tweak an effect by selecting an animation effect, and then clicking the Effect Options button (shown in the margin). A list of options, similar to the one shown in Figure 13-9, appears.

For even more control, click the flyout button at the lower-right corner of the Animation group. This brings up a dialog box similar to the one in Figure 13-10, which lets you change a wide variety of effect options, add a sound to the animation, change the color of the object after the animation completes, and specify how you want text animated (All at Once, One Word at a Time, or One Letter at a Time). Depending on the type of effect, additional controls may appear in this dialog box.

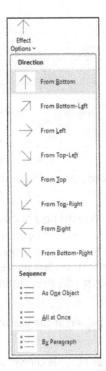

FIGURE 13-9: Choosing effect options.

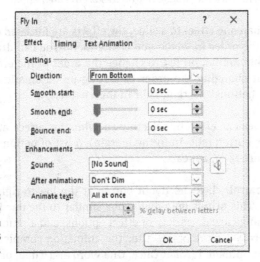

FIGURE 13-10: Using the animation settings dialog box.

More about animating text

The most common reason for animating text is to draw attention to your text one paragraph at a time while you show your presentation. One way to do this is to create an entrance effect for the text placeholder and then adjust the effect settings so that the entrance effect is applied one paragraph at a time. When you do that, your slide initially appears empty except for the title. Click once, and the first paragraph appears. Talk about that paragraph for a while, and then click again to bring up the second paragraph. You can keep talking and clicking until all the paragraphs have appeared. When you click again, PowerPoint calls up the next slide.

Another approach is to use an emphasis effect instead of an entrance effect. This sort of effect allows all the paragraphs to display initially on the slide. When you click the mouse, the emphasis effect is applied to the first paragraph — it changes colors, increases in size, spins, whatever. Each time you click, the emphasis effect is applied to the next paragraph in sequence.

Either way, you must first add the effect for the text placeholder and then call up the Effect Settings dialog box by clicking the down arrow next to the effect in the advanced animation list and then choosing Effect Options. Doing this summons the settings dialog box for the text object. Click the Text Animation tab to see the animation settings (see Figure 13-11).

FIGURE 13-11: Animating text.

The Group Text drop-down list, found on the Text Animation tab of the animation settings dialog box, controls how paragraphs appear when you click the mouse during the show, based on the paragraph's outline level. If you have only one outline level on the slide, choosing By 1st Level Paragraphs will do. If you have two or more levels, By 1st Level Paragraphs causes each paragraph to be animated along with any paragraphs that are subordinate to it. If you'd rather animate the second-level paragraphs separately, choose By 2nd Level Paragraphs instead.

CHAPTER 13 **Animating Your Slides** 183

The other controls on this tab let you animate each paragraph automatically after a certain time interval or display the paragraphs in reverse order.

In the following sections, I explain how to make text jiggle and use the Animation Painter.

Making text jiggle

One of my favorite cute little animations is to make text — especially a short heading — jiggle. Not a lot, but just a little. The effect works best if the text has a funny typeface, such as Comic Sans or Jokerman. By using a very small motion path and setting the timing options to repeat until the end of the slide, you can make the text jiggle just a little bit the entire time the slide is on-screen:

1. **Type the text that you want to jiggle and use the Font drop-down list to choose an appropriately silly typeface.**

   Jokerman is a favorite font for jiggling text.

2. **Use the Zoom control at the lower-right corner of the screen to zoom in to 400 percent.**

   You want to zoom way in so you can draw a very small motion path.

3. **On the Animations tab of the Ribbon, click Add Animation and then choose Custom Path from the Motion Paths section of the gallery.**

   You probably have to scroll the gallery to see this option.

   The cursor changes to a little pencil.

4. **Draw a tightly knit scribble pattern directly in the center of the text.**

   Just wiggle the pencil cursor back and forth and up and down in an area of just a few pixels. Go back and forth quite a few times to make the jiggle effect appear to be random.

5. **Zoom back out to normal size.**

6. **In the Animation task pane, click the arrow next to the animation you just created and then choose Timing.**

   The animation settings dialog box appears, letting you set the timing options.

7. **Change the Duration to 2 seconds; from the Repeat drop-down, select Until End of Slide; and then click OK.**

8. **Run the slide show to check the effect.**

   You may have to try this several times before you get an effect you like, adjusting the random scribbles or the duration of the animation. Don't be afraid to experiment!

Using the Animation Painter

The Animation Painter makes it easy to copy a complete animation effect from one object to another. To use the Animation Painter, follow these steps:

1. **Use the techniques presented throughout this chapter to apply an animation effect to one of the objects in your slide show.**

2. **Select the object you've animated.**

3. **In the Advanced Animation group of the Animation tab on the Ribbon, click the Animation Painter button.**

   The mouse pointer changes to a little paintbrush.

4. **Click the object you want to apply the animation to.**

   The animation that you created for the object selected in Step 2 is applied to the object you clicked on in this step.

TIP

If you want to apply the animation to more than one object, double-click the Animation Painter button in Step 3. Then you can repeat Step 4 as many times as you want to copy the animation to multiple objects. When your animation frenzy has come to a close, press the Esc key.

Timing your animations

Most animations are initiated by mouse clicks. However, you can set up several animations to activate automatically — in sequence or all at the same time. To do so, you must use PowerPoint's animation timing features.

The first trick to controlling animation timing is to get the effects listed in the advanced animation list in the correct order. Effects are added to the list in the order you create them. If you plan carefully, you may be able to create the effects in the same order that you want to animate them. More likely, you'll need to change the order of the effects. Fortunately, you can do that easily enough by dragging the effects up or down in the Animation pane.

After you get the effects in the right order, choose an option from the Start dropdown list that's near the top of the Animation pane to set the Start setting for each effect. This setting has three options:

» **Start on Click:** Starts the effect when you click the mouse or press Enter.

» **Start with Previous:** Starts the effect when the effect immediately above it starts. Use this option to animate two or more objects simultaneously.

» **Start after Previous:** Starts the effect as soon as the preceding effect finishes.

Starting with the first effect in the list, click each effect to select it and then choose the Start setting for the effect. If all the effects except the first are set to With Previous or After Previous, the entire slide's animations run automatically after you start the first effect by clicking the mouse.

For example, Figure 13-12 shows a slide with three polygons drawn to resemble pieces of a puzzle, with the pieces animated to create the impression that the puzzle assembles itself. (This figure shows the slide at four stages of the animation so you can see how the pieces come together.)

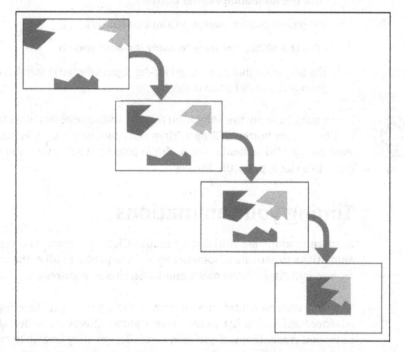

FIGURE 13-12:
An animated puzzle.

TIP

To find out how to draw the shapes that are animated in this illustration, turn to Chapter 16.

Follow these steps to set up an animated puzzle like the one shown in Figure 13-12:

1. **Draw the shapes that you want to use for your puzzle.**

    The shapes representing your puzzle pieces should fit snugly together, as the three shapes in Figure 13-13 do. (In the figure, I have selected the shape at the upper-left corner of the puzzle.)

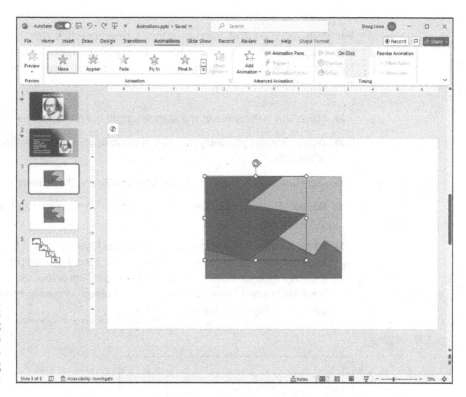

FIGURE 13-13:
Three shapes that fit snugly to create the self-assembling puzzle effect.

2. **Add a Fly In entrance effect for the upper-left piece with the following settings:**

   - **Start (on the Timing tab):** On Click
   - **Duration (on the Timing tab):** 2 Seconds
   - **Direction (on the Effect tab):** From Top-Left

3. **Add a Fly In entrance effect for the upper-right piece with the following settings:**

   - **Start (on the Timing tab):** With Previous
   - **Duration (on the Timing tab):** 2 Seconds
   - **Direction (on the Effect tab):** From Top-Right

4. **Add a Fly In entrance effect for the bottom piece with the following settings:**

   - **Start (on the Timing tab):** With Previous
   - **Duration (on the Timing tab):** 2 Seconds
   - **Direction (on the Effect tab):** From Bottom

For even more control over an effect's timings, click the flyout button at the lower-right corner of the Animation group and then select the Timing tab. A dialog box similar to the one in Figure 13-14 appears. Here's the lowdown on the timing settings:

- **Start:** This is the same as the Start setting in the Animation pane.
- **Delay:** This lets you delay the start of the animation by a specified number of seconds.
- **Duration:** This is the same as the Speed setting in the Animation pane.
- **Repeat:** This lets you repeat the effect so the object is animated several times in succession.
- **Rewind when Done Playing:** Certain effects leave the object in a different condition than the object was in when you started. For example, the object may change color or size or move to a new position on the slide. If you select the Rewind when Done Playing option, the object is restored to its original condition when the animation finishes.

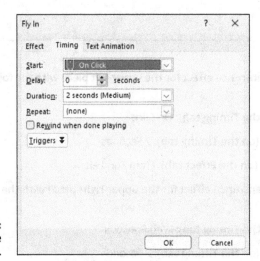

FIGURE 13-14: Establishing the timing settings.

IN THIS CHAPTER

» Discovering stuff about masters you have to know

» Working with masters

» Working with headers and footers

» Creating new masters

» Finding lost placeholders

» Creating templates

» Using presentation sections

Chapter 14
Masters of the Universe Meet the Templates of Doom

Want to add a bit of text to every slide in your presentation? Or maybe add your name and phone number at the bottom of your audience handouts? Or place a picture of your dog in the lower-right corner of each page of your speaker notes?

Masters are the surefire way to add something to every slide. No need to toil separately at each slide. If you want your company logo or your name to show up on every slide, just add it to the master, and it shows up automatically on every slide. If you change your mind, remove it from the master, and — *poof!* — it disappears from every slide. Very convenient.

Masters govern all aspects of a slide's appearance: background color, objects that appear on every slide, text that appears on all slides, and more.

Working with Masters

In PowerPoint, a master governs the appearance of all the slides or pages in a presentation. Each presentation has at least three masters:

- » **Slide master:** Dictates the format of your slides. You work with this master most often when you tweak your slides to cosmetic perfection.
- » **Handout master:** Controls the look of printed handouts.
- » **Notes master:** Determines the characteristics of printed speaker notes.

Each master specifies the appearance of text (font, size, and color, for example), slide background color, animation effects, and any additional text or other objects that you want to appear on each slide or page.

In addition, each master can contain one or more *layouts* that provide different arrangements of text and other elements on the slide. For example, a typical slide master might contain a Title layout and several Text layouts for various types of body text slides.

One interesting — and often useful — aspect of slide masters is that any elements you add to the master itself are also included in each layout that's associated with the master. For example, if you set the background color for the slide master, that color is used for each layout. Likewise, if you add a big blue rectangle in the upper-left corner of the slide master, that rectangle is visible in the upper-left corner of each layout.

However, you can also add elements to an individual layout. Then the element is present only for that layout. For example, you may want to add more graphical elements to the Title layout. Then those elements appear only on slides that use the Title layout.

Here are a few other points to ponder while you lie awake at night thinking about slide masters:

- » Masters aren't optional. Every presentation has them. You can, however, override the formatting of objects contained in the master for a particular slide. This capability enables you to vary the appearance of slides when necessary.
- » PowerPoint allows you to create more than one slide master in a single presentation, so you can mix two or more slide designs in your presentations. That's why I say a presentation has *at least* three masters. If you have more than one slide master, a presentation will have more than three masters

altogether. Note, however, that you can still have only one handout or notes master in each presentation. For more information about using more than one slide master, see the section, "Yes, You Can Serve Two Masters," later in this chapter.

» If you've used previous versions of PowerPoint, you may be wondering what happened to the title master. In the old days, there was actually a separate master for title slides. However, in newer versions of PowerPoint, title slides don't have their own masters. Instead, the format of title slides is controlled by a Title Slide layout that belongs to a particular slide master.

Modifying the slide master

If you don't like the layout of your slides, open the slide master and do something about it, as shown in these steps:

1. **Open Slide Master view by selecting the View tab on the Ribbon and then clicking the Slide Master button (shown in the margin), found in the Master Views group.**

   Alternatively, you can hold down the Shift key and click the Normal View button near the lower right of the screen.

2. **Behold the slide master in all its splendor.**

   Figure 14-1 shows a typical slide master. You can see the placeholders for the slide title and body text. The master can also contain background colors and other elements that are present on each slide.

   The slide master includes placeholders for three objects that appear at the bottom of each slide: the Date area, the Footer area, and the Number area. These special areas are described later in this chapter in the "Using Headers and Footers" section.

   A thumbnail of each slide master, as well as the layouts for each master, are shown on the left side of the screen.

3. **Make any formatting changes that you want.**

   Select the text you want to apply a new style to and make your formatting changes. If you want all the slide titles to be in italics, for example, select the title text and then press Ctrl+I or click the Italic button on the Formatting toolbar.

TIP

   Make sure the slide master itself is selected — not one of its layouts. That way, any changes you make will apply to all the layouts associated with the slide master.

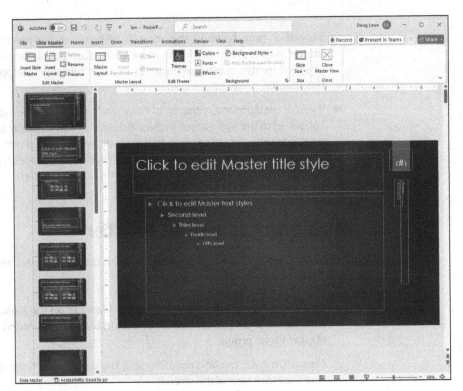

FIGURE 14-1:
Slide Master view.

4. **(Optional) To add elements that are specific to one of the layouts, select the layout and then add your changes.**

   For example, you may want to add more graphical elements or select different fonts for your title slides. To do that, select the Title Slide layout and make your changes.

5. **Click the Normal View button near the lower right of the window to return to Normal view.**

   You're done!

Notice that the body object contains paragraphs for five outline levels formatted with different point sizes, indentations, and bullet styles. If you want to change the way an outline level is formatted, this is the place to do so.

TIP

You can type all you want in the title or object area placeholders, but the text that you type doesn't appear on the slides. The text that appears in these placeholders is provided only so you can see the effect of the formatting changes you apply. (To insert text that appears on each slide, see the later section, "Adding recurring text or other elements.")

TIP

You can edit any other object on the master by clicking it. Unlike the title and object area placeholders, any text you type in other slide master objects appears exactly as you type it on each slide.

Working with the Slide Master and Edit Master tabs

When you switch to Slide Master view, an entirely new tab appears on the Ribbon. This new tab — appropriately called Slide Master — is shown in Figure 14-2.

FIGURE 14-2: The Slide Master tab.

Throughout this chapter, I show you how to use many of the controls on this tab. For now, here's a quick overview of each group on this tab and the controls found in them:

» **Edit Master:** The controls in this group let you edit the slide master. You can click the Insert Slide Master button to create a new slide master, or you can click the Insert Layout button to add a new layout element to an existing master. You can also click the Delete and Rename buttons to delete or rename masters or layouts. For information about the Preserve button, see the section "Preserving your masters," later in this chapter.

» **Master Layout:** The controls in this group let you edit a layout by adding or removing placeholders, the title, and footer elements.

» **Edit Theme:** The controls in this group let you apply a theme to a master or a layout. (For more information about themes, flip to Chapter 12.)

» **Background:** The controls in this group let you set the background for a master or a layout. (See Chapter 12 for more information.)

» **Size:** The controls in this group let you select Standard, Widescreen, or a custom slide size.

» **Close:** This group contains a Close Master View button that returns you to Normal view.

Adding recurring text or other elements

To add recurring text to each slide, follow this procedure:

1. **If it isn't displayed already, open the slide master by clicking the Slide Master button (shown in the margin) in the Master Views group on the Views tab on the Ribbon.**

2. **Add a text box to the slide master by selecting the Insert tab on the Ribbon and then clicking the Text Box button (found in the Text group).**

   Click where you want to add the text.

3. **Type the text that you want to appear on each slide.**

   For example, "Call 1-800-555-BARD today! Don't delay! Poets and playwrights are standing by!"

4. **Format the text however you want.**

   For example, if you want bold, press Ctrl+B or click the Bold button on the Formatting toolbar. (See Chapter 11 for more on text formatting.)

5. **Click the Normal View button to return to your presentation.**

   Now's the time to gloat over your work. Lasso some coworkers and show 'em how proud you are that you added some text that appears on each slide in your presentation.

You can add other types of objects to the slide master, too. You can add clip art, pictures, or even a video or sound clip. Anything that you can add to an individual slide can be added to the slide master.

After you place an object on the slide master, you can grab it with the mouse and move it or resize it in any way you want. The object appears in the same location and size on each slide.

To delete an object from the slide master, click it and press Delete. To delete a text object, click the object, then click again on the object frame and then press Delete.

Applying themes to your masters

You can use the Edit Theme group in the Slide Master tab on the Ribbon to change the theme applied to a slide master. *Note:* All the layouts that belong to a given master use the same theme. So, it doesn't matter whether the slide master itself or one of its layouts is selected when you change the theme; either way, the entire slide master is changed.

To change the theme for a slide master, follow these steps:

1. **If it isn't displayed already, open the slide master by clicking the Slide Master button (shown in the margin) in the Master Views group on the Views tab on the Ribbon.**

2. **Select the Slide Master tab on the Ribbon, and use the Themes drop-down list to select the theme you want to apply to the slide master.**

3. **(Optional) Use the Colors, Fonts, and Effects controls to modify the color scheme, fonts, and effects used for the theme.**

   Treat yourself to a bag of Cheetos if it works the first time. If it doesn't work, have a bag of Cheetos anyway. Then rub all that orange gunk that sticks to your fingers on the computer screen. That will apply the Cheetos Orange color scheme to your slide master — at least temporarily.

   PowerPoint themes are hefty enough that I devote an entire chapter to them. Go to Chapter 12 if you need to know how they work.

TIP

If you want to adjust the slide background, use the Background Styles control. Chapter 12 walks you through this feature.

Adding new layouts

If you don't like the standard layouts that come with PowerPoint's built-in slide master, you can add a layout and customize it any way you want. To add your own layout, just follow these steps:

1. **If it isn't displayed already, open the slide master by clicking the Slide Master button in the Master Views group on the Views tab on the Ribbon.**

2. **Select the Slide Master tab on the Ribbon, and click Insert Layout in the Edit Master group (shown in the margin).**

   A new blank layout is inserted in the current slide master.

3. **Use the Insert Placeholder drop-down list in the Master Layout group on the Slide Master tab on the Ribbon to insert whatever placeholders you want to add to the new layout.**

   This control reveals a list of placeholder types you can insert. The options are Content, Text, Picture, Chart, Table, Diagram, Media, and Clip Art.

4. **Play with the layout until you get it just right.**

   You can move and resize the placeholders to your heart's content, and you can apply any formatting or other options you want for the layout.

5. **When you're happy, click the Close Master View button to switch back to Normal view.**

CHAPTER 14 **Masters of the Universe Meet the Templates of Doom**

Modifying the handout master

Follow these simple steps to change the handout master:

1. **Open the handout master by clicking the Handout Master button (shown in the margin) in the Master Views group on the Views tab on the Ribbon.**

   The handout master rears its ugly head, as shown in Figure 14-3. Notice that it includes a special Handout Master tab on the Ribbon.

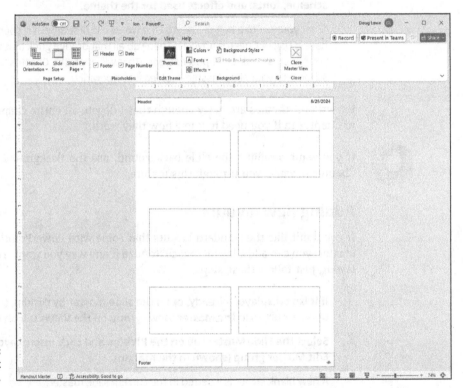

FIGURE 14-3: The handout master.

2. **Mess around with it.**

   The handout master shows the arrangement of handouts for slides printed two, three, four, six, or nine per page, plus the arrangement for printing outlines. You can switch among these different handout layouts by using the Slides-Per-Page control in the Page Setup group on the Handout Master tab.

   Unfortunately, you can't move, resize, or delete the slide and outline placeholders that appear in the handout master. You *can*, however, add or change elements that you want to appear on each handout page, such as your name and phone number, a page number, and maybe a good lawyer joke.

3. **Click the Close Master View button on the Handout Master tab on the Ribbon.**

   PowerPoint returns to Normal view.

4. **Print a handout to see whether your changes worked.**

   Handout master elements are invisible until you print them, so you should print at least one handout page to check your work.

When you print handout pages, the slides are formatted according to the slide master. You can't change the appearance of the slides from the handout master.

Modifying the notes master

Notes pages consist of a reduced image of the slide, plus any notes that you type to go along with the slide. For more information about creating and using notes pages, see Chapter 6.

When printed, notes pages are formatted according to the notes master. To change the notes master, follow these steps:

1. **Open the notes master by clicking the Notes Master button (shown in the margin) in the Master Views group on the Views tab on the Ribbon.**

   The notes master comes to life, as shown in Figure 14-4.

2. **Indulge yourself.**

   The notes master contains two main placeholders — one for your notes and the other for the slide. You can move or change the size of either of these objects, and you can change the format of the text in the notes placeholder. You also can add or change elements that you want to appear on each handout page. Also notice the convenient placement of the header, footer, date, and page number blocks.

3. **Click the Close Master View button.**

   PowerPoint returns to Normal view.

4. **Print your notes to see whether your changes worked.**

TIP

At the very least, add page numbers to your speaker notes. That way, if you drop a stack of notes pages, you can use the page numbers to quickly sort them back into order.

If public speaking gives you severe stomach cramps, add the text "Just picture them naked" to the notes master. It works for me every time.

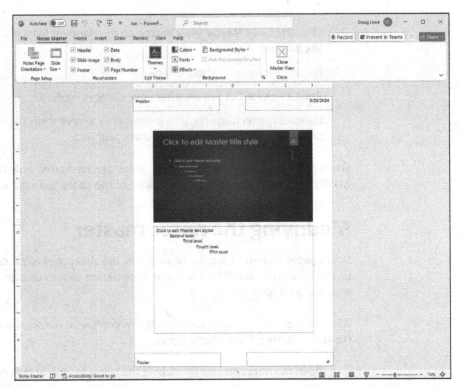

FIGURE 14-4: The notes master.

Using Masters

You don't have to do anything special to apply the formats from a master to your slide; all slides automatically pick up the master format unless you specify otherwise. So, this section really should be titled "Not Using Masters" because it talks about how to *not* use the formats provided by masters.

Overriding the master text style

To override the text style specified by a slide master, simply format the text however you want while you're working in Normal view. The formatting changes you make apply only to the selected text. The slide masters aren't affected.

REMEMBER

The only way to change one of the masters is to do it directly by switching to the appropriate master view. Therefore, any formatting changes you make while in Slide view affect only that slide.

198 PART 3 **Creating Great-Looking Slides**

TIP If you change the layout or formatting of text elements on a slide (for example, if you move the title placeholder or change the title font) and then decide that you liked it better the way it was, you can quickly reapply the text style from the slide master. Right-click the slide in the Slide Preview pane (on the left side of the screen) and then choose Reset Slide from the menu that appears.

Hiding background objects

Slide masters enable you to add background objects that appear on every slide in your presentation. You can, however, hide the background objects for selected slides. You can also change the background color or effect used for an individual slide. Here's how:

1. **Display the slide that you want to show with a plain background.**
2. **Select the Design tab on the Ribbon and then click Format Background to reveal the Format Background pane.**
3. **Check the Hide Background Graphics check box found in the Format Background pane.**

TIP Hiding background objects or changing the background color or effect applies only to the current slide. Other slides are unaffected.

If you want to remove some but not all of the background objects from a single slide, try this trick:

1. **Hide the background graphics from the slide by choosing Design ⇨ Format Background and then checking the Hide Background Graphics check box.**
2. **Open the slide master by clicking the Slide Master button (shown in the margin) in the Master Views group on the Views tab on the Ribbon.**
3. **Hold down the Shift key and then click each of the background objects that you want to appear.**
4. **Press Ctrl+C to copy these objects to the Clipboard.**
5. **Return to Normal view by clicking the Normal button at the bottom of the screen.**
6. **Press Ctrl+V to paste the objects from the Clipboard.**
7. **Select the Design tab on the Ribbon and then click the Send to Back button, found in the Arrange group, if the background objects obscure other slide objects or text.**

TIP Note that if you paste objects in this way, those objects are no longer tied to the slide master. So, if you later change the objects on the slide master, the change won't be reflected on the slides with the pasted copies of the objects.

Using Headers and Footers

Headers and footers provide a convenient way to place repeating text at the top or bottom of each slide, handout, or notes page. You can add the time and date, slide number or page number, or any other information that you want to appear on each slide or page, such as your name or the title of your presentation.

The PowerPoint slide masters include three placeholders for such information:

- » **Date area:** Display a date and time.
- » **Number area:** Display the slide number.
- » **Footer area:** Display any text that you want to see on each slide.

TIP In addition, handout and notes masters include a fourth placeholder, the *Header area*, which provides an additional area for text that you want to see on each page.

Although the Date, Number, and Footer areas normally appear at the bottom of the slide in the slide masters, you can move them to the top by switching to Slide view or Slide Master view and then dragging the placeholders to the top of the slide.

Adding a date, number, or footer to slides

To add a date, number, or footer to your slides, follow these steps:

Header & Footer

1. **Select the Insert tab on the Ribbon and then click the Header & Footer button (shown in the margin), found in the Text group.**

   The Header and Footer dialog box appears, as shown in Figure 14-5. (If necessary, select the Slide tab so that you see the slide footer options, as shown in the figure.)

2. **To display the date, select the Date and Time check box and then select the date format that you want in the list box beneath the Update Automatically radio button.**

   Alternatively, you can select the Fixed radio button and then type any text that you want in the Fixed text box. The text you type appears in the Date area of the slide master.

FIGURE 14-5:
The Header and Footer dialog box.

3. **To display slide numbers, select the Slide Number check box.**

4. **To display a footer on each slide, select the Footer check box and then type the text that you want to appear on each slide in the Footer text box.**

   For example, you can type your name, your company name, a subliminal message, or the name of your presentation.

5. **If you want the date, number, and footer to appear on every slide except for the title slide, select the Don't Show on Title Slide check box.**

6. **Click Apply to All.**

TIP

If you're going to give a presentation on a certain date in the future (for example, at a sales conference or a trade show), type the date that you'll be giving the presentation directly into the Fixed text box. You can use the same technique to post-date presentations that you never really gave but need to supply to your legal counsel to back up your alibi. (You can also type any other type of text you want to appear here.)

If you want to change the Footer areas for just one slide, click Apply instead of Apply to All. This option comes in handy for those occasional slides that contain a graphic or a block of text that crowds up against the footer areas. You can easily suppress the footer information for that slide to make room for the large graphic or text.

Adding a header or footer to notes or handout pages

To add header and footer information to notes or handout pages, follow the steps described in the preceding section, "Adding a date, number, or footer to slides," except select the Notes and Handouts tab after the Header and Footer dialog box appears. Selecting this tab displays a dialog box that's similar to the Header and Footer dialog box for Slide, except that it gives you an additional option to add a header that appears at the top of each page. After you indicate how you want to print the Date, Header, Number, and Footer areas, click the Apply to All button.

Editing the header and footer placeholders directly

If you want, you can edit the text that appears in the header and footer placeholders directly. First, display the appropriate master: slide, handout, or notes. Then click the date, number, footer, or header placeholder and start typing.

You may notice that the placeholders include special codes for the options that you indicated in the Header and Footer dialog box. For example, the date placeholder may contain the text *<date,time>* if you indicated that the date should be displayed. You can type text before or after these codes, but you should leave the codes themselves alone.

Yes, You Can Serve Two Masters

In spite of the biblical edict, Microsoft has endowed PowerPoint with the capability to have more than one slide master. This feature lets you set up two or more slide masters and then choose which master you want to use for each slide in your presentation.

The following sections explain how to use the multiple masters feature.

Creating a new slide master

To add a new master to a presentation, follow these steps:

1. **Switch to Slide Master view by selecting the View tab on the Ribbon and clicking the Slide Master button, found in the Presentation Views group.**

If you prefer, hold down the Shift key and click the Normal View button near the lower-right corner of the screen.

2. **On the Slide Master tab on the Ribbon, click the Insert Slide Master button in the Edit Master group (shown in the margin).**

Insert Slide Master

A new slide master appears, as shown in Figure 14-6. Notice that a thumbnail for the new slide master is added to the list of thumbnails on the left side of the screen and that the new slide master uses PowerPoint's default settings (white background, black text, and so forth).

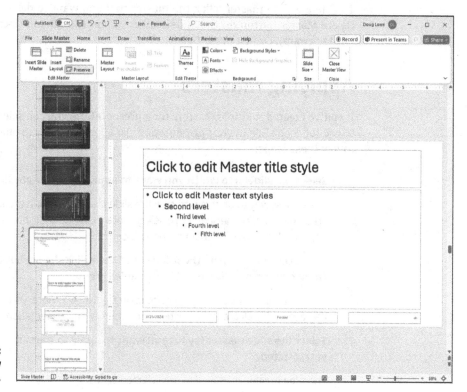

FIGURE 14-6: Creating a new slide master.

3. **Modify the new slide master to your liking.**

    You can make any formatting changes you want: Change the background color and text styles, add background objects, and so on.

4. **Click the Close Master View button on the Slide Master tab on the Ribbon to return to Normal view.**

    You can now begin using the new master that you created. (See the next section, "Applying masters," for more information.)

TIP Another way to create a new slide master is to duplicate one of your presentation's existing slide masters. When you do that, the new slide master inherits the formatting of the original one. This inheritance can save you a lot of work, especially if you want to create a new slide master that varies from an existing one in only a minor way, such as having a different background color.

To duplicate a slide master, click the master that you want to duplicate in the thumbnails on the left of the screen and then press Ctrl+D or right-click the thumbnail and choose Duplicate Layout.

To delete a slide master, click the master that you want to delete. Then click the Delete Master button on the Slide Master tab on the Ribbon (located in the Edit Master group). Or just press Delete.

Applying masters

If you've created multiple masters for a presentation, you can select which master to use for each slide in your presentation. To apply a master to one or more slides, follow these steps:

1. **Select the slide(s) to which you want to apply the alternate slide master.**

   The easiest way to do this is to click the slide that you want in the thumbnails area on the left of the screen. To select more than one slide, hold down the Ctrl key and click each slide that you want to select.

2. **Select the Home tab on the Ribbon and then click the Layout button (shown in the margin) found in the Slides group.**

   This action summons the gallery shown in Figure 14-7. Here, you can see all the layouts for all the slide masters contained in the presentation.

3. **Select the slide master layout you want to apply to the slides you selected.**

   The slide master is applied to the selected slides.

Preserving your masters

PowerPoint has a bad habit of deleting slide masters when they're no longer used in your presentation. For example, if you create a new slide master and then apply it to all the slides in your presentation, PowerPoint assumes that you no longer need the original slide master. So, the original is deleted. Poof! Your presentation is now one pickle short of a full jar.

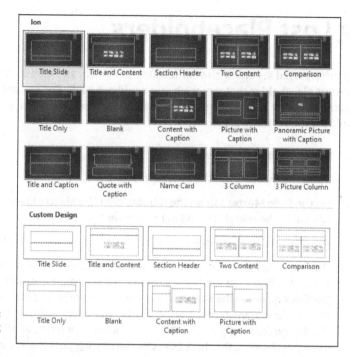

FIGURE 14-7: Choosing a layout.

You can prevent this from happening with the Preserve Master option for your slide masters. Any new slide masters that you create automatically get the Preserve Master option, so they won't be deleted. However, the slide masters that your presentations start off with don't have the Preserve Master option, so you may want to set it yourself.

 To preserve a master, switch to Slide Master view, click the thumbnail for the master that you want to preserve, and then click the Preserve button (shown in the margin) found in the Edit Master group on the Slide Master tab on the Ribbon. A little pushpin icon appears next to the master's thumbnail to show that the master will be preserved.

WARNING Don't click the Preserve button indiscriminately! If you click it for a master that already has the Preserve Master setting, Preserve Master is removed for that master. Then the master is subject to premature deletion.

Restoring Lost Placeholders

If you've played around with your masters too much, you may inadvertently delete a layout placeholder that you wish you could get back. For example, suppose you delete the footer placeholder from a master and now you want it back. No problem! Just follow these steps:

1. **Switch to Slide Master view.**

2. **Open the master with the missing placeholder.**

3. **On the Slide Master tab on the Ribbon, click the Master Layout button (shown in the margin) found in the Master Layout group.**

   Master Layout

   This step calls up the Master Layout dialog box, shown in Figure 14-8.

   TIP The Master Layout dialog box is one of the strangest dialog boxes you encounter. If you summon it for a master that still has all its placeholders, all the check boxes on the Master Layout dialog box are grayed out. So, all you can do is look at the controls, grunt, scratch your head, and then click OK to dismiss the seemingly useless dialog box. However, if you *have* deleted one or more placeholders, the check boxes for the missing placeholders are available.

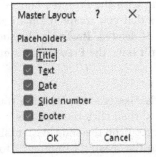

FIGURE 14-8: The Master Layout dialog box.

4. **Select the check boxes for the placeholders that you want to restore.**

5. **Click OK.**

   The missing placeholders reappear.

   TIP Note that the preceding procedure works only for actual masters, not for individual layouts. If you delete a placeholder from a layout, you must re-create it by using the Insert Placeholder command as I describe in the section "Adding new layouts," earlier in this chapter.

Working with Templates

If you had to create every presentation from scratch, starting with a blank slide, you would probably put PowerPoint back in its box and use it as a bookend. Creating a presentation is easy, but creating one that looks good is a different story. Making a good-looking presentation is tough even for the artistically inclined. For left-brained, nonartistic types, it's next to impossible.

REMEMBER

Thank heavens for themes and templates. A *theme* is simply a PowerPoint presentation with predefined slide masters. A *template* is similar to a theme, but it also includes boilerplate text. Because themes and templates are so similar, I refer to both of them simply as *templates* throughout the rest of this section.

Templates jump-start the process of creating good-looking presentations. You can create your own templates, but fortunately PowerPoint comes with a ton of them designed by professional artists who understand color combinations, balance, and all that other artsy stuff. Have a croissant and celebrate.

Templates use the special file extension .potx, but you can also use ordinary PowerPoint presentation files (.pptx) as themes or templates. You can, therefore, use any of your own presentations as a template. If you make extensive changes to a presentation's masters, you can use that presentation as a template for other presentations that you create. Or, you can save the presentation as a template by using the .potx file extension.

REMEMBER

Because a template is a presentation, you can open it and change it if you want.

Creating a new template

If none of the templates that come with PowerPoint appeals to you, you can easily create your own. All you have to do is create a presentation with the masters and the color scheme set up just the way you want, and then save it as a template. Here are a few points to remember about templates:

- >> If you want to make minor modifications to one of the supplied templates, open the template by using the Open command. Then make your changes and use the Save As command to save the template under a new name.
- >> You can also create your own presentation templates. Just create the template as a normal presentation and add however many slides you want to include.
- >> Choose a location to store all your templates. You need to know the path to this location to create new presentations based on your templates.

Creating a presentation based on a template

To create a new presentation based on a template you've created yourself, you must first configure PowerPoint to look for personal templates. To do so, choose File ⇨ Options, click Save, enter the path to your templates folder in the Default Personal Templates Location box, and click OK.

After you've configured the template location, you can create a new presentation based on one of your templates by choosing File ⇨ New and then clicking on Personal to display a list of your personal templates. For example, in Figure 14-9, you can see a template I previously created (named Monthly Report) as an template option to use for a new presentation.

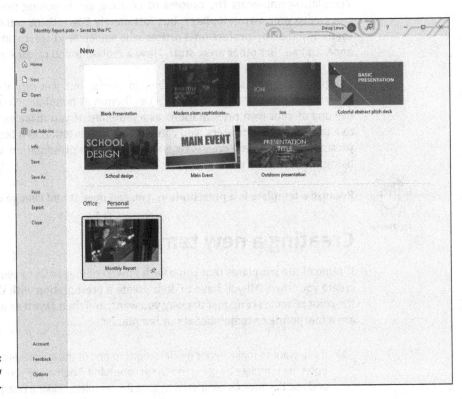

FIGURE 14-9:
Creating a new presentation.

Working with Presentation Sections

Sections let you divide a presentation into two or more groups of slides. Sections are designed for large presentations that contain a multitude of slides that can easily be combined into logical groupings.

Using sections couldn't be easier. Just follow these steps:

1. **Return to Normal view.**
2. **Select the Home tab.**
3. **Select the first slide that you want in the new section.**
4. **In the Slides group on the Home tab, click Section (shown in the margin) and then choose Add Section.**

   The dialog box shown in Figure 14-10 appears.

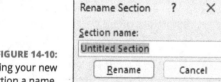

FIGURE 14-10: Giving your new section a name.

5. **Enter a name for your section, and then click Rename.**

   The new section is created and appears in the Slide thumbnail area with the name you gave it, as shown in Figure 14-11.

After you've created one or more sections in your presentation, you can

>> Select all the slides in a section by clicking the section header in the Slide Thumbnail pane.
>> Collapse or expand the sections in the Slide Thumbnail pane by clicking the arrow at the left of the section header.
>> Rename a section by right-clicking the section header and choosing Rename Section.
>> Move all the slides in a section by dragging the section header to a new location in the Slide Thumbnail pane.

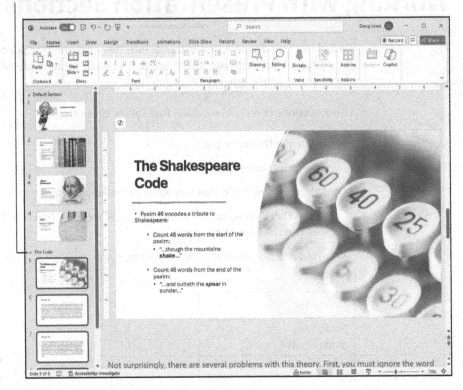

FIGURE 14-11:
The new section is added.

» Delete the slides in a section, as well as the section itself, by clicking the section header to select the section and then pressing the Delete key.

» Remove a section without deleting its slides by right-clicking the section header and choosing Remove Section.

» Go to the first slide in any section, during a slide show, by clicking the Menu icon in the lower-left corner of the slide and then choosing Go to Section and selecting the section you want to go to.

4
Embellishing Your Slides

IN THIS PART . . .

Get familiar with the different types of computer pictures, how you can insert them into a PowerPoint slide, and how you can fiddle with them to get them to look better.

Find out about the powerful drawing tools of PowerPoint.

Add a chart to your presentation and get it to look the way you want.

Add all sorts of embellishments to your slides, including one of the coolest ways to embellish your slides — special diagrams called *SmartArt*.

Craft some impressive, high-tech presentations by including and editing video and sound elements.

Insert tables into your presentations.

IN THIS CHAPTER

» Getting to know bitmap pictures and vector drawings

» Adding pictures to your presentation

» Moving, sizing, stretching, and cropping pictures

» Adding panache to your pictures

» Tackling technical details like sharpness, brightness, contrast, and color

» Compressing your pictures to save disc space

» Using 3D models in your presentation

Chapter **15**

Inserting Pictures

Face it: Most of us weren't born with even an ounce of artistic ability. Some day (soon, hopefully), the genetic researchers combing through the billions and billions of genes strung out on those twisty DNA helixes will discover the artist gene. Then, in spite of protests from the da Vincis, van Goghs, and Monets among us (who fear that their NEA grants will be threatened), doctors will splice the little gene into our DNA strands so we can all be artists. Of course, this procedure won't be without its side effects: Some will develop an insatiable craving for croissants; others will inexplicably develop Dutch accents and whack off their ears. But artists we shall be.

Until then, we have to rely on clip art pictures, pictures we've found on the internet, or pictures we have on our hard drives.

In this chapter, you find out about the different types of computer pictures and how you can insert them into a PowerPoint slide. Then, after you get your pictures into PowerPoint, you discover how you can fiddle with them to get them to look better.

Exploring the Many Types of Pictures

The world is awash with many different picture file formats. Fortunately, PowerPoint works with almost all these formats. The following sections describe the two basic types of pictures you can work with in PowerPoint: bitmap pictures and vector drawings.

Bitmap pictures

A *bitmap picture* is a collection of small dots that compose an image. Bitmap pictures are most often used for photographs and for icons and other buttons used on web pages. You can create your own bitmap pictures with a scanner, a digital camera, or a picture-drawing program such as Adobe Photoshop. You can even create crude bitmap pictures with Microsoft Paint, which is a free program that comes with Windows.

The dots that make up a bitmap picture are called *pixels.* The number of pixels in a given picture is referred to as the picture's *resolution* and is stated in terms of width and height. For example, an image that is 1,000 pixels wide and 600 pixels tall has a resolution of 1,000 x 600 pixels.

To find the total number of pixels in an image, multiply the width and height values. Thus, a 1,000-x-600-pixel image has a total of 600,000 pixels.

The term *pixel density* refers to the density of bits per inch when an image is displayed or printed. For example, a 1,000-x-600-pixel image scaled to 5 inches wide would display 200 pixels per inch. The same image scaled to 10 inches wide would display just 100 pixels per inch. The higher the pixel density, the sharper the image.

The amount of color information stored for the picture — also referred to as the picture's *color depth* — affects how many bytes of computer memory the picture requires. The color depth determines how many different colors the picture can contain. Most pictures have one of two color depths: 256 colors or 16.7 million colors. Most simple charts, diagrams, cartoons, and other types of clip art look fine at 256 colors. Photographs usually use 16.7 million colors.

Pictures with 16.7 million colors are also known as *true color* pictures or *24-bit color* pictures.

A 4-x-6-inch photograph, which has more than 2 million pixels, requires about 2MB to store with 256 colors. With true color, the size of the picture jumps to a whopping 6.4MB. Fortunately, bitmap pictures can be compressed to reduce their size without noticeably distorting the image. Depending on the actual contents of the picture, a 6MB picture may be reduced to 250KB or less.

Table 15-1 lists the bitmap file formats that PowerPoint supports, along with the file extensions usually associated with each image format.

TABLE 15-1 PowerPoint's Bitmap Picture File Formats

Format	File Extension(s)	What It Is
Windows Bitmap	BMP, DIB, or RLE	Garden-variety Windows bitmap file, used by Windows Paint and many other programs.
Graphics Interchange Format	GIF	A format commonly used for small internet pictures. GIF files can include simple animations.
JPEG File Interchange Format	JPG, JPEG, JFIF, or JPE	A common format for photographs that includes built-in compression.
Portable Network Graphics	PNG	An image format designed for internet graphics.
Tag Image File Format	TIF or TIFF	Another bitmap program most often used for high-quality photographs.
High-Efficiency Image File Format	HEIF, HEIC, or HIF	An image format that can include single images or image sequences, as well as audio and video streams.
Icon	ICO	The standard format for Windows icons. ICO files contain one or more small images at various sizes.

TIP

If you have a choice in the matter, I recommend you use JPEG images for photographs that you want to include in PowerPoint presentations because JPEG's built-in compression saves hard-drive space.

Victor, give me a vector

Besides bitmap pictures, you can also use vector drawings in PowerPoint. A *vector drawing* is a picture file that contains a detailed definition of each shape that makes up the image. Vector drawings are usually created with high-powered drawing programs, such as Adobe Illustrator.

PowerPoint supports all the most popular vector drawing formats, as I describe in Table 15-2.

TABLE 15-2 PowerPoint's Vector File Formats

File Format	Extension	What It Is
Windows Metafile	WMF	A vector format developed by Microsoft. Note that WMF files can hold bitmap as well as vector data.
Windows Enhanced Metafile	EMF	An enhanced version of the WMF format.
Compressed Windows Metafile	WMZ	A compressed version of the WMF format.
Compressed Windows Enhanced Metafile	EMZ	A compressed version of the EMF format.
Scalable Vector Graphics	SVG	A vector file format based on XML. SVG files can contain animation.

Inserting Pictures in Your Presentation

Are you sitting down? Whether you buy PowerPoint by itself or get it as part of Microsoft 365, you also get access to an online collection of thousands of clip art pictures that you can drop directly into your presentations. You can also download images from the web or use images you already have on your hard drive.

TIP

Don't overdo the pictures. One surefire way to guarantee an amateurish look to your presentation is to load it down with three cheesy clip art pictures on every slide. Judicious use is much more effective.

From the web

Here's how to insert pictures into your presentation that you download from the web:

1. **Connect to the internet.**

   You can't grab pictures from the web if you're not connected.

2. **Move to the slide on which you want to plaster the picture.**

   If you want the same picture to appear on every slide, move to Slide Master view.

Pictures

3. **Select the Insert tab on the Ribbon, click the Pictures button (shown in the margin), and then choose Online Pictures.**

   After a brief moment's hesitation, the Online Pictures dialog box appears (see Figure 15-1).

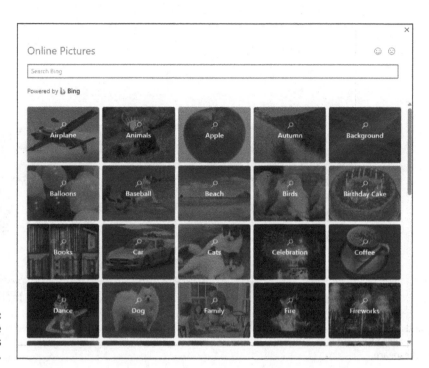

FIGURE 15-1: The Online Pictures dialog box.

4. **Type a keyword in the Search Bing text box and then press Enter.**

    For example, to search for pictures of William Shakespeare, type **Shakespeare** in the text box and then press Enter.

    PowerPoint searches Bing to locate the picture you're looking for, and then it displays thumbnails of the pictures it finds (see Figure 15-2).

5. **Click the picture that you want to use and then click Insert.**

    The picture is inserted on the current slide, as shown in Figure 15-3.

    When you insert a picture, a new tab named Picture Format appears on the Ribbon. In addition, the Design Ideas pane appears, offering suggestions for how you may want to alter the appearance of the picture you just inserted.

    Notice that when you insert a picture, the Designer automatically pops up to offer suggestions for improving the look of the picture on your slide.

WARNING

Some of the images displayed by Bing's image search may be copyrighted, so make sure you have permission from the copyright holder before using images found on Bing.

TIP

6. **Drag and resize the picture as needed.**

    To find out how, see the "Moving, Sizing, Stretching, and Cropping Pictures" section, later in this chapter.

CHAPTER 15 **Inserting Pictures** 217

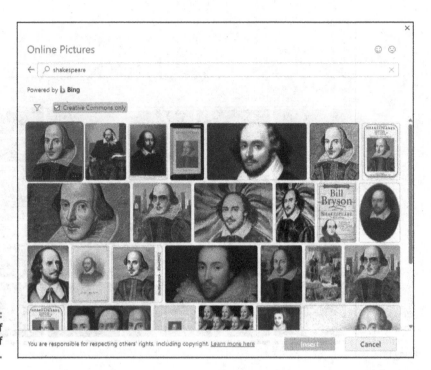

FIGURE 15-2:
Bing finds lots of images of Shakespeare.

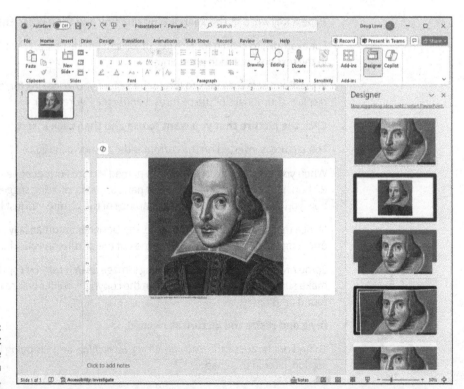

FIGURE 15-3:
PowerPoint inserts the picture on the slide.

From your computer

If you happen to already have an image file on your computer or on OneDrive that you want to insert into a presentation, PowerPoint lets you insert the file. Here's how:

1. **Move to the slide on which you want to splash a picture.**

2. **Select the Insert tab on the Ribbon and then choose Pictures ⇨ This Device.**

   The Insert Picture dialog box appears (see Figure 15-4).

FIGURE 15-4:
The Insert Picture dialog box.

3. **Dig through the bottom of your hard drive until you find the file that you want.**

   The picture you want may be anywhere. Fortunately, the Insert Picture dialog box has all the controls you need to search high and low until you find the file.

   You can also look in your OneDrive if you've saved the picture there. (Note that OneDrive is available only if you use Microsoft 365.)

   TIP

4. **Click the file and then click Insert.**

   You're done! Figure 15-5 shows how a picture appears when it has been inserted on a slide.

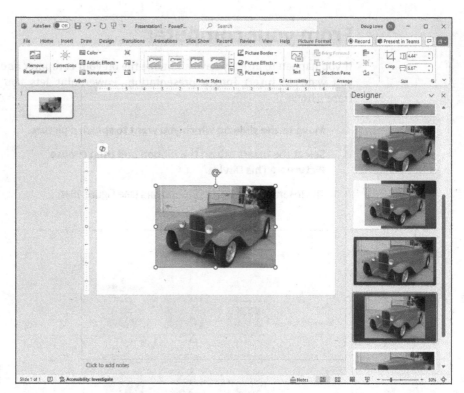

FIGURE 15-5: Nice ride!

TIP

You also can paste a picture directly into PowerPoint by way of the Clipboard. Anything that you can copy to the Clipboard can be pasted into PowerPoint. For example, you can doodle a sketch in Windows Paint, copy it, and then zap over to PowerPoint and paste it. *Voilà!* Instant picture!

From the stock library

In addition to online pictures and pictures from your own computer or OneDrive, PowerPoint provides a nice selection of professional stock images you can use without worrying about copyright details. To insert a stock image, follow these steps:

1. **Move to the slide on which you want to splash a picture.**
2. **Select the Insert tab on the Ribbon and then choose Pictures ⇨ Stock Images.**

   The dialog box shown in Figure 15-6 appears.

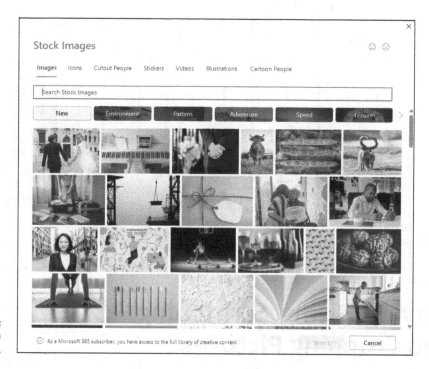

FIGURE 15-6:
Inserting a stock image.

3. **Enter a search word to look for a stock image you'd like to use.**

TIP

The tabs across the top let you select from several predefined categories: Images, Icons, Cutout People, Stickers, Videos, and Illustrations. The Cutout People category is especially interesting — it includes pictures of more than 30 individuals, each in multiple poses. The great thing about these pictures is that they have transparent backgrounds. (For more information about transparent backgrounds, see the section "Removing picture backgrounds" later in this chapter.)

4. **Click the file and then click Insert.**

You're done! Figure 15-7 shows how a picture appears after it has been inserted on a slide.

Actually, for this figure, I inserted two pictures. First, I inserted an image I found after searching on the word *office* to create the impression that we are in an office. Next, I added a cutout person (this one happens to be "Kevin"), adjusted the image size so he would fit better in the scene, and then added a shadow to make the scene a bit more realistic.

CHAPTER 15 **Inserting Pictures** 221

FIGURE 15-7: The image is inserted on the slide.

Moving, Sizing, Stretching, and Cropping Pictures

Because PowerPoint chooses an arbitrary position on the slide to insert pictures, you undoubtedly want to move the clip art to a more convenient location. You probably also want to change the size of the picture if it's too big or too small for your slide.

Follow these steps to force your inserted clip art into full compliance:

1. **Click the picture and drag it wherever you want.**

   You don't have to worry about clicking exactly the edge of the picture or one of its lines — just click anywhere in the picture and drag it around.

2. **Drag one of the eight handles to resize the picture.**

   You can click and drag any of these handles to adjust the size of the picture. When you click one of the corner handles, you can change the height and width of the picture at the same time. When you drag one of the edge handles (top, bottom, left, or right) to change the size of the picture in just one dimension, you distort the picture's outlook as you go.

TIP

When you resize a picture, the picture changes its position on the slide. As a result, you'll likely need to move it after you resize it. If you hold down the Ctrl key while dragging a handle, however, the picture becomes anchored at its center point as you resize it. Therefore, its position is unchanged and you probably won't have to move it.

Stretching a clip art picture by dragging one of the edge handles can dramatically change the picture's appearance. For example, you can stretch an object vertically to make it look tall and thin or horizontally to make it look short and fat.

Sometimes you want to cut off the edges of a picture so you can include just part of the picture in your presentation. For example, you might have a picture of two people, only one of whom you like. You can use PowerPoint's cropping feature to cut off the other person. (Note that you can crop bitmap images, but not vector pictures.)

To crop a picture, select the picture and click the Crop button located near the right side of the Picture Format tab on the Ribbon, found in the Size group. The selection handles change to special crop marks. You can then drag the crop marks around to cut off part of the picture. When you're satisfied, press the Esc key. Figure 15-8 shows three versions of a picture cropped and resized in three different ways.

FIGURE 15-8:
A picture that has been cropped.

TIP

If you decide later that you don't like the cropping, you can right-click the picture and choose Format Picture from the menu that appears. Then click the Reset button.

CHAPTER 15 **Inserting Pictures** **223**

TIP When you crop a picture, the picture still retains a basic rectangular shape. If you prefer to remove the background from an irregular shape in the picture, see the section "Removing picture backgrounds," later in this chapter.

Adding Style to Your Pictures

PowerPoint enables you to draw attention to your pictures by adding stylistic features such as borders, shadows, and reflections. Figure 15-9 shows a slide with several copies of a picture, each with a different style applied.

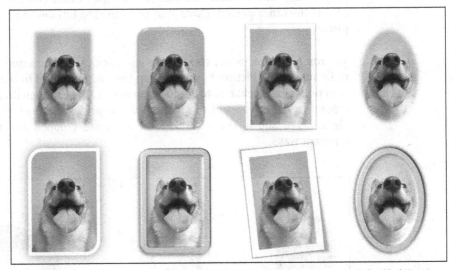

FIGURE 15-9: Pictures with style.

Holly Hildreth/Getty Image

To add a style effect to a picture, select the picture and then select the Picture Format tab on the Ribbon. Then simply select the picture style you want to apply.

PowerPoint comes with 28 predefined picture styles, as shown in Figure 15-10. Each of these styles is simply a combination of three types of formatting that you can apply to pictures: Shape, Border, and Effects. If you want, you can apply these formats individually (see the following sections).

Note that if you use one of these predefined picture styles, the picture will be updated automatically if you later change the presentation's theme. As a result, you should use one of the predefined styles whenever possible.

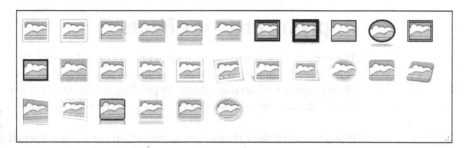

FIGURE 15-10:
The Picture Style gallery.

Applying a picture border

You can apply a border to a picture by selecting the Picture Format tab and clicking Picture Border in the Picture Styles group. This reveals the Picture Border menu, which lets you choose the border color, weight (the width of the border lines), and the pattern of dashes you want to use.

Note that if you've applied a shape to the picture, the border is applied to the shape.

Applying picture effects

The Picture Effects button in the Picture Styles group (located on the Picture Format tab) lets you apply several interesting types of effects to your pictures. When you click this button, a menu with the following options is displayed:

» **Shadow:** Applies a shadow to the picture. You can select one of several predefined shadow effects or call up a dialog box that lets you customize the shadow.

» **Reflection:** Creates a reflected image of the picture beneath the original picture.

» **Glow:** Adds a glowing effect around the edges of the picture.

» **Soft Edges:** Softens the edges of the picture.

» **Bevel:** Creates a 3-D beveled look.

» **3-D Rotation:** Rotates the picture in a way that creates a three-dimensional effect.

TIP

The best way to figure out how to use these effects is to experiment with them to see how they work. Have fun and go crazy — but remember that you don't necessarily need to share the results of your experiments!

Applying artistic effects

The Artistic Effects command applies one of several special filters to your picture in an effort to make the picture look like it was created by an artist rather than photographed with a smartphone. Depending on the nature of the original picture, the results may or may not be convincing — the only way to find out is to try!

When you click the Artistic Effects button on the Picture Format tab, you'll see a preview of how each of the available effects will transform the selected image. Each of the effects has a name, which you can see by hovering the mouse over the preview of the effect. Here's a complete list of the effects that are available:

- Blur
- Cement
- Chalk Sketch
- Crisscross Etching
- Cutout
- Film Grain
- Glass
- Glow Diffused
- Glow Edges
- Light Screen
- Line Drawing
- Marker
- Mosaic Bubbles
- Paint Brush
- Paint Strokes
- Pastels Smooth
- Pencil Grayscale
- Pencil Sketch
- Photocopy
- Plastic Wrap
- Texturizer
- Watercolor Sponge

To apply one of these effects, select the picture and select the Picture Format tab. Then click the Artistic Effects button and select the effect you want to apply.

To give you an idea of what these effects can accomplish, Figure 15-11 shows a picture with the Pencil Grayscale, Paint Strokes, and Cutout filters applied.

Pencil Grayscale   Paint Strokes   Cutout

FIGURE 15-11: Artistic effects can dramatically change the appearance of a picture.

Removing picture backgrounds

One final bit of picture editing wizardry provided by PowerPoint is the capability to remove the background from a picture. For example, Figure 15-12 shows a picture of a dog with the background removed. (Background removal works best with pictures that have a clear high-contrast distinction between the picture's subject and the background.)

FIGURE 15-12: A corgi with the background removed.

To accomplish this bit of photo-editing magic, follow these steps:

1. **Select the picture whose background you want to remove.**
2. **Select the Picture Format tab and click the Remove Background button, found in the Adjust group.**

   PowerPoint tries to determine which part of your picture is the subject of the picture and which part is the background. PowerPoint creates a bounding rectangle that contains what it believes to be the subject of the picture. Then it analyzes the colors in the picture to determine what it believes to be the background portions of the picture. The background is then displayed in purple. In addition, a special Background Removal tab appears on the Ribbon, as shown in Figure 15-13.

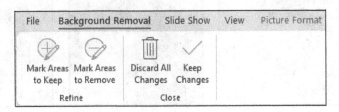

FIGURE 15-13: The Background Removal tab.

Figure 15-14 shows PowerPoint's initial attempt at removing the background from the picture of the corgi. As you can see, PowerPoint has found most of Lucy's head but managed to cut off her neck and shoulders. The result would be a disconcerting floating head.

FIGURE 15-14: PowerPoint's initial attempt at removing the background.

3. **If necessary, use the Mark Areas to Keep and Mark Areas to Remove buttons to refine the location of the picture's background.**

Mark Areas to Keep

For example, if an area that's part of the subject is shown as background, click the Mark Areas to Keep button (shown in the margin). Then either click in the area you want included or click and drag a line across a large portion of the area to be included. PowerPoint will try to discern which part of the picture you marked and include that area in the picture's subject. Note that you don't have to circle the area you want to include, nor do you have to be too precise. PowerPoint will do its best to figure out which portions of the image to include based on your mark.

Mark Areas to Remove

Similarly, if PowerPoint has mistaken part of the background for the subject, click the Mark Areas to Remove button (shown in the margin) and click or draw a line within the area that should be removed.

If PowerPoint misinterprets your mark, press Ctrl+Z to undo your action, or click the Delete Mark button and then click the mark you want to delete.

4. **Repeat Step 3 until you've successfully removed the picture's background.**

   Figure 15-15 shows the results after I've marked the parts of the corgi's body I want to keep.

FIGURE 15-15: Background removal after marking areas to keep and remove.

Keep Changes

5. **Click the Keep Changes button (shown in the margin).**

   The slide returns to normal, with the background of your picture removed.

CHAPTER 15 **Inserting Pictures** 229

Correcting Sharpness, Brightness, Contrast, and Color

Sometimes, in spite of your best efforts, your pictures just don't come out quite right. They may be too bright or too dim, too faded or too contrasty, or a bit out of focus. There are many excellent programs dedicated to the task of improving such photographs. Among the best known and most powerful is Adobe Photoshop.

However, PowerPoint includes several features that can accomplish much of what a program like Photoshop can do. One of them is the Corrections command, which can help you out when your pictures need a little tender love and care. This command, found in the Adjust section of the Picture Format tab, lets you adjust a picture's sharpness, brightness, and contrast.

To change a picture's sharpness, brightness, or contrast, click the Corrections button and choose one of the preset options from the gallery of choices that appears. Or choose the Picture Correction Options command from the bottom of the Corrections menu to reveal the Picture Corrections controls in the task pane to the right of the slide, as shown in Figure 15-16. For this image, I've adjusted the sharpness, brightness, and contrast to create a different appearance.

The Color button in the Adjust section of the Picture Format tab lets you adjust the color of your pictures. You can adjust the following aspects of a picture's color:

» **Color Saturation:** The overall amount of color in the picture

» **Color Tone:** The overall "warmth" of the picture's color

» **Recolor:** The primary color visible in the picture

To change a picture's color, click the Color button on the Picture Format tab and choose one of the options from the gallery of preset choices. Or choose the Picture Color Options command at the bottom of the Color menu. In Figure 15-17, I've adjusted the Color Saturation and Color Temperature to create a different effect.

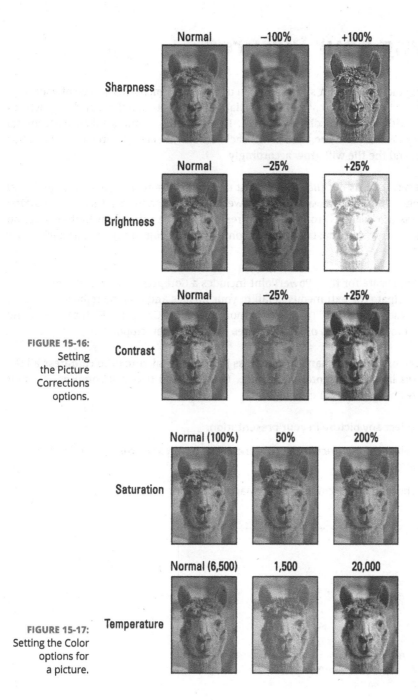

FIGURE 15-16: Setting the Picture Corrections options.

FIGURE 15-17: Setting the Color options for a picture.

Compressing Your Pictures

Adding pictures to your slide show can dramatically increase the size of your presentation's file on disc. This is especially true if you insert a bunch of pictures taken with a modern digital camera. For example, pictures taken with digital cameras are often more than 10MB each. Insert 50 such pictures into your slide show, and the file will grow accordingly.

However, it turns out that the amount of detail contained in your average digital photograph is mostly wasted in a PowerPoint slide show. That's because digital cameras are designed to create pictures that can be printed on high-resolution printers. However, most computer monitors (and projectors) have a much lower resolution.

To compensate for this, PowerPoint includes a Compress Pictures command that can eliminate the extraneous detail in your images and thereby reduce the size of your presentation files. To save even more space, the Compress Pictures command also removes any parts of your pictures that have been cropped.

You can use this command to compress just a single picture or to compress all the pictures in your presentation at once. I recommend that you compress all your pictures by following these steps:

1. **Select any picture in your presentation.**
2. **Select the Picture Format tab, and click Compress Pictures, found in the Adjust group.**

   The Compress Pictures dialog box appears (see Figure 15-18).

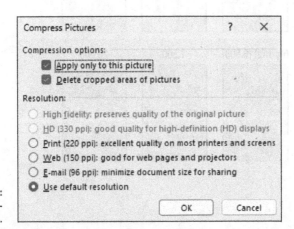

FIGURE 15-18: Compressing pictures.

3. **Deselect the Apply Only to This Picture option.**

   If you leave this option checked, only the selected picture will be compressed. Deselect this option to compress all the pictures in the presentation.

4. **Select the resolution option you want to use.**

   If you're going to display the presentation on a high-definition television, you may want to select HD resolution. For web broadcast or most projectors, Web is suitable.

5. **Click OK.**

   The images are compressed. Note that if you have a lot of pictures in your presentation, this step may take a few moments.

6. **Save your presentation.**

Working with 3D Models

A *3D model* is a three-dimensional model that realistically represents a real-world object. The 3D model can be rotated around its x-, y-, and z-axes so that you can view it from any angle.

To insert a 3D model onto a slide, select the Insert tab on the Ribbon, click the 3D Models button (shown in the margin), and choose Stock 3D Models. You'll be taken to the gallery shown in Figure 15-19. You can select one of the predefined categories or search by keyword.

I'm a space nut, so I went straight to the Space category and inserted a wonderful 3D model of the International Space Station into my presentation, as shown in Figure 15-20.

The control at the center of the model lets you rotate the model in three dimensions around its center point. It takes some getting used to, but with a bit of practice, you'll quickly figure out how to maneuver the model to any angle you like. Figure 15-21 shows a slide on which I've duplicated the model several times to create a total of six space stations, all shown from different angles.

In addition to rotating the 3D model in three dimensions, you can also use PowerPoint's standard rotation tool to rotate the model. In addition, you can resize the model just as you resize any other PowerPoint object.

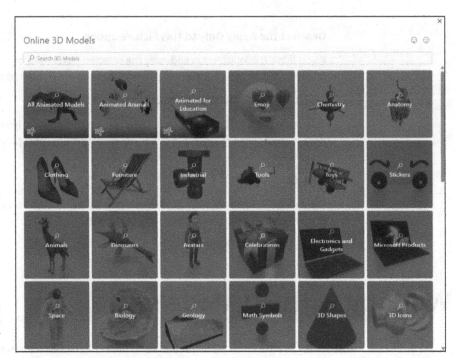

FIGURE 15-19: Locating a 3D model for your presentation.

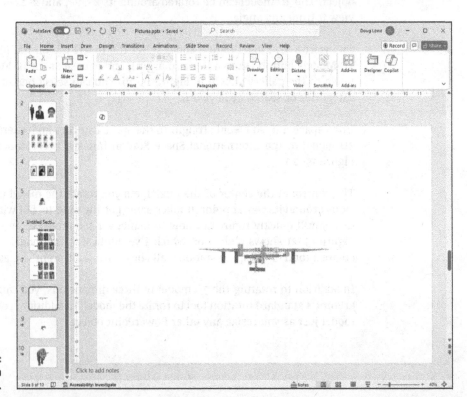

FIGURE 15-20: A 3D Model on a PowerPoint slide.

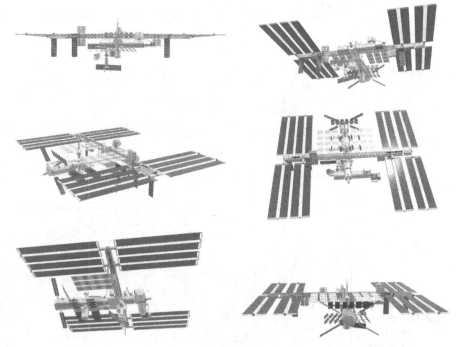

FIGURE 15-21:
A 3D model in various rotations.

 And finally, you can use the Pan & Zoom control (shown in the margin) found in the 3D Model tab on the Ribbon to further tweak your 3D model. This control allows you to zoom in or out of the model or move the model left or right relative to its center of rotation. Play with these controls a bit, and you'll see how Pan & Zoom is different than just resizing or moving the 3D model.

Morphing a 3D model

One of the most effective ways to use a 3D model in a presentation is to apply the Morph transition effect to two slides that contain the same model but in two different orientations. For example, Figure 15-22 shows two slides with two different views of the space station model. By applying the Morph transition to the second slide, the space station will gracefully reorient itself from the head-on view to the larger view angled from above, as if it's flying toward you.

 Play with the timing to get the Morph effect just right. For the Morph transition shown in Figure 15-22, I ended up setting the timing to 20 seconds, so the space station appears to be slowly approaching.

CHAPTER 15 **Inserting Pictures**   235

Slide 1

Slide 2

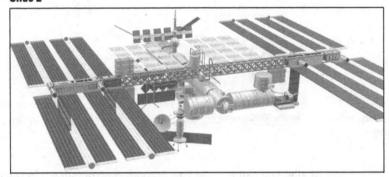

FIGURE 15-22: Morphing a 3D model is an effective presentation technique.

Using animated 3D models

Some 3D models are animated — that is, not only do the models provide three-dimensional realism, but they also move in three dimensions. You can spot an animated 3D model when you see the Animation icon (shown in the margin) as part of the model's snapshot preview when you browse available models. At the time I wrote this, Microsoft had a total of 54 animated 3D models available. Some of them are fascinating, such as the beating heart and the flying bee. Others are just fun, like the juggling octopus and the acrobatic toaster. Keep checking — there may be more to come!

When you insert an animated 3D model, a Play 3D group will be added to the 3D Model tab on the Ribbon. This group contains the Play and Pause buttons to start and stop an animation, as well as a Scenes button (shown in the margin). You can click the Scenes button to turn off animation for the model by clicking None. Some models have more than one animation to choose from. In that case, the Scenes button will let you choose which scene to play.

For fun, Figure 15-23 illustrates a slide in which I added two animated 3D models: A scary dinosaur (presumably a Tyrannosaurus rex) and a hamburger. The T. rex has a total of five scenes to choose from; the hamburger has three. I chose Scene 4 for the T. rex, which causes him to stare at the hamburger for a bit, then look toward the audience. For the hamburger, I chose Scene 1, which causes the components of the burger to expand so you can see what's in it. The effect is fun — it appears that the T. rex is annoyed that his arms are too short to grab the burger.

FIGURE 15-23:
The dinosaur and the hamburger.

> **IN THIS CHAPTER**
> » Using the PowerPoint Shape Format
> » Using predefined shapes
> » Drawing polygons or curved lines
> » Giving your shapes some style
> » Flipping and rotating objects
> » Using advanced tricks

Chapter 16
Drawing on Your Slides

A rt time! Get your crayons and glue and don an old paint shirt. You're going to cut out some simple shapes and paste them on your PowerPoint slides so that people either think that you're a wonderful artist or scoff at you for not using clip art.

This chapter covers the drawing features of PowerPoint. Once upon a time, PowerPoint had but rudimentary drawing tools — the equivalent of a box of crayons — but today PowerPoint has powerful drawing tools, sufficient for all but the most sophisticated aspiring artists.

Some General Drawing Tips

Before getting into the specifics of using each PowerPoint drawing tool, the following sections describe a handful of general tips for drawing pictures.

Zooming in

When you work with the PowerPoint Shape Format, you may want to increase the zoom factor so you can draw more accurately. I often work at 200 percent, 300 percent, or even 400 percent when I'm drawing. To change the zoom factor, use the Zoom slider located in the lower-right corner of the screen.

TIP

Before you change the zoom factor to edit an object, select the object that you want to edit. This way, PowerPoint zooms in on that area of the slide. If you don't select an object before you zoom in, you may need to scroll around to find the right location.

Note that on a touchscreen device, you can zoom in and out by using a two-fingered pinch gesture. And on a device with a mouse, you can quickly zoom by holding down the Ctrl key while spinning the mouse wheel.

Displaying the ruler, gridlines, and guides

PowerPoint provides three on-screen features that can help you line up your drawings:

» **Ruler:** Horizontal and vertical rulers appear at the top and to the left of the slide.

» **Gridlines:** A grid of evenly spaced dots appears directly on the slide.

» **Guides:** A pair of horizontal and vertical lines intersect on your slide like crosshairs in a target.

You can activate any or all of these features by selecting the View tab on the Ribbon and selecting the Ruler, Gridlines, and Guides check boxes. Figure 16-1 shows PowerPoint with the rulers, gridlines, and guides displayed.

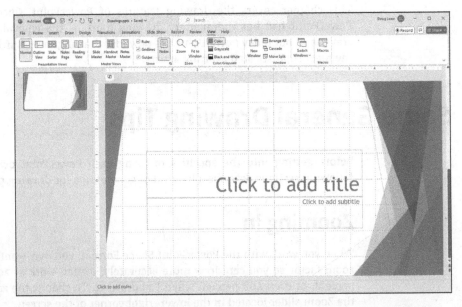

FIGURE 16-1: PowerPoint with the rulers, gridlines, and guides on.

When you work with drawing objects, the ruler is positioned so that zero is at the middle of the slide. When you edit a text object, the ruler changes to a text ruler that measures from the margins and indicates tab positions.

For more information about using the gridlines or guides, see the section "Using the grids and guides," later in this chapter.

Sticking to the color scheme

You can assign individual colors to each object that you draw, but the purpose of the PowerPoint color schemes (see Chapter 12) is to talk you out of doing that. If possible, let solid objects default to the color scheme's fill color, or, if you must change the fill color, change it to one of the alternative colors provided by the scheme. The beauty of doing this is that if you change the color scheme later, the fill color for objects changes to reflect the new fill color. After you switch to a color that's not in the theme, however, the object ignores any subsequent changes to the theme.

Saving frequently

Drawing is tedious work. You don't want to spend two hours working on a particularly important drawing only to lose it all just because a comet strikes your building or an errant Scud missile lands in your backyard. You can prevent catastrophic loss from incidents such as these by pressing Ctrl+S or by frequently clicking the Save button as you work. And always wear protective eyewear.

PowerPoint has a feature called AutoSave that automatically saves your presentation every few seconds, so you don't have to be so diligent about manually saving your work. If you're using the Microsoft 365 version of PowerPoint and your presentation is stored on OneDrive, the AutoSave feature is enabled by default. If your presentation is stored on a local disk, you can turn on AutoSave using the AutoSave switch (shown in the margin) at the upper-left corner of the PowerPoint window.

Remembering Ctrl+Z

REMEMBER

In my opinion, Ctrl+Z — the ubiquitous Undo command — is the most important keyboard shortcut in any Windows program, and PowerPoint is no exception. Remember that you're never more than one keystroke away from erasing a boo-boo. If you do something silly — like forgetting to group a complex picture before trying to move it — you can always press Ctrl+Z to undo your last action. Ctrl+Z is my favorite and most frequently used PowerPoint key combination. (For left-handed mouse users, Alt+Backspace does the same thing.) And if you aren't ready to climb on a chair shrieking at the first sign of a mouse, try clicking the handy Undo button on the Quick Access Toolbar (QAT).

Drawing Simple Objects

Shapes

To draw an object on a slide, select the Insert tab on the Ribbon. Then click the Shapes button (shown in the margin) to reveal a gallery of shapes you can choose from (see Figure 16-2). Finally, select the shape you want to draw from the Shapes gallery.

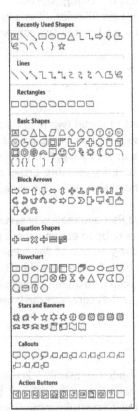

FIGURE 16-2:
The Shapes gallery.

You can find detailed instructions for drawing with the more important tools in the Shapes gallery in the following sections. Before I get to that, though, I want to give you some pointers to keep in mind:

- » **Choosing a location:** Before you draw an object, move to the slide on which you want to draw the object. If you want the object to appear on every slide in the presentation, display the slide master by choosing Slide Master in the Master Views section of the View tab on the Ribbon or by Shift+clicking the Normal View button.

- » **Fixing a mistake:** If you make a mistake while drawing a shape, the Undo button (shown in the margin) on the QAT can usually correct the mistake for you.

- » **Holding down the Shift key:** If you hold down the Shift key while drawing a shape, PowerPoint forces the shape to be *regular* (that is, rectangles are squares, ellipses are circles, and lines are constrained to horizontal or vertical or 45-degree diagonals).

Drawing straight lines

You can use the Line button to draw straight lines on your slides. Here's how:

1. **Select the Insert tab, click the Shapes button, and then click the Line button (shown in the margin) in the Shapes gallery.**
2. **Point the cursor to where you want the line to start.**
3. **Click the mouse and drag the cursor to where you want the line to end.**
4. **Release the mouse button when you reach your destination.**

After you've drawn the shape, the Ribbon displays the Shape Format tab (see Figure 16-3). You can then use the controls in the Shape Styles group to change the fill, outline, and effects applied to the line.

FIGURE 16-3: The Shape Format tab on the Ribbon.

After you've drawn a line, you can adjust it by clicking it and then dragging the handles that appear on each end of the line.

You can force a line to be perfectly horizontal or vertical by holding down the Shift key while you draw. If you hold down the Shift key and drag diagonally while you draw the line, the line will be constrained to perfect 45-degree angles.

CHAPTER 16 **Drawing on Your Slides** 243

Drawing rectangles, squares, ovals, and circles

To draw a rectangle, follow these steps:

1. **Select the Insert tab, click the Shapes button found in the Illustrations group, and then click the Rectangle button (shown in the margin).**

2. **Point the cursor to where you want one corner of the rectangle to be positioned.**

3. **Click and drag to where you want the opposite corner of the rectangle to be positioned.**

4. **Release the mouse button.**

The steps for drawing an oval are the same as the steps for drawing a rectangle except that you click the Oval button rather than the Rectangle button.

TIP

To draw a square or circle, select the Rectangle button or the Oval button but hold down the Shift key while you draw.

REMEMBER

You can adjust the size or shape of a rectangle or circle by clicking it and dragging any of its love handles (the small circles you see at the corners of the shape — officially called *sizing handles*).

Creating Other Shapes

Rectangles and circles aren't the only two shapes that PowerPoint can draw automatically. The Shapes gallery includes many other types of shapes you can draw, such as pentagons, stars, and flowchart symbols.

The Shapes gallery (refer to Figure 16-2) organizes shapes into the following categories:

> » **Recently Used Shapes:** The top section of the gallery lists as many as 24 of the shapes you've used most recently. The shapes found in this section change every time you draw a new shape.

> » **Lines:** Straight lines, curved lines, lines with arrowheads, scribbly lines, and free-form shapes that can become polygons if you want. The free-form shapes are useful enough to merit their own section, "Drawing a polygon or free-form shape," later in this chapter.

- **Rectangles:** Basic rectangular shapes, including not just a regular rectangle but also rectangles with corners lopped off.
- **Basic Shapes:** Squares, rectangles, triangles, crosses, happy faces, lightning bolts, hearts, clouds, and more.
- **Block Arrows:** Fat arrows pointing in various directions.
- **Equation Shapes:** Shapes for drawing simple math equations.
- **Flowchart:** Various flowcharting symbols.
- **Stars and Banners:** Shapes that add sparkle to your presentations.
- **Callouts:** Text boxes and speech bubbles like those used in comic strips.
- **Action Buttons:** Buttons that you can add to your slides and click during a slide show to go directly to another slide or to run a macro.

Drawing a shape

The following steps explain how to draw a shape:

1. **Select the Insert tab and click the Shapes button found in the Illustrations group on the Insert tab of the Ribbon.**

   The Shapes gallery appears.

2. **Select the shape you want to insert.**

   When you select one of the shapes, the Shapes gallery disappears and PowerPoint is poised to draw the shape you selected.

3. **Click the slide where you want the shape to appear and then drag the shape to the desired size.**

   Hold down the Shift key while drawing the Shape to create an evenly proportioned shape.

   When you release the mouse button, the Shape object takes on the current fill color and line style.

4. **(Optional) Start typing if you want the shape to contain text.**

   After you've typed your text, you can use PowerPoint's formatting features to change its typeface, size, color, and so on (see Chapter 11).

Some shapes — especially the stars and banners — cry out for text. Figure 16-4 shows how you can use star shapes to add jazzy bursts to a slide.

FIGURE 16-4:
Use a star shape to make your presentation look like a late-night infomercial.

You can change an object's shape at any time. First, select the shape. Then select the Shape Format tab on the Ribbon, click the Edit Shape button found in the Insert Shapes group, and choose Change Shape from the menu that appears.

TIP

Many shape buttons have an extra handle shaped like a yellow diamond that enables you to adjust some aspect of the object's shape. For example, the block arrows have a handle that enables you to increase or decrease the size of the arrowhead. The location of these handles varies depending on the shape you're working with. Figure 16-5 shows how you can use these extra handles to vary the shapes produced by six different shapes. For each of the six shapes, the first object shows how the shape is initially drawn; the other two objects show how you can change the shape by dragging the extra handle. (Note that the yellow handles aren't shown in this figure. When you select a shape that has one of these adjustment handles, the handles will appear.)

Drawing a polygon or free-form shape

Mr. Arnold, my seventh-grade math teacher, taught me that a *polygon* is a shape that has many sides and has nothing to do with having more than one spouse (one is certainly enough for most people). Triangles, squares, and rectangles are polygons, but so are hexagons, pentagons, and any unusual shapes whose sides all consist of straight lines. Politicians are continually inventing new polygons when they revise the boundaries of congressional districts.

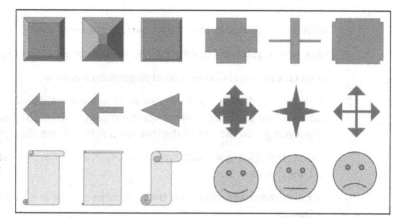

FIGURE 16-5: You can create interesting variations by grabbing the extra handles on these shapes.

One of the most useful shapes in the Shapes gallery is the Freeform Shape tool. It's designed to create polygons, but with a twist: Not all the sides have to be straight lines. The Freeform Shape tool lets you build a shape whose sides are a mixture of straight lines and free-form curves. Figure 16-6 shows three examples of shapes that I created with the Freeform Shape tool.

FIGURE 16-6: Three free-form shapes.

Follow these steps to create a polygon or free-form shape:

1. **Select the Freeform Shape tool (shown in the margin) from the Shapes gallery.**

   You can find the Shapes gallery in the Shapes group on the Insert tab of the Ribbon.

   When you select the Freeform Shape tool, the cursor changes to a crosshair pointer.

CHAPTER 16 **Drawing on Your Slides** 247

2. **Click where you want to position the first corner of the object.**

3. **Click where you want to position the second corner of the object.**

4. **Keep clicking wherever you want to position a corner.**

5. **(Optional) To draw a free-form side on the shape, hold down the mouse button when you click a corner and then drag to draw the free-form shape. When you get to the end of the free-form side, release the mouse button.**

   You can then click again to add more corners. The bottom shape in Figure 16-6 has one free-form side.

6. **To finish the shape, click near the first corner — the one that you created in Step 2.**

   You don't have to be exact. If you click anywhere near the first corner that you put down, PowerPoint assumes that the shape is finished.

   You're finished! The object assumes the line and fill color from the slide's color scheme.

REMEMBER

You can reshape a polygon or free-form shape by double-clicking it and then dragging any of the love handles that appear on the corners.

If you hold down the Shift key while you draw a polygon, the sides are constrained to 45-degree angles. I drew the upper-right shape in Figure 16-6 this way. How about a constitutional amendment requiring Congress to use the Shift key when it redraws congressional boundaries?

You also can use the Freeform Shape tool to draw a multisegmented line called an *open shape*. To draw an open shape, you can follow the steps in this section, except that you skip Step 6. Instead, double-click or press Esc when the line is done.

Drawing a curved line or shape

Another useful tool is the Curve Shape tool, which lets you draw curved lines or shapes. Figure 16-7 shows several examples of curved lines and shapes drawn with the Curve Shape tool.

Here's the procedure for drawing a curved line or shape:

1. **Select the Curve Shape tool (shown in the margin) from the Shapes gallery.**

   You can find the Shapes gallery in the Shapes group on the Insert tab.

   When you select the Curve Shape tool, the cursor changes to a cross-hair pointer.

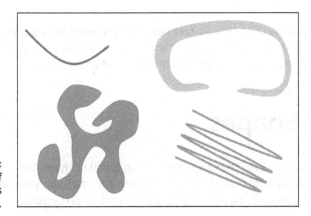

FIGURE 16-7: Examples of curved lines and shapes.

2. **Click where you want the curved line or shape to begin.**

3. **Click where you want the first turn in the curve to appear.**

   The straight line turns to a curved line, bent around the point where you clicked. As you move the mouse, the bend of the curve changes.

4. **Click to add turns to the curve.**

   Each time you click, a new bend is added to the line. Keep clicking until the line is as twisty as you want.

5. **To finish a line, double-click where you want the end of the curved line to appear. To create a closed shape, double-click over the starting point, where you clicked in Step 2.**

Creating a text box

A text box is a special type of shape that's designed to place text on your slides. To create a text box, select the Insert tab, click the Text Box button found in the Text group, and then click where you want one corner of the text box to appear and drag to where you want the opposite corner, just like you're drawing a rectangle. When you release the mouse button, you can type text.

You can format the text that you type in the text box by highlighting the text and using the usual PowerPoint text formatting features, most of which are found on the Home tab. (For more information about formatting text, see Chapter 11.)

You can format the text box itself by using Shape Fill, Shape Outline, Shape Effects, and other tools available on the Shape Format tab (see the next section). By default, text boxes have no fill or line color, so the box itself is invisible on the slide — only the text is visible.

TIP Most shapes also function as text boxes. If you want to add text to a shape, just click the shape and start typing. The text appears centered over the shape. (The only shapes that don't accept text are lines and connectors.)

Styling Your Shapes

The second section of the Shape Format tab is called Shape Styles. It lets you control various stylistic features of your shapes. For example, you can set a fill color, set the outline, and add effects such as shadows or reflections.

You can set these styles individually, or you can choose one of the preselected shape styles that appears in the Shape Styles group. Note that the styles that appear in the Shape Styles group vary depending on the type of shape you've selected and the theme used for the presentation. For example, if you select a line, various predefined line styles are displayed. But if you select a rectangle, the styles appropriate for rectangles are displayed.

Setting the shape fill

The Shape Fill control found in the Shape Styles group of the Shape Format tab lets you control how shapes are filled. The simplest type of fill is a solid color. But you can also use a picture, a gradient fill, or a texture to fill the shape. A handy Eyedropper tool lets you set the fill of the selected object to match the fill of any other object.

Selecting solid colors, pictures, gradients, and textures for shapes is similar to setting the fill for backgrounds and themes (see Chapter 12).

Setting the shape outline

The Shape Outline control found in the Shape Styles group of the Shape Format tab lets you change the style of line objects or the border for solid shape objects. You can change the following settings for the outline:

>> **Color:** Sets the color used for the outline.

>> **Weight:** Sets the thickness of the line.

>> **Dashes:** Sets the dashing pattern used for the lines that outline the object. The default uses a solid line, but different patterns are available to create dashed lines.

>> **Arrows:** Sets the arrowheads of the line. Lines can have arrowheads at either or both ends. Arrowheads are used mostly on line and arc objects.

For maximum control over the outline style, choose the More command from the menu that appears when you click the flyout button (shown in the margin) at the bottom right of the Shape Styles group. This summons the Format Shape pane, as shown in Figure 16-8. From here, you can control all aspects of a line's style — its color, width, dash type, cap type, arrowheads, and more.

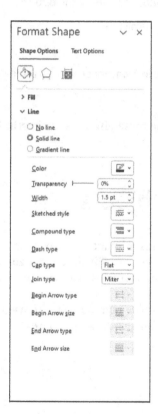

FIGURE 16-8: Formatting the line style.

Applying shape effects

The Shape Effects button on the Shape Format tab on the Ribbon lets you apply several interesting types of effects to your shapes. When you click this button, a menu with the following effect options is displayed:

- » **Shadow:** Applies a shadow to the picture. You can select one of several predefined shadow effects, or you can call up a dialog box that lets you customize the shadow.
- » **Reflection:** Creates a reflected image of the picture beneath the original picture.
- » **Glow:** Adds a glowing effect around the edges of the picture.
- » **Soft Edges:** Softens the edges of the picture.
- » **Bevel:** Creates a beveled effect.
- » **3-D Rotation:** Rotates the picture in a way that creates a three-dimensional effect.

The best way to discover how to use these effects is to experiment with them to see how they work.

Flipping and Rotating Objects

To *flip* an object means to create a mirror image of it. To *rotate* an object means to turn it about its center. PowerPoint lets you flip objects horizontally or vertically, rotate objects in 90-degree increments, or freely rotate an object to any angle.

Rotation works for text boxes and shape text. So, you can use rotation to create vertical text or text skewed to any angle you want. However, flipping an object doesn't affect the object's text.

Flipping an object

PowerPoint enables you to flip an object vertically or horizontally to create a mirror image of the object. To flip an object, follow these steps:

1. **Select the object that you want to flip.**
2. **Select the Shape Format tab, click the Rotate button found in the Arrange group, and then choose Flip Horizontal or Flip Vertical.**

Rotating an object 90 degrees

You can rotate an object in 90-degree increments by following these steps:

1. **Select the object that you want to rotate.**

   ⟲ Rotate ˅ **Select the Shape Format tab, click the Rotate button (shown in the margin) found in the Arrange group, and then choose Rotate Right or Rotate Left.**

2. **To rotate the object 180 degrees, click the appropriate Rotate button again.**

Using the rotate handle

Remember how all the bad guys' hideouts were slanted in the old *Batman* TV show? The rotate handle lets you give your drawings that same kind of slant. With the rotate handle, you can rotate an object to any arbitrary angle just by dragging it with the mouse.

The rotate handle is the circular handle that appears when you select an object that can be rotated. The rotate handle appears above the object, connected to the object by a line, as shown in Figure 16-9. You can rotate an object to any angle simply by dragging the rotate handle.

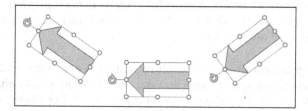

FIGURE 16-9: The rotate handle lets you rotate an object to any arbitrary angle.

The following steps show you how to use the rotate handle:

1. **Click the object that you want to rotate.**
2. **Drag the rotate handle in the direction that you want to rotate the object.**

   As you drag, an outline of the object rotates around. When you get the object's outline to the angle you want, release the mouse button, and the object is redrawn at the new angle.

TIP To restrict the rotation angle to 15-degree increments, hold the Shift key while dragging around the rotation handle.

Drawing a Complicated Picture

When you add more than one object to a slide, you may run into several problems. What happens when the objects overlap? How do you line up objects so that they don't look like they were thrown at the slide from a moving car? And how do you keep together objects that belong together?

The following sections show you how to use PowerPoint features to handle overlapped objects and how to align and group objects.

Changing layers

Whenever you have more than one object on a slide, the potential exists for objects to overlap one another. Like most drawing programs, PowerPoint handles this problem by layering objects like a stack of plates. The first object that you draw is at the bottom of the stack, the second object is on top of the first object, the third object is atop the second object, and so on. If two objects overlap, the one that's at the highest layer wins; objects below it are partially covered. (Note that PowerPoint's layers aren't nearly as powerful as layers in other programs, such as Adobe Illustrator or AutoCAD. All they really do is set the stacking order when objects are placed on top of one another.)

So far, so good. But what if you don't remember to draw the objects in the correct order? What if you draw a shape that you want to tuck behind a shape that you've already drawn, or what if you want to bring an existing shape to the top of the pecking order? No problem. PowerPoint enables you to change the stacking order by moving objects toward the front or back so that they overlap just the way you want.

The Shape Format tab provides two controls that let you move an object forward or backward in the layer order:

>> **Bring to Front:** Brings the chosen object to the top of the stack. Note that this button has a down arrow next to it. If you click this down arrow, a menu appears with two subcommands: Bring to Front and Bring Forward. The Bring Forward command moves the object just one step closer to the top of the heap, whereas the Bring to Front command moves the object all the way to the top.

- **Send to Back:** Sends the chosen object to the back of the stack. Again, this button has a down arrow next to it, which leads to two subcommands: Send to Back and Send Backward. The Send Backward command moves the object just one step closer to the bottom of the pile, whereas Send to Back sends it all the way to the bottom.

Layering problems are most obvious when objects have a fill color. If an object has no fill color, objects behind it are allowed to show through. In this case, the layering doesn't matter much.

To bring an object to the top of another object, you may have to use the Bring Forward command several times. Even though the two objects appear to be adjacent, other objects may occupy the layers between them.

Line 'em up

Nothing looks more amateurish than objects dropped randomly on a slide with no apparent concern for how they line up with each other. The Shape Format tab includes an Align button that brings up a menu with the following commands:

- Align Left
- Align Center
- Align Right
- Align Top
- Align Middle
- Align Bottom
- Distribute Horizontally
- Distribute Vertically

The first three commands (Align Left, Align Center, and Align Right) align items horizontally; the next three commands (Align Top, Align Middle, and Align Bottom) align items vertically.

You can also distribute several items so they're spaced evenly. Select the items that you want to distribute, click the Draw button, choose Align or Distribute, and then choose Distribute Horizontally or Distribute Vertically. PowerPoint adjusts the spacing of the objects that appear between the two outermost objects selected.

TIP

Another quick way to align one item to another is to simply drag the first item until it's close to the alignment you want. When the item reaches the correct alignment, a magic guideline appears to indicate that you've found the correct alignment. If you release the mouse button while this magic guideline is visible, the object will be snapped into alignment.

Using the grids and guides

To help you create well-ordered slides, PowerPoint lets you display a grid of evenly spaced lines over the slide. These lines aren't actually part of the slide, so your audience won't see them when you give your presentation. They exist simply to make the task of lining things up a bit easier.

In addition to the grid, PowerPoint also lets you use guides. The guides are two lines — one horizontal, the other vertical — that appear on-screen. Although the gridlines are fixed in their location on your slides, you can move the guides around as you want. Any object that comes within a pixel's breadth of one of these guidelines snaps to it. Like the grid, the guides don't show up when you give your presentation. They appear only when you're editing your slides. Guides are a great way to line up objects in a neat row.

To display the grid or guides, click the dialog box launcher in the lower-right corner of the Show section of the View tab on the Ribbon. The Grid and Guides dialog box, shown in Figure 16-10, appears.

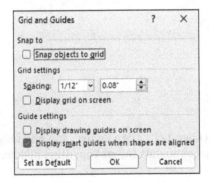

FIGURE 16-10: The Grid and Guides dialog box.

To activate the grid, select the Snap Objects to Grid check box and then adjust the grid spacing to whatever setting you want. If you want to actually see the grid on-screen, select the Display Grid on Screen check box.

To fire up the guides, select the Display Drawing Guides on Screen check box. After the guides are visible, you can move them around the slide by clicking and dragging them.

You can also deselect Display Smart Guides When Shapes Are Aligned to disable the guidelines that appear when you move shapes into alignment with each other. This feature is useful, however, so I recommend that you leave this box checked.

Group therapy

A *group* is a collection of objects that PowerPoint treats as though they were one object. Using groups properly is one key to putting simple shapes together to make complex pictures without becoming so frustrated that you have to join a therapy group. ("Hello, my name is Doug, and PowerPoint drives me crazy.")

To create a group, follow these steps:

1. **Select all the objects that you want to include in the group.**

   You can do this by holding down the Shift key and clicking each of the items or by clicking and dragging the resulting rectangle around all the items.

2. **Right-click one of the selected objects and then choose Group ⇨ Group from the menu that appears.**

You can also find the Group command on the Shape Format tab of the Ribbon, but it's much easier to find by right-clicking.

To take a group apart so that PowerPoint treats the objects as individuals again, follow these steps:

1. **Right-click the group you want to break up.**
2. **Choose Group ⇨ Ungroup.**

If you create a group and then ungroup it so you can work on its elements individually, you can easily regroup the objects. Here's how:

1. **Right-click one of the objects that was in the original group.**
2. **Choose Group ⇨ Regroup.**

   PowerPoint remembers which objects were in the group and automatically includes them.

PowerPoint enables you to create groups of groups. This capability is useful for complex pictures because it enables you to work on one part of the picture, group it, and then work on the next part of the picture without worrying about accidentally disturbing the part that you've already grouped. After you have several such groups, select them and group them. You can create groups of groups of groups and so on, ad nauseam.

IN THIS CHAPTER

» Getting to know charts

» Adding a chart to your presentation

» Changing a chart's type

» Working with data in charts

» Changing the layout of a chart

» Changing the style of a chart

» Embellishing your chart with titles, legends, and other stuff

» Representing hierarchical data with Treemap and Sunburst charts

» Plotting data geographically with a Map chart

Chapter 17
Charting for Fun and Profit

One of the best ways to prove a point is with numbers, and one of the best ways to present numbers is in a chart. With PowerPoint, adding a chart to your presentation is easy. And getting the chart to look the way you want is usually easy, too. It takes a little bit of pointing and clicking, but it works. This chapter shows you how.

The charts depicted in this chapter are based on one of my favorite Broadway musicals, *The Music Man*. It's the story of a grifter named Harold Hill, who, in 1912, convinces the residents of the small town of River City, Iowa, that their little town is in terrible trouble on account of a pool table recently installed in their community. Hill's solution: a boys' band, complete with instruments, music, uniforms, and — of course — music lessons from none other than Professor Hill himself who — of course — knows absolutely nothing about music. The musical debuted on Broadway in 1957 and recently concluded a successful Broadway revival with Hugh Jackman in the lead role.

Understanding Charts

If you've never tried to add a chart to a slide, the process can be a little confusing. A *chart* is simply a series of numbers rendered as a graph. You can supply the numbers yourself, or you can copy them from a separate file, such as an Excel spreadsheet. You can create all kinds of different charts, ranging from simple bar charts and pie charts to exotic doughnut charts and radar charts. Very cool, but a little confusing to the uninitiated.

The following list details some of the jargon that you have to contend with when you're working with charts:

- **Graph or chart:** Same thing. These terms are used interchangeably. A graph or chart is nothing more than a bunch of numbers turned into a picture. After all, a picture is worth a thousand numbers.

- **Chart type:** PowerPoint supports several chart types: bar charts, column charts, pie charts, line charts, scatter charts, area charts, radar charts, Dunkin' Donuts charts, and others. You can even create cone charts that look like something that fell off a Mister Softee truck. Different types of charts are better suited to displaying different types of data.

- **Chart layout:** A predefined combination of chart elements, such as headings and legends, that lets you easily create a common type of chart.

- **Chart style:** A predefined combination of formatting elements that controls the visual appearance of a chart.

- **Datasheet:** Supplies the underlying data for a chart. After all, a chart is nothing more than a bunch of numbers made into a picture. Those numbers come from the datasheet, which is actually an Excel spreadsheet. When you create a chart, PowerPoint automatically starts Excel (if it isn't already running) and uses Excel to hold the numbers in the datasheet.

- **Series:** A collection of related numbers. For example, a chart of quarterly sales by region may have a series for each region. Each series has four sales totals, one for each quarter. Each series is usually represented by a row on the datasheet, but you can change the datasheet so each column represents a series. Most chart types can plot more than one series. Pie charts can plot only one series at a time, however. The name of each series can be displayed in a legend.

- **Axes:** The lines on the edges of a chart. The *x*-axis is the line along the bottom of the chart; the *y*-axis is the line along the left edge of the chart. The *x*-axis usually indicates categories. Actual data values are plotted along the *y*-axis. Microsoft Graph automatically provides labels for the *x*-axis and *y*-axis, but you can change them.
- **Legend:** A box used to identify the various series plotted on the chart. PowerPoint can create a legend automatically if you want one.

Adding a Chart to Your Presentation

To add a chart to your presentation, you have several options:

- Create a new slide by using a layout that includes a *Content placeholder* (an object that reserves space for content on the slide). Then click the Chart icon in the Content placeholder to create the chart.
- Use the Insert tab to insert a chart into any slide.
- Create the chart separately in Excel and then paste the chart into PowerPoint. This is the most common method if the chart is based on data that's already stored in an Excel workbook.

Adding a new slide with a chart

To insert a new slide that contains a chart, follow these steps:

1. **Move to the slide that you want the new slide to follow.**
2. **Select the Home tab and then click the New Slide button in the Slides group.**

   A list of slide layouts appears.
3. **Click one of the slide layouts that includes a Content placeholder.**

   Several slide types include a Content placeholder. When you click the one you want, a slide with the selected layout is added to your presentation, as shown in Figure 17-1. (In this case, I chose the Title and Content layout.)

   As you can see, the Content placeholder includes eight little icons for inserting different types of content.

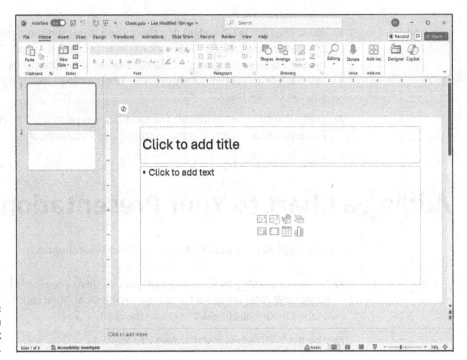

FIGURE 17-1:
A slide with a Content placeholder.

 4. **Click the Chart icon (shown in the margin).**

The Chart icon is the one on the far right side of the second row of icons. Clicking the Chart icon summons the Insert Chart dialog box, as shown in Figure 17-2.

5. **Select the type of chart you want to create.**

   You can select any of the following chart types:

   - *Column:* Data is shown as vertical columns. The columns can be displayed side-by-side or stacked, and you can pick various shapes for the columns, including simple bars, 3-D blocks, cylinders, cones, and pyramids.
   - *Line:* The data is shown as individual points linked by various types of lines.
   - *Pie:* The data is shown as slices in a circular pie.
   - *Bar:* The same as a column chart, except the columns are laid out horizontally instead of vertically.
   - *Area:* Similar to a line chart, but the areas beneath the lines are shaded.
   - *X Y (Scatter):* Plots individual points using two values to represent the *x*- and *y*-coordinates.
   - *Map:* Plots data geographically (for this to work, the chart data must include geographic regions, such as country names, state names, or zip codes).
   - *Stock:* Plots high/low/close values.

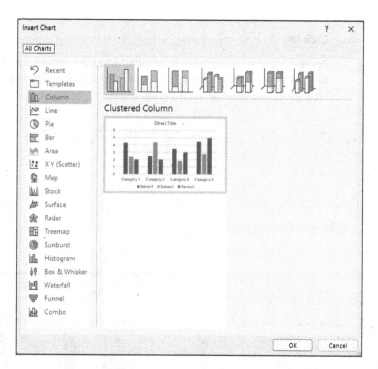

FIGURE 17-2: The Insert Chart dialog box.

- *Surface:* Similar to a line chart but represents the data as a three-dimensional surface.

- *Radar:* Plots data relative to a central point rather than to the *x*-axis and *y*-axis.

- *Treemap:* Charts hierarchical data as nested rectangles. (For more information, see the section "Using Treemap and Sunburst Charts," later in this chapter.)

- *Sunburst:* Charts hierarchical data as a series of concentric rings each divided into wedges. (For more information, see the section "Using Treemap and Sunburst Charts," later in this chapter.)

- *Histogram:* Charts the distribution of data.

- *Box & Whisker:* A chart type of interest mostly to statistics nerds, it graphically shows how data is clustered around its median value.

- *Waterfall*: A variation of a bar chart that shows how successive additions or subtractions from a starting value lead to an ending value.

- *Funnel:* Plots data as stacked horizontal bars that are centered over each other. If the data is sorted from largest to smallest, the effect looks like a funnel.

- *Combo:* Lets you combine different chart types in a single chart.

For this example, I selected a Column chart.

6. **Click OK.**

   PowerPoint whirs and grinds for a moment and then inserts the chart into the slide, as shown in Figure 17-3. The data is displayed in a separate Excel-like editing window, as show in the figure.

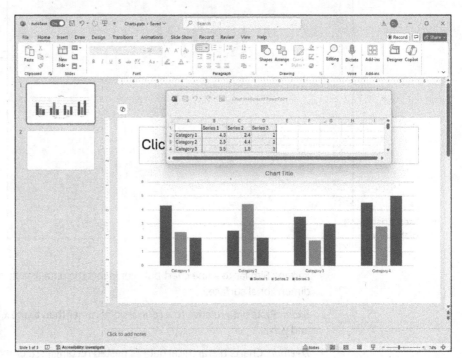

FIGURE 17-3: A chart after it has been inserted into PowerPoint.

7. **Change the sample data to something more realistic.**

   As you can see, the data for the chart is shown in a separate spreadsheet window that resembles Excel. You need to edit the data in this spreadsheet to provide the data you want to chart. Notice that any changes you make to the spreadsheet data are automatically reflected in the chart. (For more information, turn to the section "Working with Chart Data," later in this chapter.)

8. **Customize the chart any way you want.**

   For example, you can change the chart layout or style, as described later in this chapter. Figure 17-4 shows a finished chart.

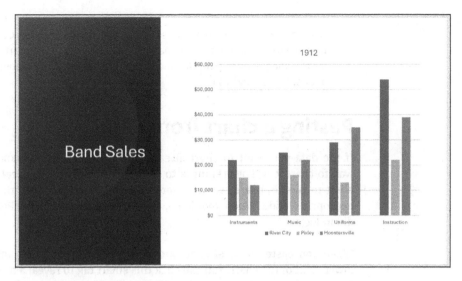

FIGURE 17-4:
A finished chart.

Adding a chart to an existing slide

If you prefer, you can add a chart to an existing slide by following these steps:

1. **Move to the slide on which you want to place the chart.**

2. **Select the Insert tab and click the Chart button found in the Illustrations group.**

   The Insert Chart dialog box appears (refer to Figure 17-2).

3. **Select the type of chart you want to create and then click OK.**

   PowerPoint pops up a little Excel window with sample data and then inserts a chart based on sample data. (See the section "Changing the Chart Type," later in this chapter, for more information about chart types.)

4. **Change the sample data to something more realistic.**

   For more information about working with chart data, turn to the section "Working with Chart Data," later in this chapter.

5. **Finish the chart by setting the chart layout and style.**

   For more information, see the sections "Changing the Chart Layout" and "Changing the Chart Style," later in this chapter.

6. **Rearrange everything.**

   The chart undoubtedly falls on top of something else already on the slide. You probably need to resize the chart by selecting it and then dragging it by the love handles. You can move the chart like any other object: Just click and drag it to a new location. You may also need to move, resize, or delete other objects to make room for the chart or change the layer order of the chart or other surrounding objects. (You can find information about these manipulations in Chapters 15 and 16.)

Pasting a chart from Excel

If the data you want to chart already exists in an Excel workbook, the easiest way to chart it in PowerPoint is to first create the chart in Excel. Then copy the chart to the Clipboard, switch over to PowerPoint, and paste the chart into the appropriate slide. When you do so, the chart appears in PowerPoint exactly as it did in Excel.

When you paste an Excel chart into PowerPoint, a smart tag appears near the lower right of the chart. You can click this smart tag to reveal a menu that lets you indicate whether you want to keep the original formatting of the chart or use the theme in the PowerPoint presentation.

In addition, the smart tag lets you indicate whether the chart should be embedded or linked. If you embed the chart, PowerPoint creates a copy of the Excel data and stores it as a workbook object within your PowerPoint file. This effectively severs the chart in the PowerPoint presentation from the original workbook, so any changes you make to the data in the original workbook aren't reflected in the PowerPoint chart.

On the other hand, if you link the chart, PowerPoint copies the chart into the PowerPoint presentation but creates a link to the data in the original Excel workbook. Then any changes you make to the data in the original Excel workbook are reflected in the chart.

One final option on the smart tag lets you insert the chart as a picture. If you choose this option, PowerPoint converts the chart to a collection of PowerPoint shape objects, with no link to the original Excel chart or data.

Changing the Chart Type

PowerPoint enables you to create 15 basic types of charts. Each chart type conveys information with a different emphasis. Sales data plotted in a column chart might emphasize the relative performance of different regions, for example, and the same data plotted as a line chart might emphasize an increase or decrease in sales over time. The type of chart that's best for your data depends on the nature of the data and which aspects of it you want to emphasize.

Fortunately, PowerPoint doesn't force you to decide the final chart type up front. You can easily change the chart type at any time without changing the chart data. These steps show you how:

1. **Click the chart to select it.**

   When you select a chart, two new tabs appear on the Ribbon: Chart Design and Format.

2. **Select the Chart Design tab (see Figure 17-5).**

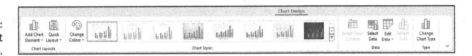

FIGURE 17-5: The Chart Design tab.

3. **Click the Change Chart Type button (shown in the margin) found in the Type group.**

   PowerPoint displays a gallery of chart types.

4. **Click the chart type that you want.**

5. **Click OK.**

   You're done.

Working with Chart Data

The data that provides the numbers plotted in a PowerPoint chart is stored in an Excel workbook. Depending on how you created the chart, this Excel workbook can be either a separate workbook document or embedded within your PowerPoint document. Either way, you can work with Excel whenever you want to modify the chart data.

To change the data on which a chart is based, select the chart and then select the Chart Design tab. This tab includes a group called Data, which provides four controls that let you perform various tricks on the data, as I describe in the following sections.

Switching rows and columns

The first control in the Data group of the Chart Design tab is called Switch Row/Column (shown in the margin). It changes the orientation of your chart in a way that can be difficult to describe but is easy to visualize. Look back at the chart in Figure 17-4. It's based on the following data:

	River City	Pixley	Hoostersville
Instruments	$22,000	$15,000	$12,000
Music	$25,000	$16,000	$22,000
Uniforms	$29,000	$13,000	$35,000
Instruction	$54,000	$22,000	$39,000

As shown in Figure 17-4, the rows are used to determine the data categories. Thus, the chart displays the data for Instruments, Music, Uniforms, and Instruction along the x-axis.

If you click the Switch Row/Column button, the chart changes, as shown in Figure 17-6. Here, the chart categorizes the data by city, so sales for River City, Pixley, and Hoostersville are shown along the x-axis. (Yes, I know that in the old TV series *Green Acres*, the town was called Hootersville. But Mrs. Douglas called it "Hoostersville," which makes me smile.)

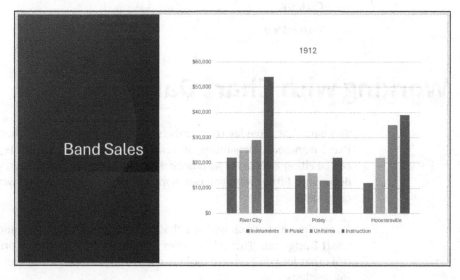

FIGURE 17-6: A chart with the rows and columns switched.

TIP

If the Switch Row/Column button is grayed-out, it's because the Excel data on which the chart is based is not open. Click the Edit Data button and then return to PowerPoint and the Switch Row/Column button will come to life.

Changing the data selection

The Select Data button (shown in the margin) found in the Data group of the Chart Design tab lets you change the selection of data that your chart is based on. When you click this button, you're escorted to Excel, and the dialog box shown in Figure 17-7 is displayed.

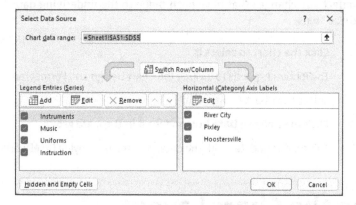

FIGURE 17-7: The Select Data Source dialog box.

This dialog box lets you do three basic tasks:

» **Change the data range.** You can change the range of data that's used for the chart by using the Chart Data Range text box.

» **Switch rows and columns.** You can switch rows and columns by clicking the Switch Row/Column button. This has the same effect as clicking the Switch Row/Column button back in PowerPoint.

» **Modify ranges and series.** You can play with the individual ranges that contain the data for each series. You can use the Add, Edit, and Remove buttons to add a new series, edit the range used for an existing series, or delete a series, respectively. And you can change the order in which the series are presented by clicking the buttons with the up and down arrows.

Editing the source data

To change the actual data values on which a chart is based, click the Edit Data button (shown in the margin) in the Data group of the Chart Design tab. This action launches a little Excel-like window to display the chart data. You can then make any changes you want. When you return to PowerPoint (by clicking anywhere in the PowerPoint window), the chart is updated to reflect your changes.

You can open the data in a full Excel window by clicking the arrow beneath the Edit Data button and choosing Edit in Excel.

Refreshing a chart

If a chart is linked to a separate Excel workbook, you can update the chart to reflect any changes that have been made to the underlying data. To do so, follow these steps:

1. **Click the chart to select it.**

   The Ribbon expands to include the Chart Design and Format tabs.

2. **Select the Chart Design tab.**
3. **Click the Refresh Data button found in the Data group.**

   The chart is updated with the data from the underlying Excel workbook.

Changing the Chart Layout

A *chart layout* is a predefined combination of chart elements such as legends, titles, and so on. Microsoft studied thousands of charts and talked to chart experts to come up with galleries of the most common layouts for each chart type.

To change the layout for a chart, follow these steps:

1. **Click the chart to select it.**

   The Ribbon expands to include the Chart Design and Format tabs.

2. **Select the Chart Design tab.**
3. **Click the Quick Layout button (shown in the margin) found in the Chart Layouts group.**

   The Quick Layout Gallery opens, as shown in Figure 17-8.

4. **Click the layout you want to use.**

   The layout you select is applied to the chart. Figure 17-9 shows the Band Sales chart with a different layout applied.

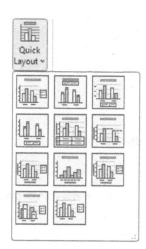

FIGURE 17-8:
The Quick Layout Gallery for column charts.

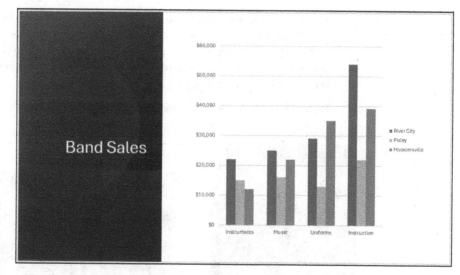

FIGURE 17-9:
Changing the layout changes the appearance of a chart.

Changing the Chart Style

A *chart style* is a predefined combination of formatting elements, such as colors and shape effects. Microsoft provides a large assortment of chart styles to choose from. For example, Figure 17-10 shows the Chart Style gallery for column charts.

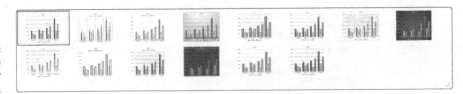

FIGURE 17-10:
The Chart Style gallery for column charts.

To change the style for a chart, follow these steps:

1. **Click the chart to select it.**

   The Ribbon expands to include the Chart Design and Format tabs (refer to Figure 17-5).

2. **Select the Chart Design tab.**

3. **Select the style you want to use from the Chart Styles group.**

   The Chart Styles group displays the most commonly used styles for the chart type. If the style you want to use isn't visible in this group, you can click the More button to display a gallery of all available styles. (The More button is the down-arrow button at the bottom of the scroll bar that appears at the right side of the Chart Styles group.)

   Figure 17-11 shows the Band Sales chart with a different chart style.

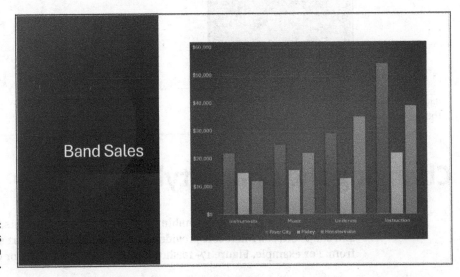

FIGURE 17-11:
The Band Sales chart in a different style.

272 PART 4 **Embellishing Your Slides**

Embellishing Your Chart

PowerPoint enables you to embellish a chart in many ways: You can add titles, labels, legends, and who knows what else. The easiest way to add these elements is by selecting a chart layout, as I describe in the earlier section "Changing the Chart Layout." However, you can create your own unique chart layout by adding these elements individually.

Add Chart Element

To do that, select the chart and then click the Add Chart Element button (shown in the margin), which appears next to the chart. A list of chart elements appears, as shown in Figure 17-12. You can then select the chart elements you want to appear on your chart. (Note that each type of chart has its own set of options, so peruse the possibilities when you work with different chart types.)

FIGURE 17-12: Adding elements to a chart.

The following paragraphs describe the elements you can add to your charts:

» **Axes:** Sometimes an axe is what you'd like to use to fix your computer. But in this case, *axes* refer to the *x*- and *y*-axes on which chart data is plotted. The *x*-axis is the horizontal axis of the chart, and the *y*-axis is the vertical axis. For 3-D charts, a third axis — *z* — is also used. The Axes control lets you show or hide the labels used for each chart axis.

» **Axis titles:** These titles describe the meaning of each chart axis. Most charts use two axes titles: the Primary Horizontal Axis Title and the Primary Vertical Axis Title.

» **Chart titles:** A chart title describes the chart's contents. It normally appears at the top of the chart, but you can drag it to any location.

» **Data Labels:** Let you add labels to the data points on the chart. For maximum control over the data labels, choose More Options to display the Format Data Labels pane, as shown in Figure 17-13.

FIGURE 17-13: The Format Data Labels pane.

TIP

For most slide types, data labels add unnecessary clutter without adding much useful information. Use labels only if you think that you must back up your chart with exact numbers.

» **Data Table:** The *data table* is a table that shows the data used to create a chart. Most charts don't include a data table, but you can add one if you think your audience will benefit from seeing the raw numbers. For example, the version of the Band Sales chart shown in Figure 17-11 includes a data table.

» **Error Bars:** Adds a graphical element that indicates a range of values for each point rather than a single point. The size of the range can be calculated as a fixed value, a percentage of the point value, or a standard deviation.

» **Gridlines:** *Gridlines* are light lines drawn behind a chart to make it easier to judge the position of each dot, bar, or line plotted by the chart. You can turn gridlines on or off via the Gridlines button.

» **Legends:** A *legend* identifies the data series that appear in the chart. When you click the Legend button, a menu with several choices for the placement of the legend appears. You can also choose More Legend Options to display the Format Legend pane, as shown in Figure 17-14. From this dialog box, you can set the position of the legend, as well as control various formatting options for the legend, such as the fill and border style. (Note that you can also drag the legend to move it to another location in the chart.)

FIGURE 17-14: The Format Legend pane.

TIP

PowerPoint enables you to create a legend, but you're on your own if you need a myth or fable.

» **Trendline:** Allows you to add line elements that show the trend of one or more data points, using one of several methods to calculate the trend.

Using Treemap and Sunburst Charts

Both the Treemap and Sunburst chart types are designed to represent hierarchical data. The data I've been using for the charts in this chapter so far represent band sales data with one row for each city and four columns to subdivide each city's sales according to type — instrument sales, music sales, uniform sales, and instruction sales. The data table looks like this:

City	Instruments	Music	Uniforms	Instruction
River City	20.4	37.4	90	75
Pixley	50.6	36.6	35	102
Hoostersville	45.9	45.6	46.5	88

To represent this same data in a way that can be used by the Treemap and Sunburst chart types, eliminate the separate columns for Instruments, Music, Uniforms, and Instruction. Instead, use three columns — City, Product, and Sales — like this:

City	Product	Sales
River City	Instruments	20.4
River City	Music	37.4
River City	Uniforms	90
River City	Instruction	75
Pixley	Instruments	50.6
Pixley	Music	36.6
Pixley	Uniforms	35
Pixley	Instruction	102
Hoostersville	Instruments	45.9
Hoostersville	Music	45.6
Hoostersville	Uniforms	46.5
Hoostersville	Instruction	88

TECHNICAL STUFF

If you're into database technology, you'll recognize that the data in the second table resembles a *relational database*. This way of organizing hierarchical data is common in Microsoft Access and other types of database servers.

When your data is in the correct format, you can create a Treemap or Sunburst chart. Figure 17-15 shows a Treemap chart of this data. As you can see, each city is represented by a large rectangle; the products are smaller rectangles nested inside the larger rectangles. The size of the inner rectangles is proportional to the sales values. Thus, the Instruction rectangle for Hoostersville is larger than the other three rectangles.

A Sunburst chart is similar to a Treemap chart, but instead of using rectangles, the Sunburst chart uses concentric rings, as shown in Figure 17-16. Here, the inner ring represents the cities and the outer ring represents the products sold.

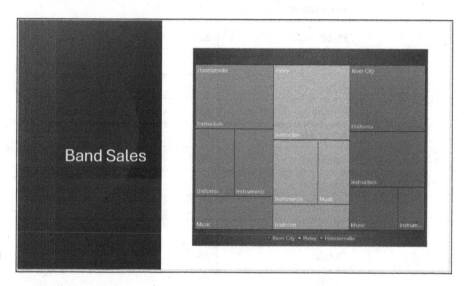

FIGURE 17-15: A Treemap chart.

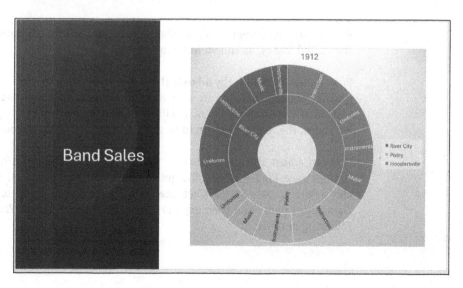

FIGURE 17-16: A Sunburst chart.

CHAPTER 17 **Charting for Fun and Profit** 277

Using Map Charts

A *Map chart* plots data geographically. PowerPoint extrapolates geographic data from the data table and searches Bing's vast collection of maps to try to plot the data to a map. For this to work properly, your data table must include real-world geographic data that PowerPoint can recognize. Examples include the names of countries, names of states, and zip codes.

As a simple example, suppose you have a spreadsheet that contains two columns, labeled State and Sales. The following table shows the first ten values for such a table:

State	Sales
Alabama	22
Alaska	2
Arizona	32
Arkansas	80
California	30
Colorado	27
Connecticut	17
Delaware	12
Florida	66
Georgia	92

PowerPoint can recognize these state names and render the data using a map of the United States, as shown in Figure 17-17.

PowerPoint automatically adjusts the scope of the map to accommodate the geographic regions included in your data. For example, if you use country names instead of state names, the map will expand to include the entire globe. If you use zip codes, the map will zoom in to show just the zip codes in your data.

You can adjust the appearance of the map by tinkering with the map's Series Options (see Figure 17-18). To get to these settings, right-click the chart and chose Format Data Series. Click the Series Options icon at the top of the Format Data Series pane, and then expand the Series Options group. You can adjust the following options:

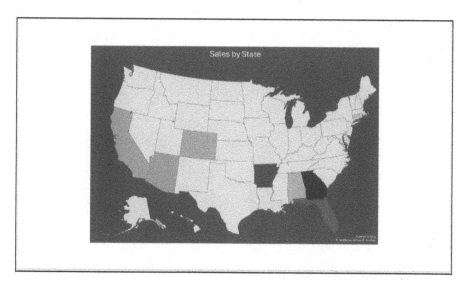

FIGURE 17-17: A Map chart.

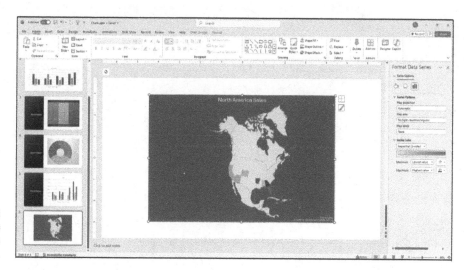

FIGURE 17-18: Editing a map chart's Series Options.

» **Map Projection:** Sets the type of map projection used for the chart. PowerPoint supports three map projection types: Mercator, Miller, and Robinson. Cycle through these choices until you find the one that works best for your chart.

» **Map Area:** Use this option to set the scope of the map. The options available here depend on the range of the geographic data in the data series but may include options such as County, State/Province, Country, or World.

» **Map Labels:** This option lets you indicate whether you want all data series labels included or just those that fit.

You can also use the Format Data Series pane to adjust the colors used for the map.

CHAPTER 17 **Charting for Fun and Profit** 279

> **IN THIS CHAPTER**
> » Looking at the SmartArt feature
> » Creating diagrams using SmartArt
> » Editing a SmartArt diagram
> » Changing SmartArt text
> » Creating organization charts

Chapter **18**

Working with SmartArt

You'll hear nothing but yawns from the back row if your presentation consists of slide after slide of text and bulleted lists with an occasional bit of clip art thrown in for good measure. Mercifully, PowerPoint is well equipped to add all sorts of embellishments to your slides. This chapter shows you how to work with one of the coolest ways to embellish your slides: special diagrams called SmartArt.

Understanding SmartArt

PowerPoint includes a nifty little feature called SmartArt, which lets you add several different types of useful diagrams to your slides. With SmartArt, you can create List, Process, Cycle, Hierarchy, Relationship, Matrix, Pyramid, and Picture diagrams. And each of these basic diagram types has multiple variations. In all, you can choose from 185 variations.

The diagrams created by SmartArt consist of multiple elements, such as shapes and lines. SmartArt itself takes care of drawing these elements in a coordinated fashion, so you don't have to draw the separate elements manually.

The basic idea behind SmartArt diagrams is to represent bulleted lists as a diagram of interconnected shapes. Although many different types of SmartArt diagrams are available, they all work the same way. The only real difference among the various SmartArt diagram types is how they graphically represent the bullets. For example, consider the following bulleted list:

» Arrive

» Work

» Lunch

» More work

» Leave

Figure 18-1 shows this list represented by a SmartArt diagram. All I did to create this diagram was select the text, right-click, choose Convert to SmartArt, and then select the Descending Process SmartArt diagram type.

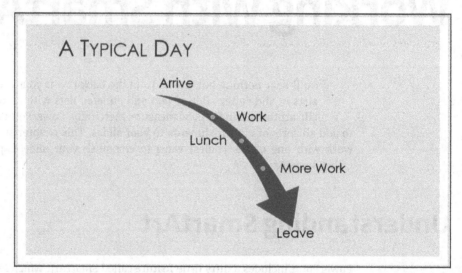

FIGURE 18-1: A simple SmartArt diagram.

Note that many of the SmartArt diagram types can display two or more outline levels in your bulleted list. For example, suppose you have the following list:

» Arrive
- Stop for coffee on the way.
- Try not to be late.

» Work
- Coffee break at 10:00.
- Look smart!

» Lunch

- Best part of the day!
- No more than two hours!

» More work

- Coffee break at 3:00.
- Try to stay awake at 4:00.

» Leave

- Leave early today?

Figure 18-2 shows how this list appears when formatted as an Increasing Arrows Process chart. As you can see, the second-level bullets are incorporated as text within the diagram.

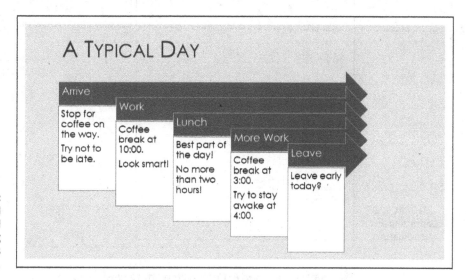

FIGURE 18-2: How second-level text is displayed in an Increasing Arrows Process chart.

One of the most useful aspects of SmartArt is that you can easily change from one type of diagram to another. So, if you decide that a diagram doesn't convey the message you intend, you can try changing the diagram type to see whether the message is clearer.

Creating a SmartArt Diagram

The easiest way to create a SmartArt diagram is to create a new slide, enter the bulleted list as if you were going to display the list as normal text, and then convert the text to SmartArt. Just follow these steps:

1. **Create a new slide with the Title and Content layout.**

2. **Type your bulleted list.**

   Use one or two levels of bullets, but try to keep the list as short and concise as you can.

3. **Right-click anywhere in the list and choose Convert to SmartArt.**

   A menu of SmartArt diagram types appears (see Figure 18-3).

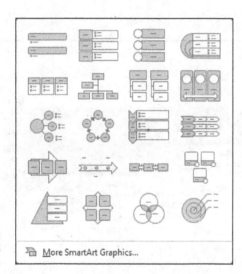

FIGURE 18-3:
Converting text to SmartArt.

4. **Select the SmartArt type you want to use.**

   If the SmartArt type doesn't appear in the menu, you can choose More SmartArt Graphics to display the Choose a SmartArt Graphic dialog box (see Figure 18-4), which lets you choose from about a million different SmartArt diagram types. PowerPoint offers eight basic categories of SmartArt diagrams; these diagram types are pictured and described in Table 18-1.

5. **Click OK.**

   The diagram is created.

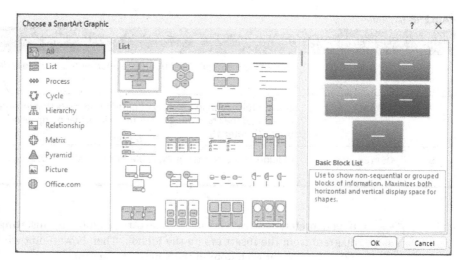

FIGURE 18-4:
The Choose a SmartArt Graphic dialog box.

6. **Modify the diagram however you see fit.**

   For more information, see the section "Tweaking a SmartArt Diagram," later in this chapter.

   You're done! Well, you're never really done. You can keep tweaking your diagram until the end of time to get it perfect. But at some point, you have to say, "Enough is enough," and call it finished.

TABLE 18-1 Types of Diagrams You Can Create

Icon	Diagram Type	Description
	List	Shows a simple list. Some of the list diagrams show information that doesn't have any particular organization; others display information in a way that implies a sequential progression, such as steps in a task.
	Process	Shows a process in which steps flow in a sequential fashion.
	Cycle	Shows a process that repeats in a continuous cycle.
	Hierarchy	Shows hierarchical relationships, such as organization charts.
	Relationship	Shows how items are conceptually related to one another. Included in this group are various types of radial and Venn diagrams.
	Matrix	Shows four items arranged into quadrants.

(continued)

TABLE 18- *(continued)*

Icon	Diagram Type	Description
	Pyramid	Shows how elements build upon one another to form a foundation.
	Picture	Shows information in a variety of different formats that incorporate picture objects into the chart design. (For more information on working with pictures, turn to Chapter 15.)
	Office.com	Additional SmartArt types available from Microsoft's `Office.com` website.

> **TIP** If you prefer, you can create a SmartArt diagram by inserting the SmartArt diagram from the Insert tab on the Ribbon. Then PowerPoint will prompt you to enter the text for each item in the SmartArt diagram.

Tweaking a SmartArt Diagram

After you've created a SmartArt diagram, you can adjust its appearance in many ways. The easiest way is to change the SmartArt style that's applied to the diagram. A *SmartArt style* is simply a collection of formatting elements, such as colors and shape effects, that are assigned to the various elements of a SmartArt diagram.

Microsoft provides a large assortment of SmartArt styles to choose from. For example, Figure 18-5 shows the style gallery for Pyramid diagrams.

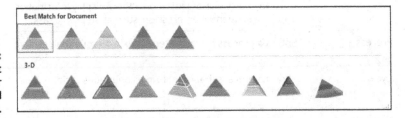

FIGURE 18-5: The SmartArt style gallery for Pyramid diagrams.

To change the quick style for a SmartArt diagram, follow these steps:

1. **Click the diagram to select it.**

   The SmartArt Design tab appears on the Ribbon (see Figure 18-6).

2. **Select the SmartArt Design tab.**

FIGURE 18-6:
The SmartArt
Design tab.

3. **Select the style you want to use from the SmartArt Styles group.**

   The SmartArt Styles group displays the most commonly used styles for the diagram type. If the style you want to use isn't visible in this group, you can click the More button to display a gallery like the one shown in Figure 18-5.

Note that the SmartArt Design tab also includes controls that let you modify the SmartArt diagram by adding additional shapes or bullet items or changing the chart type. You can also reset the diagram to its original appearance by clicking the Reset Graphic button found in the Reset group of the SmartArt Design tab.

Editing the SmartArt Text

When you create a SmartArt diagram from an existing bulleted list, the bullet text is replaced by the diagram. After you've converted the text to SmartArt, what do you do if you need to modify the text?

To modify SmartArt text, simply select the SmartArt diagram. Then click the little left-arrow icon that appears on the left edge of the diagram's selection box. This action reveals a flyout window called the Text pane (see Figure 18-7), in which you can edit the bullet points. (On a tablet, you can simply tap the text to edit it.)

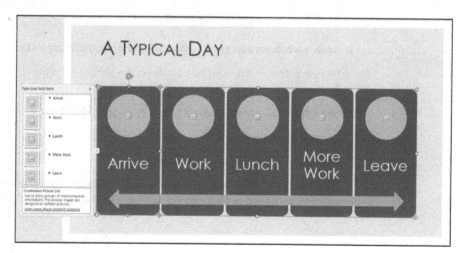

FIGURE 18-7:
Editing SmartArt
bullet text.

FLOWCHARTS, ANYONE?

One type of diagram that people often want to create with PowerPoint is a flowchart. Although SmartArt doesn't have an option for creating flowcharts, you can easily create flowcharts by using PowerPoint's AutoShapes. For example, take a look at the following flowchart, which I created with just a few minutes' work.

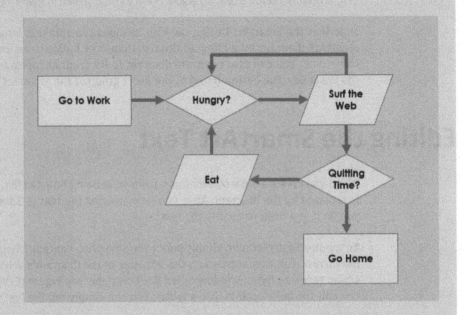

To create a flowchart like this, follow these basic steps:

1. **Draw each flowchart shape using basic shape objects (see Chapter 16).**

    Use the shapes in the Flowchart section of the Shapes gallery to create the shapes for the flowchart, and use arrows to connect the shapes.

2. **Enter text into each flowchart shape by clicking the shape and typing.**

    If necessary, adjust the text font and size.

3. **Adjust the alignment of your shapes.**

    Here's where the flowcharting AutoShapes really shine: The connectors stay attached to the shapes even when you move the shapes around! Pretty slick, eh?

Working with Organization Charts

Organization charts — you know, those box-and-line charts that show who reports to whom, where the buck stops, and who got the lateral arabesque — are an essential part of many presentations.

The hierarchical SmartArt diagrams are ideal for creating organization charts. You can create diagrams that show bosses, subordinates, coworkers, and assistants. You can easily rearrange the chain of command, add new boxes or delete boxes, and apply fancy 3-D effects. Figure 18-8 shows a finished organization chart.

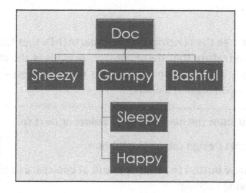

FIGURE 18-8: A finished organization chart.

The bullet list I used to create this chart looked like this before I converted it to SmartArt:

- Doc
  - Sneezy
  - Grumpy
    - Sleepy
    - Happy
  - Bashful

Notice that Dopey isn't in this list. That's because Dopey is in a special kind of box on the chart, called an *Assistant*. You find out how to add Assistant boxes in the later section "Adding boxes to a chart."

Keep in mind that organization charts are useful for more than showing employee relationships. You also can use them to show any kind of hierarchical structure. For example, back when I wrote computer programs for a living, I used organization charts to plan the structure of my computer programs. They're also great for recording family genealogies, although they don't have any way to indicate that Aunt Millie hasn't spoken to Aunt Beatrice in 30 years.

Adding boxes to a chart

You can add a box to an organization chart by calling up the Text pane and editing the text. (See "Editing the SmartArt Text," earlier in this chapter, for tips on how to do that.)

Alternatively, you can use the controls on the SmartArt Design tab on the Ribbon to add boxes. One nice feature that these controls provide is the capability to add an *Assistant*, which is a box that appears outside the hierarchical chain of command. Here's how to add boxes to a chart:

1. **Click the box you want the new box to be below or next to.**
2. **Select the SmartArt Design tab on the Ribbon.**
3. **Click the Add Shape button to reveal a menu of choices, and then select one of the following options:**

   - *Add Shape Before:* Inserts a new box at the same level as the selected box, immediately to its left
   - *Add Shape After:* Inserts a new box at the same level as the selected box, immediately to its right
   - *Add Shape Above:* Inserts a new box above the selected box
   - *Add Shape Below:* Inserts a new box beneath the selected box
   - *Add Assistant:* Inserts a new box beneath the selected box, but the new box is connected with a special elbow connector to indicate that the box is an Assistant, not a subordinate

4. **Click the new box and then type whatever text you want to appear in the box.**
5. **If necessary, drag the box to adjust its location.**

Deleting chart boxes

To delete a box from an organization chart, select the box and press Delete. PowerPoint automatically adjusts the chart to compensate for the lost box.

When you delete a box from an organization chart, you should observe a moment of somber silence — or throw a party. It all depends on whose name was in the box, I suppose.

Changing the chart layout

PowerPoint lets you choose from four methods of arranging subordinates in an organization chart branch:

- **Standard:** Subordinate shapes are placed at the same level beneath the superior shape.
- **Both Hanging:** Subordinates are placed two per level beneath the superior with the connecting line between them.
- **Left Hanging:** Subordinates are stacked vertically beneath the superior, to the left of the connecting line.
- **Right Hanging:** Subordinates are stacked vertically beneath the superior, to the right of the connecting line.

Figure 18-9 shows an organization chart that uses all four of these layouts. Sneezy, Grumpy, and Bashful use Standard layout. Sleepy and Happy use Both Hanging layout. Groucho, Harpo, and Chico use Left Hanging layout, and Manny, Moe, and Jack use Right Hanging layout.

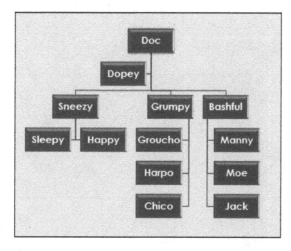

FIGURE 18-9: An organization chart that uses all four layout types.

To change the layout of a branch of your chart, click the shape at the top of the branch, select the SmartArt Design tab on the Ribbon, click the Layout button in the Create Graphic group, and choose the layout type you want to use.

> **IN THIS CHAPTER**
>
> » Adding interesting sound effects to your presentation
>
> » Spicing up your presentation with video
>
> » Reducing the size of audio and video files

Chapter 19
Lights! Camera! Action! (Adding Sound and Video)

One of the cool things about PowerPoint is that it lets you create slides that contain not only text and pictures but also sounds and even movies. You can add sound effects, such as screeching brakes or breaking glass, to liven up dull presentations. You can even add your own applause, making your presentation like a TV sitcom or game show. You can also add a musical background or a narration to your presentation.

Additionally, you can insert a film clip from *The African Queen* or a picture of the space shuttle launching if you think that will help keep people awake. This chapter shows you how to add those special effects.

This chapter is short because you can't do as much with audio and video in PowerPoint as you can with professional video-editing software such as Adobe Premiere Pro. Still, PowerPoint does allow you to paste audio and video elements into your slide show, giving you the power to craft some impressive high-tech presentations. And PowerPoint allows you to perform basic edits on the videos you insert.

Adding Sound to a Slide

A sterile *beep* used to be the only sound you could get from your computer. Nowadays, you can make your computer talk almost as well as the computers in the *Star Trek* movies, or you can give your computer a sophomoric sense of audible distaste. At last, the computer can be as obnoxious as the user!

Investigating sound files

Computer sounds are stored in *sound files*, which come in two basic varieties:

» **Audio files:** Audio files contain digitized recordings of real sounds. These sounds can be sound effects, such as cars screeching, guns firing, or drums rolling; music; or even quotes from movies or TV shows. (Imagine Darth Vader saying to your audience, "I find your lack of faith disturbing.")

Audio files come in two distinct varieties:

- *Uncompressed:* This type of audio file (including the standard Windows WAV format) provides pristine, clean sound (and packs a large file size to prove it). Both Windows and PowerPoint come with a collection of WAV files that provide simple sound effects, such as swooshes, blips, applause, and drumrolls.

- *Compressed:* For longer sound clips, such as complete songs, the most common formats are MP3 and M4A.

» **MIDI files:** MIDI files contain music stored in a form that your computer's music synthesizer can play. Think of it like sheet music for your digital piano player. Windows comes with several MIDI files, and you can download many more from the internet. MIDI files have the file extension .mid.

To insert a sound into a PowerPoint presentation, all you have to do is paste one of these sound files into a slide. Then when you run the presentation in Slide Show view, you can have the sounds play automatically during slide transitions, or you can play them manually by clicking the Sound button.

Fortunately, the national shortage of sound files ended years ago. PowerPoint comes with a handful of useful sound files, including drumrolls, breaking glass, gunshots, and typewriter sounds. Windows comes with some useful sounds, too. But a virtually unlimited supply of sounds is available at your disposal via the internet. Search the web for something general, like "WAV file collection," or something specific, such as "Star Trek sounds."

MP3 AND THE INTERNET

MP3 files are a compressed form of WAV files that allow entire songs to be squeezed into a reasonable amount of hard-drive space. For example, the Steppenwolf song "Wild Thing" weighs in at just under 2.5MB in an MP3 file. The same file in WAV format requires a whopping 26MB — more than ten times the space!

Napster, the online file exchange system that let users swap MP3 files, popularized the MP3 format in the early 2000s. Of course, this file swapping bothered the music industry, which sued because it said users were illegally trading copyrighted music without paying for it, which of course they were, and we (oops, I mean *they*) all knew it.

These days, the most popular sources for legally obtaining audio files are Amazon, Bandcamp, Google Play, Apple Music, and YouTube Music. You can legally download music from these sources, and you can still find plenty of online sources to trade music under the table. Another popular way to obtain audio files is to rip them from a music CD. Windows Media Player has the built-in capability to do this. (Note that you can't use music streamed from services such as Amazon Prime or Spotify in your presentations.)

Keep in mind, however, that the legality of using copyrighted music in your PowerPoint presentations is questionable. So, if you use hot audio files you got from the internet or ripped from a CD, don't blame me if one day you wake up and find your house surrounded by federal agents and a CNN news crew referring to you as a "dangerous copyright abuser" and your house as a "compound." They'll probably even interview your ninth-grade English teacher, who will tell the nation that all you could talk about when you were a troubled teen was stealing Aerosmith music from the internet and using it in illegal PowerPoint presentations.

Inserting an audio sound object

In this section, I explain how to insert a sound object onto a slide. You can configure the sound object to play automatically whenever you display the slide, or you can set it up so that it will play only when you click the sound object's icon. Note that if you want the sound to play automatically and the sound is a WAV file, it's easier to add it to the slide transition (see Chapter 13) than to add it as a separate object.

To insert a sound file from your hard drive onto a PowerPoint slide, follow these steps:

1. **Move to the slide to which you want to add the sound.**
2. **Select the Insert tab on the Ribbon, click the Audio button found in the Media group, and then choose Audio on My PC.**

    The Insert Audio dialog box appears (see Figure 19-1).

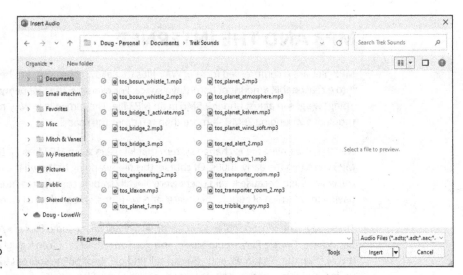

FIGURE 19-1:
The Insert Audio dialog box.

3. **Select the audio file that you want to insert.**

   You may have to rummage around your hard drive to find the folder that contains your sound files. (In Figure 19-1, I've navigated to a folder named Trek Sounds, where I have conveniently stored some *Star Trek* sound effect files I previously downloaded from the internet.)

4. **Click the Insert button.**

   The audio file is inserted into the current slide, along with a toolbar of controls that let you play the sound (see Figure 19-2).

TIP

You can also record a sound directly from PowerPoint. To do this, you'll need a microphone. To record a sound, click the Audio button on the Insert tab on the Ribbon and choose Record Audio. The dialog box shown in Figure 19-3 appears. When you're ready to start recording, click the red Record button. When you're finished, click the Stop button (the square icon).

Here are a few other random thoughts on adding sounds to your slides:

REMEMBER

» To play a sound while working in Normal view, double-click the sound icon. However, to play the sound during a slide show, click only once.

» You can also play audio files as a part of the slide transition (see Chapter 13).

» If you change your mind and decide that you don't want any sounds, you can easily remove them. To remove a sound, click the sound's icon (which resembles a speaker) and press Delete.

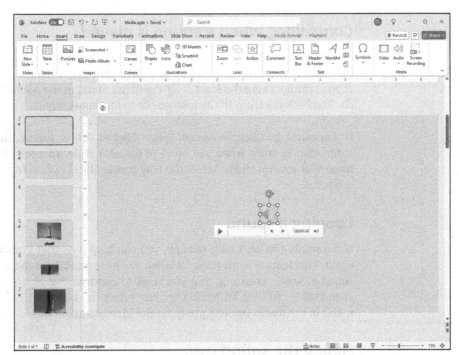

FIGURE 19-2:
A sound inserted into a slide.

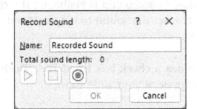

FIGURE 19-3:
Recording an audio clip.

Setting audio options

You can control several important aspects of how an audio file is played by selecting the file and then selecting the Playback tab, shown in Figure 19-4. This tab contains several controls that let you edit the way the sound file is played. The following sections explain how to use the most important of these tools.

FIGURE 19-4:
The Playback tab.

CHAPTER 19 **Lights! Camera! Action! (Adding Sound and Video)** 297

Controlling when a sound is played

By default, sounds are not played until you click the sound icon that appears on the slide. If you want a sound to play automatically when the slide is displayed, change the option in the Start drop-down list found in the Audio Options group on the Playback tab from In Click Sequence to Automatically.

If you select In Click Sequence, When Clicked On, or Automatically, the sound automatically stops when you move to the next slide. To allow the sound to continue over several slides, select the Play across Slides option from the Start drop-down list.

Looping a sound

If the sound file isn't long enough, you can loop it so that it plays over and over again. This feature is most useful when you have a subtle sound effect, such as the sound of waves crashing, that you want to continue for as long as you leave the slide visible. To loop an audio clip, just select the Loop Until Stopped check box found in the Audio Options group on the Playback tab.

Hiding the sound icon

By default, the icon representing an audio clip is visible on the slide during your slide show. Assuming that you've set the sound to play automatically, you probably don't want the icon visible.

The Audio Options group includes a check box titled Hide During Show, which hides the sound icon when you present your slide show.

Fading the sound in and out

The Fade In and Fade Out controls let you gradually fade your audio clip in and out. By default, these controls are both set to 0, so the audio clip begins and ends at full volume. By changing either or both of these controls to a value such as 2 seconds or 3 seconds, you can smoothly fade the sound in or out for a more subtle effect.

Trimming an audio clip

Clicking the Trim Audio button brings up the Trim Audio dialog box, shown in Figure 19-5. This dialog box enables you to select just a portion of the audio clip to play in your presentation by letting you choose start and end times. You can choose the start and end times by dragging the green start pointer or the red end pointer over the image of the audio file's waveform. (You can often tell where to stop or end the audio clip by looking at the waveform that's displayed in the Trim

Audio dialog box.) You can also enter the time (in seconds) in the Start Time and End Time boxes. (Ideally, you should select the start and end trim points during silent portions of the audio file, to avoid abrupt starts and ends.)

FIGURE 19-5: The Trim Audio dialog box.

Adding Video to Your Slides

Video doesn't just belong on YouTube. You can easily add video clips to your presentations and play them at will. I'm not sure why you would want to, but hey, who needs a reason?

Adding a motion clip to a slide is similar to adding a sound clip. A crucial difference exists, however, between motion clips and sound bites: Video is meant to be *seen* (and sometimes *heard*). An inserted motion clip should be given ample space on your slide.

REMEMBER

If you think that sound files are big, wait 'til you see how big movie clips are. Ha! They consume hard-drive space the way an elephant consumes veggies. The whole multimedia revolution is really a conspiracy started by hard-drive manufacturers.

Finding a video to add to your presentation

With PowerPoint, you can add videos from three sources:

» **This Device,** which is the most likely place for video files you've scavenged from the internet, recorded on your smartphone and uploaded to your computer, or created yourself with software such as Microsoft's own Video Editor, which comes with Windows

» **Stock Videos,** which provides a set of short professional videos from Microsoft that you can use without worrying about copyright issues

» **Online Videos,** which lets you use videos from sources such as Vimeo or YouTube

Inserting a video clip

The following steps show you how to add a video clip that already exists on your computer. The steps for adding a stock video or an online video are similar:

1. **Move to the slide on which you want to insert the movie.**

    Hopefully, you left a big blank space on the slide to insert the movie. If not, rearrange the existing slide objects to make room for the movie.

2. **Select the Insert tab on the Ribbon, click Video found in the Media group, and then choose This Device.**

    The Insert Video dialog box appears, as shown in Figure 19-6.

    You can also choose Stock Video or Online Video, which lets you grab a professionally produced video or a video from Vimeo, YouTube, or another online video source. (Keep in mind that the same copyrights that apply to images and audio also apply to online videos.)

FIGURE 19-6: The Insert Video dialog box.

3. **Select the movie that you want to insert.**

    In Figure 19-6, I've navigated to a location where I previously saved a video file of the launch of Apollo 11 in 1969. You may need to scroll the list to find the movie you're looking for or navigate your way to a different folder.

4. **Click the Insert button.**

   The movie is inserted on the slide, as shown in Figure 19-7.

FIGURE 19-7: A movie inserted on a slide.

5. **Resize the movie if you want and drag it to a new location on the slide.**

   Actually, the movie shown in Figure 19-7 has already been resized; PowerPoint usually inserts videos smaller than you want.

To play the movie while you're working on the presentation in Normal view, double-click the movie. During a slide show, a single click does the trick, unless you set the movie to play automatically. In that case, the movie runs as soon as you display the slide.

Setting video options

You can set various options for playing video files via the Playback tab on the Ribbon, shown in Figure 19-8. As you can see, this tab contains several controls that let you edit the way the video file is played. The following sections explain how to use the most important of these tools.

CHAPTER 19 **Lights! Camera! Action! (Adding Sound and Video)** 301

FIGURE 19-8:
The Playback tab.

Controlling when a video is played

By default, videos play when you click the Play button that appears beneath the video frame. If you want the video to start automatically when you display the slide, change the option in the Start drop-down list found in the Video Options group on the Playback tab from On Click to Automatically.

Looping a video

If the video is short, you may want to repeat it over and over again until you move to the next slide. To do so, select the Loop Until Stopped check box found in the Video Options group on the Playback tab.

Trimming a video clip

The Trim Video button summons the Trim Video dialog box, which is shown in Figure 19-9. Here, you can select the portion of the video clip you want to play in your presentation. You can choose the start and end points of the video by dragging the start pointer or the red end pointer over the image of the video's soundtrack wave, which appears immediately beneath the video frame. Or you can enter the time (in seconds) in the Start Time and End Time boxes.

TIP

Note that you can only trim videos that you've actually downloaded to your computer. You can't trim online videos.

Playing the video full screen

If you want the video to take over the entire screen, select the Play Full Screen check box found in the Video Options group on the Playback tab. Note that this option works best for high-quality videos. If the video is of lower quality, it may not look good when it's played in full-screen mode.

Fading the video's sound in and out

The Fade In and Fade Out controls for video clips, found in the Editing group on the Playback tab, work just as they do for audio clips (which I describe earlier in this chapter). In other words, they affect the video's soundtrack, not the video image itself. You can use these controls to gradually fade the video's sound in and out.

FIGURE 19-9:
The Trim Video dialog box.

Adding a bookmark

A *bookmark* is a marked location within the playback of a video file that can be used to trigger an animation effect. For example, a few seconds into the video of the Apollo 11 launch shown in the previous two figures, the announcer says "Liftoff!" and the rocket begins to rise. It's a simple matter to create a bookmark at that exact point in the video playback. Then you can use that bookmark to trigger an animation that causes the word *Liftoff!* to appear beneath the video, as shown in Figure 19-10.

Here are the steps for creating a video bookmark and animating an object when the video playback reaches the bookmark:

1. **Add a video to the slide.**

    For this example, I added a video of the Apollo 11 launch that I downloaded from the Internet.

2. **Select the video object and then select the Playback tab (refer to Figure 19-8).**

3. **Click the Play button that appears beneath the video frame.**

    The video begins to play.

CHAPTER 19 Lights! Camera! Action! (Adding Sound and Video) 303

FIGURE 19-10:
Using a bookmark to trigger an animation effect.

4. **When the video reaches the point where you want to insert the bookmark, click the Add Bookmark button (shown in the margin) found on the Playback tab.**

   The bookmark is created. A small dot appears in the progress bar beneath the video frame to mark the location of the bookmark.

5. **Create an object on the slide that you'll animate when the bookmark is reached during playback.**

   For this example, I created a text box with the text "Liftoff!"

6. **Select the Animations tab.**

7. **Select the object you created in Step 5, click the Add Animation button found in the Advanced Animation group on the Animations tab, and select the animation effect you want.**

   For this example, I chose the Appear effect to cause the object to appear.

8. **Click the Trigger button found in the Advanced Animation group on the Animations tab, choose On Bookmark, and then choose the bookmark you created in Step 4.**

   Doing this sets up the animation so it's triggered automatically when the bookmark in the video is reached.

   You're done!

304 PART 4 Embellishing Your Slides

Here are a few additional points to ponder concerning bookmarks:

- **You can create more than one bookmark in a single video.** Each bookmark can be used as an animation trigger.

Remove Bookmark

- **To remove a bookmark, click the small circle that represents the bookmark in the video's slider bar.** Then click the Remove Bookmark button (shown in the margin) found in the Bookmarks group of the Playback tab.

For more information about creating animations, see Chapter 13.

Compressing Media

If your presentation's file size is too large, you can trim it down by compressing media files contained in the presentation. Doing so will reduce the quality of the media files but shrink the presentation file.

To compress the media files in a presentation, follow these simple steps:

1. **Select the File tab on the Ribbon and then select Info in the menu on the left.**

   The Info page appears. If the presentation contains media, the Info page will include a Compress Media icon.

2. **Click the Compress Media icon (shown in the margin).**

   A drop-down menu of compression options appears.

3. **Select the compression option you want to use.**

   The options include Full HD (1080p), HD (720p), and Standard (480p). The lower the resolution you choose, the smaller the presentation will become.

4. **Wait until the compression is finished.**

   A progress box indicates the progress of the compression. When the compression is finished, a message indicates how much disk space you saved.

5. **Click Close to dismiss the progress box.**

> **IN THIS CHAPTER**
> » Adding a table to a slide
> » Setting the table with borders, shading, and other fancy things
> » Adjusting the table's layout
> » Styling your tables

Chapter 20
Adding Tables to Your Slides

Tables are a great way to present lots of information in an orderly fashion. For example, if you want to create a slide that shows how many people like or hate various computer presentation programs, a table is the way to go. Or if you're considering purchasing some new computer equipment and you want to list the prices for five different computer configurations from three different vendors, a table is the best way to do that. In this chapter, I show you how to add professional-looking tables to your slides.

Creating a Table in a Content Placeholder

Basic tables are simple to create in PowerPoint. The easiest way to create a slide that contains a table is to use the Title and Content slide layout. Just follow these steps:

1. **Select the Home tab on the Ribbon and then click the New Slide button found in the Slides group.**

    A new slide is created with the Title and Content layout.

2. **Click the Table icon in the center of the Content placeholder.**

   The Insert Table dialog box appears (see Figure 20-1).

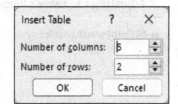

FIGURE 20-1:
The Insert Table dialog box.

3. **Set the number of rows and columns you want for the table and then click OK.**

   The table appears, as shown in Figure 20-2.

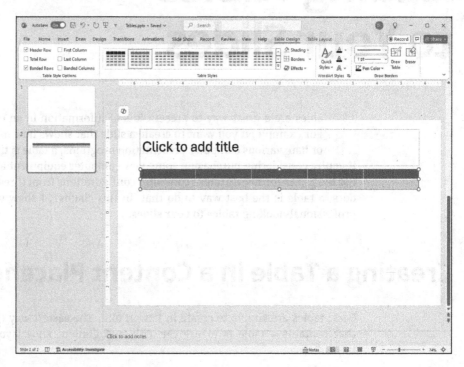

FIGURE 20-2:
An empty table, waiting for data.

4. **Type information into the table's cells.**

   You can click any cell in the table and start typing. Or you can move from cell to cell by pressing the Tab key or the arrow keys.

308 PART 4 Embellishing Your Slides

5. **Play with the formatting if you want.**

   You can use the Table Design tab on the Ribbon to control the formatting for the table (see the section "Adding Style to a Table," later in this chapter).

6. **Stop and smell the roses.**

   When you're done, you're done. Admire your work.

Figure 20-3 shows an example of a finished table.

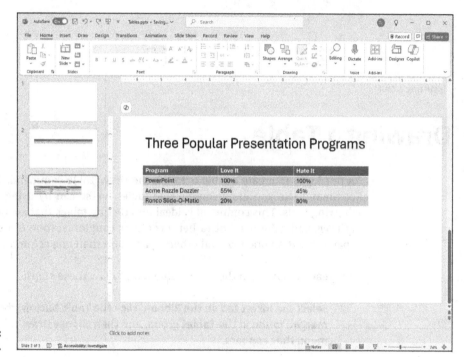

FIGURE 20-3: A finished table.

Inserting a Table on a Slide

You can use the Table button (shown in the margin), which is on the Insert tab on the Ribbon, to insert a table on an existing slide. When you click this button, a gridlike menu appears that enables you to select the size of the table you want to create, as shown in Figure 20-4. You can use this technique to create a table as large as ten columns and eight rows.

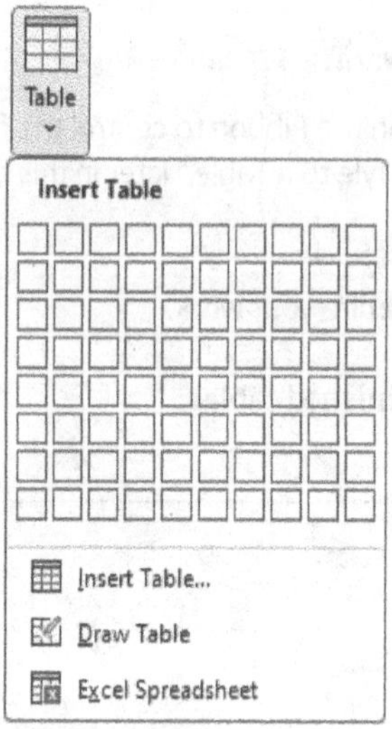

FIGURE 20-4: Inserting a table.

Drawing a Table

A third way to create a table is to use the Draw Table command. The Draw Table command lets you draw complicated tables on-screen by using a simple set of drawing tools. This command is ideal for creating tables that are not a simple grid of rows and columns, but rather a complex conglomeration in which some cells span more than one row and others span more than one column.

To create a table with the Draw Table tool, follow these steps:

1. **Select the Insert tab on the Ribbon, click the Table button (shown in the margin) found in the Tables group, and then choose Draw Table from the menu that appears.**

   PowerPoint changes the cursor to a little pencil.

2. **Draw the overall shape of the table by dragging the mouse to create a rectangular boundary for it.**

   When you release the mouse button, a table with a single cell is created, as shown in Figure 20-5. Notice also in this figure that the Table Design tab is displayed on the Ribbon.

3. **Click the Draw Table button (shown in the margin) found in the Draw Borders group on the Table Design tab.**

   The mouse pointer changes to a little pencil when you click this button.

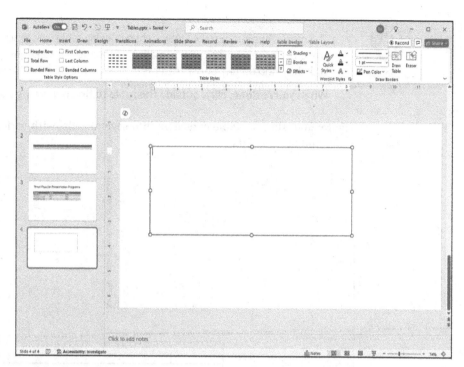

FIGURE 20-5:
Drawing a table.

4. **Carve the table into smaller cells.**

   To do that, just drag lines across the table. For example, to split the table into two rows, point the cursor somewhere along the left edge of the table and then click and drag a line across the table to the right edge. When you release the mouse button, the table splits into two rows.

   You can continue to carve the table into smaller and smaller cells. For each slice, point the cursor at one edge of where you want the new cell to begin and click and drag to the other edge.

5. **If you want to change the line size or style drawn for a particular segment, use the Pen Style and Pen Weight drop-down controls in the Draw Borders group on the Table Design tab.**

   You can change the style of a line you've already drawn by tracing over the line with a new style.

6. **If you make a mistake while drawing the table cells, click the Eraser button in the Draw Borders group and erase the mistaken line segment.**

   Or just press Ctrl+Z or click the Undo button on the Quick Access Toolbar (QAT).

   If you want to draw additional segments after using the Erase tool, click the Draw Table button.

CHAPTER 20 **Adding Tables to Your Slides** 311

TIP

The most common mistake I make when drawing table cells is accidentally creating diagonal borders. If you make this common mistake, just press Ctrl+Z, click the Undo button, or use the eraser to erase the diagonal border.

7. **When you're done, click outside the table to finish drawing the table.**

Figure 20-6 shows a table carved up into several cells, with various types of line styles and line weights.

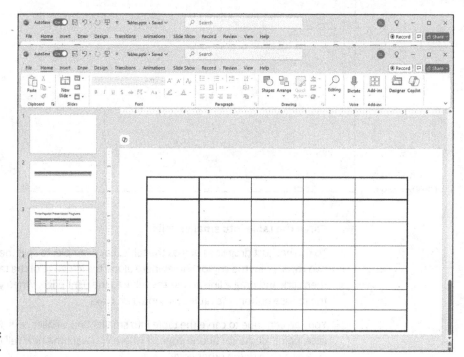

FIGURE 20-6: A finished table.

Adding Style to a Table

After you've created a table, you can set its style by using the controls on the Table Design tab on the Ribbon. The easiest way to format a table is by applying one of PowerPoint's predefined table styles.

Before you apply a style, however, use the check boxes that appear in the Table Design Options group on the Table Design tab on the Ribbon. These check boxes determine whether PowerPoint uses special formatting for certain parts of the table:

- **Header Row:** Indicates whether the style should format the first row differently from the other rows in the table
- **Total Row:** Indicates whether the style should format the last row differently from the other rows in the table
- **Banded Rows:** Indicates whether alternating rows should be formatted differently
- **First Column:** Indicates whether the style should format the first column differently from the other columns in the table
- **Last Column:** Indicates whether the style should format the last column differently from the other columns in the table
- **Banded Columns:** Indicates whether alternating columns should be formatted differently

After you've set the Quick Style options, you can apply a Table Style to the table by clicking the style you want to apply (refer to Figure 20-5). If the style doesn't appear in the Table Styles group on the Table Design tab on the Ribbon, click the More button to reveal the Table Styles gallery, shown in Figure 20-7. This gallery displays all the built-in styles provided with PowerPoint.

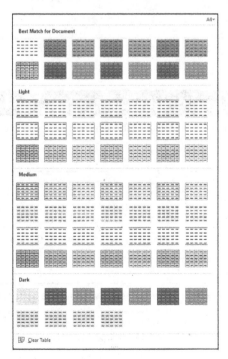

FIGURE 20-7: The Table Styles gallery.

In addition to using one of the preselected table styles, you can format each cell and line in your table by using the following controls in the Table Styles group on the Table Design tab:

- » **Shading:** Sets the background color for the selected cells.
- » **Borders:** Lets you control which edges of the selected cells have borders.
- » **Effects:** Applies bevels, shadows, and reflections. (Note that you can apply bevels to individual cells, but shadows and reflections apply to the entire table.)

Working with the Layout Tab

When you select a table, a special Table Layout tab is available, as shown in Figure 20-8. The controls on this tab let you adjust the layout of your table in various ways. Table 20-1 lists the function of each of these controls.

FIGURE 20-8: The Table Layout tab on the Ribbon.

TABLE 20-1 The Layout Tab

Control	Group	Name	What It Does
Select	Table	Select	Activates the selection cursor so you can select cells
View Gridlines	Table	View Gridlines	Shows or hides table gridlines
Delete	Rows & Columns	Delete	Deletes a row, a column, or the entire table
Insert Above	Rows & Columns	Insert Above	Inserts a new row above the current row

Control	Group	Name	What It Does
Insert Below	Rows & Columns	Insert Below	Inserts a new row below the current row
Insert Left	Rows & Columns	Insert Left	Inserts a new column to the left of the current column
Insert Right	Rows & Columns	Insert Right	Inserts a new column to the right of the current column
Merge Cells	Merge	Merge Cells	Merges adjacent cells to create one large cell
Split Cells	Merge	Split Cells	Splits a merged cell into separate cells
Height:	Cell Size	Height	Sets the row height
Width: 2.14"	Cell Size	Width	Sets the column width
Distribute Rows	Cell Size	Distribute Rows	Adjusts the height of the selected rows to distribute the rows evenly
Distribute Columns	Cell Size	Distribute Columns	Adjusts the width of the selected columns to distribute the columns evenly
	Alignment	Align Left	Left-aligns the text
	Alignment	Center	Centers the text
	Alignment	Align Right	Right-aligns the text
	Alignment	Align Top	Vertically aligns the text with the top of the cell
	Alignment	Align Middle	Vertically aligns the text with the middle of the cell
	Alignment	Align Bottom	Vertically aligns the text with the bottom of the cell

(continued)

TABLE 20-1 *(continued)*

Control	Group	Name	What It Does
Text Direction	Alignment	Text Direction	Changes the direction of the text in a cell
Cell Margins	Alignment	Cell Margins	Sets the cell margins
Height: 6.19"	Table Size	Height	Sets the overall height of the table
Width: 10.71"	Table Size	Width	Sets the overall width of the table
Lock Aspect Ratio	Table Size	Lock Aspect Ratio	Fixes the ratio between height and width so that when you change the height or width individually, both values are adjusted to maintain the same ratio
Bring Forward	Arrange	Bring Forward	Brings the table to the front of the slide
Send Backward	Arrange	Send Backward	Sends the table to the back of the slide
Selection Pane	Arrange	Selection Pane	Displays a selection pane that lists the objects you can select on the slide
Align	Arrange	Align	Aligns the table on the slide

5 Working with Others

IN THIS PART . . .

Find out about PowerPoint's collaboration features.

Save your presentations in formats other than the standard PowerPoint file format.

IN THIS CHAPTER

» Considering the joys of collaboration

» Getting your mind around OneDrive

» Collaborating with Teams

» Editing a presentation while other people are editing it, too

» Adding comments to a presentation

Chapter 21
Collaborating on Presentations

"Works well with others" is more than standard fare for rookie résumés. It's also one of the PowerPoint mantras. Many presentations are not designed by and for a single presenter, but by a team of presenters. Fortunately, PowerPoint includes several simple features that let a team of people collaborate to create a presentation. This chapter shows you how to use those features.

Understanding Collaboration

Most dictionaries define the word *collaborate* something like this:

> To work cooperatively together to produce an outcome or result. *The three collaborated on a novel.*

Few of us would consider our PowerPoint presentations to be literary works, and we often (unfortunately) find that working together with other people is different from working *cooperatively* together with other people. Still, we often find the need to collaborate with others to create a presentation.

The old-fashioned way to collaborate on a presentation is to split the presentation into sections and have each person work on one of the sections. Each person creates their own slides in a separate presentation file, and someone takes charge of merging the separate files into a single presentation. Then the result is sent via email to each person on the team for review, and again, someone takes charge of gathering the comments and updating the presentation to address each reviewer's concerns.

With Microsoft 365, the old way is just that: the old way. The new way is to use features of Microsoft 365 that let multiple people work simultaneously in a single presentation file. Team members can still comment on each other's work, and the team needs some way to settle disagreements. But gone are the days of composing slides in separate presentations, merging them, and sending out drafts of the final presentation via email for review.

Microsoft provides three distinct platforms that enable this type of real-time collaboration:

» **OneDrive:** OneDrive is a cloud-based storage feature that lets you save files to Microsoft's servers rather than on your computer's local hard drive. Files stored in OneDrive are private by default, so you need to take explicit action to share OneDrive files. You can find out more about OneDrive later in this chapter, in the section "Working with OneDrive"

» **Teams:** Teams is a complete collaboration platform that's designed specifically to enable groups of people to collaborate on projects. In addition to just sharing files, Teams lets you have running conversations about the project, create project schedules and to-do lists, and much more. Note that files stored in Teams are inherently shared with other team members, so you don't have to do anything special to a file to enable collaboration and sharing. You can find out more about Teams later in this chapter, in the section "Working with Teams."

» **SharePoint:** SharePoint is a platform for creating internal websites. It's often used to create a company *intranet*, which is like the internet except it's internal to a company. SharePoint sites are often used by teams of people to manage a specific project. SharePoint is beyond what I can cover in this book, so you won't find any specific information in this chapter about SharePoint. However, most of what you learn about Teams in this chapter applies equally to SharePoint.

OneDrive storage is available for all Microsoft 365 users. Teams and SharePoint require business subscriptions; the personal and family versions of Microsoft 365 do not include Teams or SharePoint.

Note also that in some corporate environments, OneDrive may not be available, and some other type of cloud storage platform such as Dropbox or Google Drive may be used instead.

TECHNICAL STUFF

There's a close relationship between Teams and SharePoint. In fact, Teams relies on SharePoint for much of its internal workings. Any files that you store in Teams are also available in SharePoint, and vice versa. That's why what you learn about Teams in this chapter applies to SharePoint as well.

Working with OneDrive

OneDrive is a cloud storage system that lets you store files on Microsoft's servers and access them much like you access files on your computer's local disk. All Microsoft 365 subscriptions come with 1TB of OneDrive storage. For an additional $9.99 per month, you can double that to 2TB.

When you install Microsoft 365 on your computer, OneDrive is automatically added to Windows Explorer, as shown in Figure 21-1. Here, you can see that files on OneDrive are organized into folders just as they are on a local disk drive. You can copy files to OneDrive simply by dragging them into the appropriate OneDrive folder. And you can use all the familiar Windows Explorer techniques to delete, copy, move, or rename files.

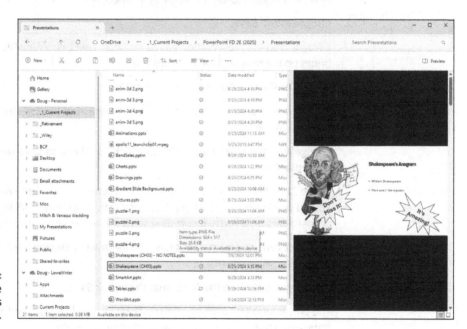

FIGURE 21-1: Viewing OneDrive in Windows Explorer.

Notice the circled green check marks next to each file in Figure 21-1. These indicate the *synchronization status* of each file. Windows keeps a local copy of OneDrive files whenever possible so it doesn't have to download files from Microsoft's servers. If you make changes to a file, you may see the status change to a pair of circular blue arrows (shown in the margin). This indicates that OneDrive is in the process of synchronizing the local and cloud copies of the file.

As I mention earlier in this chapter, OneDrive is an inherently private storage system. Files that you store in OneDrive are, by default, accessible only to you. However, you can enable sharing and collaboration for individual files or folders. In this section, I explain how to save your files to OneDrive — that's a prerequisite for sharing presentations. Later, in the section "Sharing a OneDrive presentation," I show you how to share a presentation you've stored in OneDrive.

Here are the basic steps for saving a presentation to your OneDrive storage from within PowerPoint:

1. **Create a presentation you'd like to save to OneDrive.**

   Start by creating a new presentation from scratch. Then, before you've done any editing to the presentation, continue with the remaining steps to get your new presentation safely tucked away in OneDrive.

2. **Choose File ⇨ Save.**

   Because the new presentation has never been saved, choosing File ⇨ Save brings up the familiar Save As dialog box.

3. **Select OneDrive – Personal as the location.**

   For example, Figure 21-2 shows the Save As page after I've selected OneDrive – Personal as the location.

4. **Navigate to the OneDrive folder to which you'd like to save the presentation.**

   Figure 21-3 shows that I've navigated to OneDrive > _1_Current Projects > PowerPoint FD 2E (2025) > Presentations. On your system, you'll see a different set of folders or, if you're just getting started with OneDrive, no folders at all.

    Note that you can create new folders in OneDrive by clicking the New Folder button (shown in the margin).

5. **If necessary, change the filename; then click Save.**

   The presentation is saved to your OneDrive. After the file is saved, you're returned to the presentation so you can continue editing.

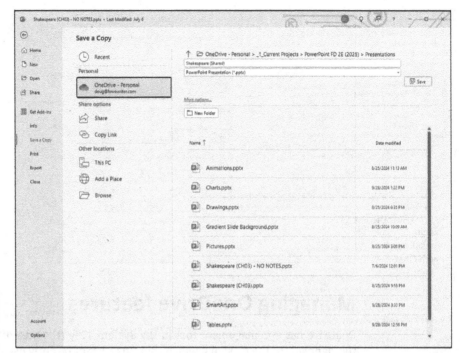

FIGURE 21-2: Saving a presentation to OneDrive.

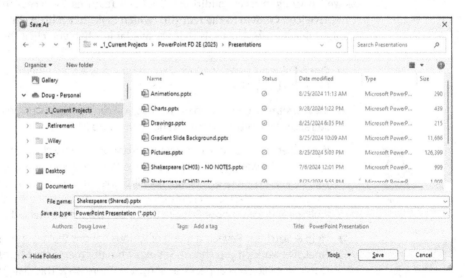

FIGURE 21-3: Navigating to a OneDrive folder.

TIP

If you prefer to work in the traditional Save As dialog box, you can reach it by clicking the Browse button (shown in the margin). This brings up the Save As dialog box, as shown in Figure 21-4.

CHAPTER 21 **Collaborating on Presentations** 323

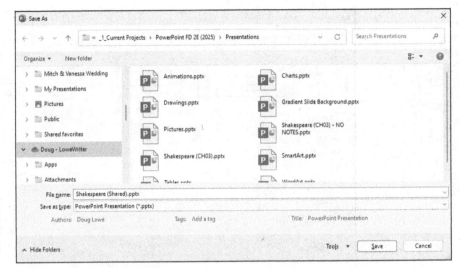

FIGURE 21-4:
Using the traditional Save As dialog box with OneDrive.

Managing OneDrive features

OneDrive has a management tool in the System Tray (the area of small icons on the right side of the taskbar), which contains a list of recently used OneDrive files, as well as icons to access additional OneDrive features. To access this tool, click the OneDrive icon (shown in the margin), which looks like a little cloud. The following paragraphs describe the tools that are available when you click the OneDrive icon:

» **Open Folder:** Opens Windows Explorer to browse your OneDrive storage (refer to Figure 21-1).

» **View Online:** Opens a web browser so you can manage your OneDrive storage via its web interface, as shown in Figure 21-5.

If you open a PowerPoint presentation from Online view, the presentation will be opened in the web-based version of PowerPoint, as shown in Figure 21-6. The web-based version has most, but not all, of the features of the desktop version. To switch to the desktop version, click Editing (to the right of the Help tab in the Ribbon), and then choose Open in Desktop App from the menu that appears.

» **Help & Settings:** Reveals a menu of various options that let you control how OneDrive works. If you choose Settings from this menu, the Microsoft OneDrive dialog box appears, as shown in Figure 21-7. This dialog box lets you control various OneDrive features:

- **Settings:** Lets you control whether OneDrive automatically starts when you log in to Windows, what kind of notifications you should receive from OneDrive, and whether OneDrive should be concerned about saving space on your local disk drive by only downloading files when you need them.

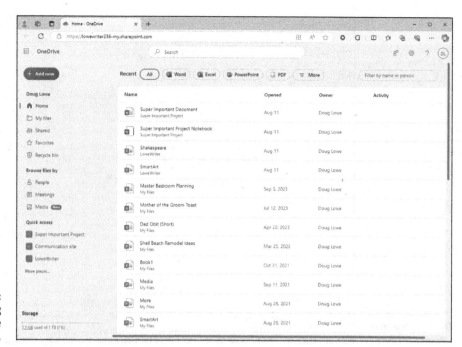

FIGURE 21-5: Managing OneDrive via the web.

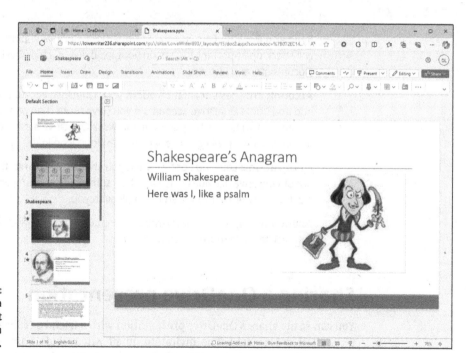

FIGURE 21-6: Editing a PowerPoint presentation in online view.

FIGURE 21-7: OneDrive settings.

- **Sync and Backup:** Lets you choose whether OneDrive should automatically back up important folders on your local disk, such as Desktop, Documents, and Pictures.

- **Account:** Provides information about your OneDrive account, and lets you add additional OneDrive accounts if you have more than one. (It's not uncommon to have both personal and work OneDrive accounts. If you add a work account, it will get a separate blue cloud icon in the System Tray.)

- **Notifications:** Lets you control when you should receive notifications about OneDrive activities, such as when something is wrong with synchronization or when someone shares a file with you.

- **About:** Provides version information about OneDrive, as well as links you can click to learn more about OneDrive.

Sharing a OneDrive presentation

You can easily share a OneDrive presentation with a friend or colleague by sending an invitation via email. The invitation email will include a link that opens the presentation in a web-based version of PowerPoint called the PowerPoint Web

App. From the PowerPoint Web App, the user can view the presentation. If the user has PowerPoint installed on their computer, the user can also open the presentation in PowerPoint, edit the presentation, add comments (as I describe in the section "Using Commands" later in this chapter), and save the edited presentation in the original OneDrive location.

To send an invitation, follow these steps:

1. **Save your presentation to OneDrive.**
2. **Choose File ⇨ Share.**

    The Send Link dialog box appears, as shown in Figure 21-8. From this dialog box, you can craft an email message that will be sent to the people with whom you'd like to share the presentation.

FIGURE 21-8: Sharing a presentation.

3. **Type one or more names or email addresses in the To text box.**

    If you type a name, Microsoft 365 attempts to find that person within your organization. If Microsoft 365 doesn't recognize the name, you'll have to type a full email address instead.

    Press the Enter key after each name or email address to include more than one person.

4. **Review the link settings and change them if necessary.**

   The default link setting is Anyone with the Link Can Edit. To change this setting, either click the current link setting near the top of the Send Link dialog box or click the pencil icon and choose Link Settings from the menu that appears. Either way, the Link Settings dialog box appears, as shown in Figure 21-9.

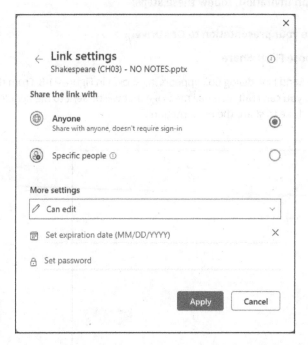

FIGURE 21-9: Adjusting link settings.

The first two options in the Link Settings dialog box control who can use the link:

- **Anyone with the Link:** This option means that anyone who has the link can access the file. Use this option with caution, because the people to whom you send the link can easily forward the link to other people, who can forward it to other people, until eventually Kevin Bacon has your link. (How many degrees of separation are you from Kevin Bacon?)

- **Specific People:** This option allows only the people you list to have access.

Under More Settings, you can choose the following options:

- **Can Edit or Can View:** The Can Edit option allows recipients to edit the presentation. If you click this option and change it to *Can View*, the recipients can view but not edit the presentation.

- **Set Expiration Date:** Sets an expiration date for the link. After the expiration date, the link won't work.

WARNING

- **Set Password:** Requires a password to access the file. You'll need to provide the password to those you want to grant access to.

  Don't include the password with the same email in which you send the link! If you do, anyone who forwards the link will also forward the password, negating the benefit of using a password in the first place.

5. **Click Apply.**

   The changes you made are applied, and you're returned to the Send Link dialog box.

6. **If you want, type a message in the Message text box.**

   The message is included in the email that is sent to the recipients.

7. **Click Send.**

   A confirmation message appears, indicating that the email has been sent.

Figure 21-10 shows what a typical shared link email looks like. In this case, I've shared the presentation Shakespeare.pptx with Kristen Gearhart. Kristen can click either the presentation or the Open button in the email to open the presentation.

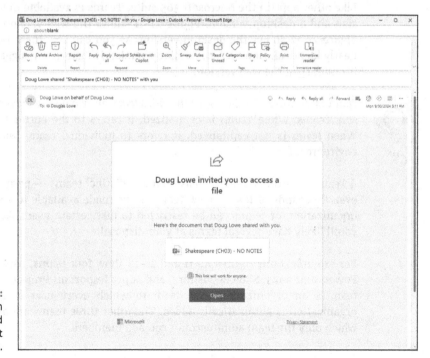

FIGURE 21-10: An invitation to a shared PowerPoint presentation.

CHAPTER 21 **Collaborating on Presentations** 329

Two additional options are available in the Send Link dialog box:

- » **Copy Link:** This option copies the link to the Clipboard. Use it if you'd rather not send the presentation by email. After you've copied the link to the Clipboard, you can paste the link to an email you compose yourself or in a message thread in Teams or another messaging platform.

- » **Outlook:** This option opens an empty Outlook message with the link pasted into the message body. You can then complete the message however you see fit. You'll need to add recipients, change the subject line, and add additional information to the message body before you click Send to deliver the message.

Working with Teams

Microsoft Teams (usually just called Teams) is an online collaboration platform that enables groups of users to work on projects together. In Teams, you can create *teams* that everyone involved in a project can join.

Like other apps in the Microsoft 365 suite, Teams is available in both a web version and a desktop version. Figure 21-11 shows the web version of Teams, and Figure 21-12 shows the desktop version. As you can see, these two versions are nearly identical. However, the desktop version is faster, so I suggest that you use it rather than the web version.

Don't be confused by the use of the word *teams* in two distinct ways within Microsoft Teams. When *Teams* is capitalized, it refers to the entire Teams platform. When *teams* is not capitalized, it refers to individual teams within the Teams environment.

A Teams environment can consist of many distinct teams — perhaps hundreds or even thousands of teams. Each team can be made available to every user of the organization, or teams can be restricted to just certain users. As a Teams user, you'll likely have several teams at your disposal.

For example, both Figures 21-11 and 21-12 show four teams, named LoweWriter, PowerPoint 2025, Slide Repository, and Super Important Project. The LoweWriter team is an organization-wide team to which every user of the LoweWriter organization is automatically added. The other three teams are private teams to which only the team administrator can add members.

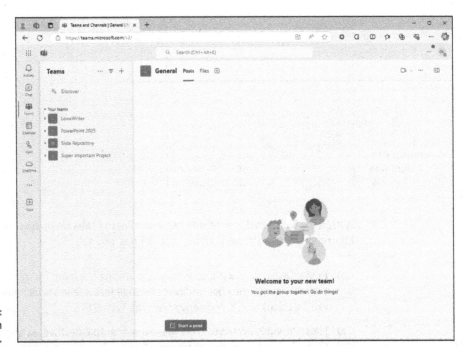

FIGURE 21-11:
The web version of Teams.

FIGURE 21-12:
The desktop version of Teams.

Within a team, you can create one or more *channels*, which allow the members of the team to focus their attention on different aspects of their work. Every team automatically has a channel named General. In Figure 21-13, I've expanded the contents of the PowerPoint 2025 team so that you can see that it contains an additional channel named Presentations.

CHAPTER 21 **Collaborating on Presentations** 331

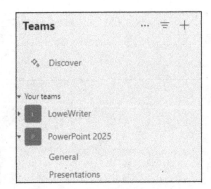

FIGURE 21-13:
A team with two channels.

Within each channel, content is organized using tabs near the top of the screen. In Figure 21-14, the Presentations channel has two tabs:

» **Posts:** Displays running conversations among the team members. The Posts tab is similar to the chat or direct message features in social media platforms like Facebook and X (formerly known as Twitter).

» **Files:** Provides access to a file system similar to OneDrive, as shown in Figure 21-14. However, the files you store in Teams are not saved in your OneDrive storage. Instead, they're saved in dedicated storage on Microsoft's cloud storage that automatically enables shared access for all members of the team. So, whenever you save a PowerPoint presentation or any other file to the Files tab, all members of the team have access to the file.

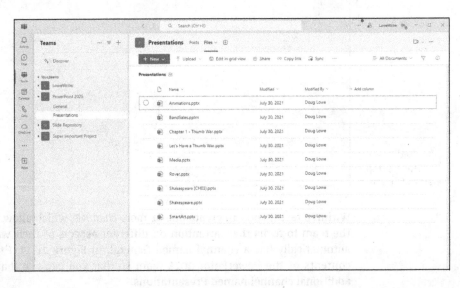

FIGURE 21-14:
The Files tab in the Presentations channel.

Collaborating in Real Time

One of the truly outstanding features of PowerPoint in Microsoft 365 is that it lets two or more people edit a presentation at the same time. You may think this would be unworkable, but in reality it works very well.

To collaborate in real time on a presentation stored in OneDrive, you must first share the presentation as I describe in the earlier section "Sharing a OneDrive presentation." If the presentation is stored in Teams, nothing special needs to be done. When two or more users open a PowerPoint presentation at the same time in Teams, all the users can simultaneously edit the presentation.

As each user edits the presentation, changes are automatically made visible on each of the other users' screens. It can be a little disconcerting at first, but you'll soon get used to seeing words type themselves and pictures resize and move themselves around as other users are editing the file at the same time as you.

PowerPoint gives you visual clues about who's editing what, as shown in Figure 21-15. As you can see, Kristen (KG) is editing the body content of a slide while I'm editing the title. The body content is outlined in green to indicate that another user is currently editing it, and an icon with Kristen's initials (KG) is displayed in the area where Kristen is working.

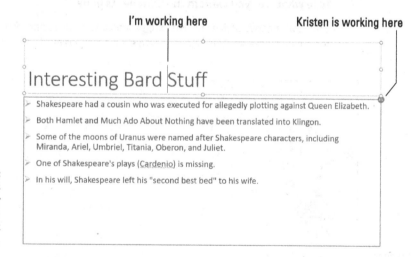

FIGURE 21-15:
Two users simultaneously editing a PowerPoint presentation.

TIP

To be safe, you should avoid editing the same slide that someone else is editing. If two users make conflicting changes to a single slide, PowerPoint will display the two versions of the slide in question when you save the presentation and allow you to choose which version to save.

Using Comments

In addition to editing a document, collaboration sometimes involves reviewing slide content and recording comments that raise concerns, suggesting changes, or simply annoying other collaborators. PowerPoint provides a feature called *Comments* just for this purpose.

A comment is a lot like a sticky note. The beauty of comments is that you can turn them on and off. So, you can view the comments while you're editing your presentation, and you can turn them off when it's time for the show.

To add a comment to a presentation, follow these steps:

1. **Call up the slide to which you want to add a comment.**
2. **Click where you want the comment to appear.**

   You can click anywhere in the slide.
3. **Select the Review tab on the Ribbon and then click the New Comment button found in the Comments group.**

   A comment bubble appears on the slide, and the Comments pane opens to the right of the slide.
4. **Type whatever you want in the Comments pane.**

   Offer some constructive criticism, suggest an alternative approach, or just comment on the weather. Figure 21-16 shows a completed comment.

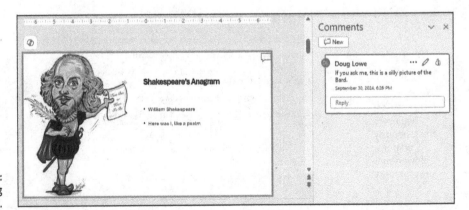

FIGURE 21-16: Creating a comment.

5. **If you want, move the comment bubble.**

    You can move the comment closer to the slide item on which you're commenting by dragging the comment tag around the slide.

Here are some additional thoughts concerning working with comments:

- To view a comment, click the comment bubble.
- To change a comment, click the comment in the Comments pane and then edit the text in the comment until you're satisfied.
- You can move a comment by dragging it. Note that comments are not attached to any particular slide object or text. Therefore, if you move a comment near the text or object that the comment applies to and then edit the slide so the text or object moves, the comment will *not* move along with the text or object. You have to manually move the comment if you want it to stay near the text or object it applies to.
- To delete a comment, click the comment to select it and then press Delete.
- To delete all the comments on a particular slide, click the down arrow beneath the Delete button on the Review tab. Then choose Delete All Markup on the Current Slide.
- To delete all the comments in a presentation, click the down arrow beneath the Delete button and choose Delete All Markup in This Presentation.
- You can quickly scan through all the comments in a PowerPoint presentation by using the Previous and Next buttons on the Review tab on the Ribbon.
- You can use the Show Comments button on the Review tab to show or hide comments from a presentation.

IN THIS CHAPTER

» Exporting to PDF

» Recording an audio narration

» Creating a video of your presentation

Chapter 22

Exporting Your Presentation to Other Formats

This chapter shows you how to use a variety of PowerPoint features that let you save your presentations in formats other than the standard PowerPoint file format. You can save your presentation as a PDF file, which can then be viewed using Adobe Acrobat. Or you can turn your entire presentation into an animated GIF that rapidly flies through your slides in a small thumbnail format. If you prefer, you can create a feature-length video narrated by none other than Morgan Freeman! (If Morgan isn't available, you can narrate it yourself.)

You can also create a self-contained presentation file that can be viewed with a free PowerPoint viewer, convert a presentation to a Word document that you can give to your attendees as handouts, or upload a video of your presentation to Microsoft's video service, Microsoft Stream.

All these features are available when you choose File ➪ Export.

Creating a PDF File

PDF, which stands for *Portable Document Format*, is a popular format for exchanging files. PowerPoint can export a presentation to a PDF file. Note that when you export to a PDF, you may lose some of the functionality of your presentation, such as the ability to play media. In any event, here are the steps:

1. **Select the File tab.**
2. **Click Export.**

   The Export options appear, as shown in Figure 22-1.

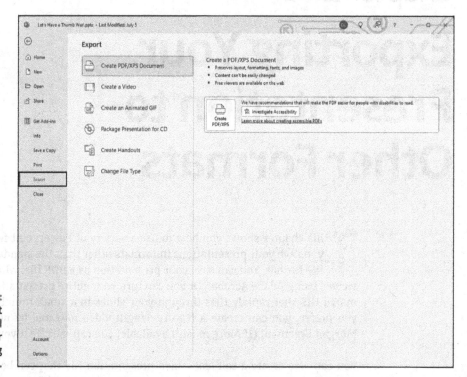

FIGURE 22-1:
PowerPoint provides several options for exporting presentations.

3. **Click the Create PDF/XPS button (shown in the margin).**

   The Publish as PDF or XPS dialog box appears, as shown in Figure 22-2.

TECHNICAL STUFF

XPS is a page-layout format that Microsoft invented back in 2006 in hopes of replacing the PDF format that was created by Adobe 15 years earlier. XPS never really caught on, and there's little reason to use it. But Microsoft continues to support it as an alternative to PDF.

FIGURE 22-2:
Creating a PDF document.

4. **Navigate to the location where you want to save the file, and change the filename if you want.**

   The default is to save the file in the same folder as the PowerPoint presentation, using the same name but with the .pdf extension.

5. **Select the appropriate optimization setting.**

   The two choices are Standard, which is appropriate for printing or in-person viewing, and Minimum Size, which is appropriate for posting to the internet.

6. **Click Publish.**

   The presentation is converted to a PDF.

TIP

If you want to fiddle with the options used to create the PDF, click the Options button before you click Publish. This brings up the Options dialog box, which is shown in Figure 22-3. Here, you can select which slides you want to publish, which content you want to publish (the slides, your notes, handouts, or an outline of the presentation), and a few other interesting options.

CHAPTER 22 **Exporting Your Presentation to Other Formats**

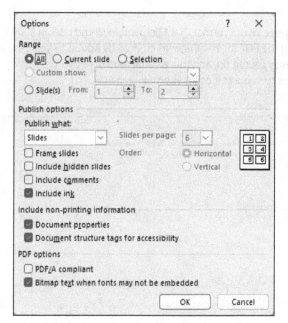

FIGURE 22-3: Setting PDF options.

Crafting a Video

PowerPoint is great for preparing presentations to give in person. But what about giving presentations when you can't be there? Wouldn't it be great if you could easily create a video of your slides that included the audio of your narration? Then anyone could watch the presentation later, when you couldn't be there.

Good news: You can! In fact, creating a video version of your presentation is a snap. First, you set up the timing you want for each slide and for each animation within each slide. You can even add a voice narration to each slide. After the timings and narration are all set up, you just click a few times with the mouse, and your presentation is converted to video.

PowerPoint includes a nifty feature that lets you record a slide show, which you can then save as a video. The recording re-creates all the slide transitions and animation elements (such as bullet points appearing), along with your own narration and, if you have a camera connected to your computer, your smiling face.

Note that you can also record PowerPoint's built-in laser pointer. Then, when you play back the show or create a video, the pointer will dance across the screen automatically! (For more information about using the laser pointer, see Chapter 7.)

TIP

Before you actually record your presentation, first make sure that you, the presentation, and your computer are ready. Here are some helpful tips:

- **Finish your presentation.** Finalize all your slides, transitions, and animation effects before you start recording.

- **Prepare your narration.** Give careful thought to your narration. Make sure to include all the salient points you want to make with each slide. You may want to write it out in speaker notes (see Chapter 6) or as a separate Word document.

- **Get your equipment ready.** You'll need a good microphone — preferably a headset with a mic or a lapel mic so that your hands will be free while you record. If you're going to use a camera, make sure the lighting is good. And be sure to tidy up a bit. *Remember:* This is for posterity.

Using the Record Tab

When you record a slide show, you work with the controls that reside on the Record tab on the Ribbon, which is shown in Figure 22-4.

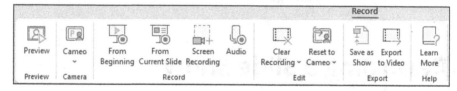

FIGURE 22-4: The Record tab.

The following list describes each of the controls on the Record ribbon tab:

- **Preview:** Displays a preview of what you've recorded so far. You'll use this button to ensure that your recording is perfect before you export it to a video file.

- **Cameo:** Lets you control how the cameo — that is, the image captured from your computer's camera — will appear on the slides.

- **From Beginning:** Use this button to kick off your recording session. You'll be taken to Presenter view (see Chapter 7). Once there, you can click the Record button to start your recording. Run through your entire presentation as if you were giving it to a live audience. When you're finished, click the Stop button and then take a deep breath. You made it! You can then use the Preview button to review the recording.

» **From Current Slide:** If the recording for one of your slides isn't quite right, you can call up that slide and click this button to rerecord just that one slide.

» **Screen Recording:** This button lets you record an action or a procedure on your computer and play it back on a slide. To use this feature, move to the slide on which you want to add the screen recording, and then click the Screen Recording button. I find this to be a very useful feature, especially for slide shows that will be used for training.

» **Audio:** Lets you record a short snippet of sound that will be inserted directly into the current slide.

» **Clear Recording:** Click this button to erase either your entire recording or everything from the current slide.

» **Reset to Cameo:** Drops the narration but keeps the video from your original cameo feed.

» **Save as Show:** Saves the Presentation as a PowerPoint Show, which is a special format used to present a slide show.

» **Export to Video:** Exports the slide show to a video format.

» **Learn More:** Displays additional Help information about creating PowerPoint recordings.

Recording a Slide Show

Here are the basic steps for recording a slide show:

1. **Select the Record tab, and then choose the From Beginning button (shown in the margin).**

   PowerPoint switches to Presenter view (see Figure 22-5), which I describe in Chapter 7.

2. **Click the Record button to begin recording the slideshow.**

   A countdown appears on the screen — 3 . . . 2 . . . 1 — and then the recording begins.

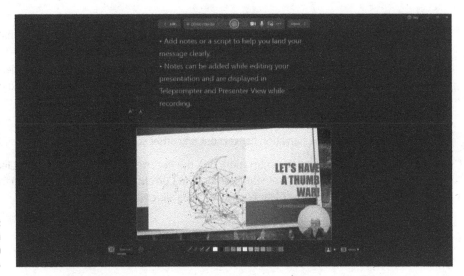

FIGURE 22-5:
Recording a slideshow in Presenter view.

3. **Speak your narration into the microphone.**

   If you want to advance to a new slide or call up a new animation element (such as a bullet point), press Enter or click the mouse button.

   If you want to use the laser pointer on a slide, hold down the Ctrl key and then click and hold the mouse button and use the mouse to control the laser pointer. When you release the mouse button, the laser pointer disappears. (For more information about working the laser pointer, see Chapter 7.)

   If you need to pause the recording at any time, click the Pause button at the upper left of the screen in Presenter view. The recording is suspended; you can click Record again to resume recording.

4. **When you're finished recording, click the Stop button.**

   Recording automatically ends when you exit the last slide, so you can skip this step if you record the entire presentation.

From Current Slide

5. **If you messed up on any slide, open that slide and then click the From Current Slide button (shown in the margin). Then rerecord the narration for that slide and press Esc to stop recording.**

   You can rerecord more than one slide in this way; just press Enter or click the mouse to advance through all the slides you want to rerecord. Press Esc to stop recording.

CHAPTER 22 Exporting Your Presentation to Other Formats

TIP

Here are some additional things to keep in mind about narrations:

» As you record the narration, leave a little gap between each slide. PowerPoint records the narration for each slide as a separate sound file and then attaches the sound to the slide. Unfortunately, you get cut off if you talk right through the slide transitions.

» The narration cancels out any other sounds you placed on the slides.

» To delete a narration, click the Record Slide Show button, click Clear, and then click either Clear Narration on Current Slide (to delete narration from just one slide) or Clear Narration on All Slides (to delete all narration).

The Part of Tens

IN THIS PART . . .

Find ten PowerPoint commandments — obey these commandments and it shall go well with you, with your computer, and even with your projector.

Produce readable slides.

Prevent your audience from falling asleep during your presentation.

Chapter 23
Ten PowerPoint Commandments

And the hapless Windows user said, "But who am I to make this presentation? For I am not eloquent, but I am slow of speech and of tongue, and my colors clasheth, and my charts runneth over." And Microsoft answered, "Fear not, for unto you this day is given a program, which shall be called PowerPoint, and it shall make for you slides, which shall bring forth titles and bullets and, yea, even diagrams."

—Presentations 1:1

And so it came to pass that these ten PowerPoint commandments were passed down from generation to generation. Obey these commandments and it shall go well with you, with your computer, and yea, even with your projector.

I. Thou Shalt Frequently Savest Thy Work

Every two or three minutes, press Ctrl+S. It takes only a second to save your file, and you never know when you'll be the victim of a rotating power outage (even if you don't live in California).

Note that if you store your presentations in Microsoft's OneDrive cloud storage or on Teams, PowerPoint will automatically save your work every few seconds. However, I urge you not to rely on this feature. Instead, stay in the habit of frequently saving your work.

II. Thou Shalt Storeth Each Presentation in Its Proper Folder

Whenever you save a file, double-check the folder that you're saving it to. It's all too easy to save a presentation in the wrong folder and then spend hours searching for the file later. You'll wind up blaming the computer for losing your files.

III. Thou Shalt Not Abuseth Thy Program's Formatting Features

Yes, PowerPoint lets you set every word in a different font, use 92 different colors on a single slide, and fill every last pixel of empty space with clip art. If you want your slides to look like ransom notes, go ahead. Otherwise, keep things simple.

IV. Thou Shalt Not Stealeth Copyrighted Materials

Given a few minutes with Google or any other search engine, you can probably find just the right picture or snippet of clip art for any presentation need that arises. But keep in mind that many of those pictures, clip art drawings, and media files are copyrighted. Don't use them if you don't have permission.

V. Thou Shalt Abideth by Thine Color Scheme, Auto-Layout, and Template

Microsoft hired a crew of out-of-work artists to pick the colors for the color schemes, arrange things with the slide layouts, and create beautifully crafted templates. Humor them. They like it when you use their stuff. Don't feel chained to the prepackaged designs, but don't stray far from them unless you have a good artistic eye.

VI. Thou Shalt Not Abuse Thine Audience with an Endless Array of Cute Animations or Funny Sounds

PowerPoint animations are cute and sometimes quite useful. But if you include a goofy animation on every slide, pretty soon your audience will just think you're strange.

VII. Keep Thy Computer Gurus Happy

If you have a friend or coworker who knows more about computers than you do, keep them happy. Throw them an occasional Twinkie or bag of Cheetos. Treat computer nerds like human beings. After all, you want them to be your friends.

VIII. Thou Shalt Backeth Up Thy Files Day by Day

Yes, every day. One of these days, you'll come to work only to discover a pile of rubble where your desk used to be. A federal agent will pick up what's left of your computer's keyboard and laugh. But if you back up every day, you won't lose more than a day's work.

Note that if you save your files on OneDrive, Microsoft will take care of backing them up for you. That's one of the main benefits of using cloud storage for your important documents. However, it's still a good idea to back up your files locally.

IX. Thou Shalt Fear No Evil, for Ctrl+Z Is Always with Thee

March ahead with boldness. Not sure what a button does? Click it! Click it twice if it makes you feel powerful! The worst it can do is mess up your presentation. If that happens, you can press Ctrl+Z to set things back the way they should be.

If you *really* mess things up, just close the presentation without saving. Then open the previously saved version. After all, you did obey the first commandment, didn't you?

X. Thou Shalt Not Panic

You're the only one who knows you're nervous. You'll do just fine. Imagine the audience naked if that helps. (Unless, of course, you're making a presentation to a nudist club and they actually *are* naked, in which case try to imagine them with their clothes on.)

Chapter 24
Ten (or So) Tips for Creating Readable Slides

This chapter gives you a few random tips and pointers that will help you produce readable slides.

Try Reading the Slide from the Back of the Room

The number-one rule of creating readable slides is that everyone in the room must be able to read them. If you're not sure, there's one sure way to find out: Try it. Fire up the projector or TV, call up the slide, walk to the back of the room, and see whether you can read it. If you can't, make an adjustment. Even if you plan on presenting online, don't be tempted to cram so much information on each slide that your viewers can't easily read them.

REMEMBER

Everyone's eyesight may not be as good as yours. If you have perfect vision, squint a little when you get to the back of the room to see how the slide may appear to someone whose vision isn't perfect.

If a projector isn't handy, make sure you can read your slides from 10 or 15 feet away from your computer's monitor.

Avoid Small Text

If you can't read a slide from the back of the room, it's probably because the text is too small. The rule to live by is that 24-point type is the smallest you should use for text that you want people to read. In a Word document, 12-point type may be perfectly readable, but it's way too small for PowerPoint.

No More Than Five Bullets, Please

Did you ever notice how David Letterman used two slides to display his Top Ten lists? Dave's producers knew that ten items is way too many for one screen. Five is just right. You may be able to slip in six now and again, but if you're up to seven or eight, try breaking the slide into two slides.

Avoid Excessive Verbiage Lending to Excessively Lengthy Text That Is Not Only Redundant But Also Repetitive and Reiterative

See what I mean? Maybe the heading should have been "Be Brief."

Use Consistent Wording

One sign of an amateur presentation is wording in bulleted lists that isn't grammatically consistent. Consider this list:

- » Profits will be improved.
- » Expanding markets.
- » It will reduce the amount of overseas competition.
- » Production increase.

Each list item uses a different grammatical construction. The same points made with consistent wording have a more natural flow and make a more compelling case:

- » Improved profits
- » Expanded markets
- » Reduced overseas competition
- » Increased production

While you're at it, use active voice rather than passive voice whenever possible. Here's an even stronger form of the bulleted list:

- » Improve profits.
- » Expand markets.
- » Reduce overseas competition.
- » Increase production.

Avoid Unsightly Color Combinations

The professionally chosen color schemes that come with PowerPoint are designed to create slides that are easy to read. If you venture away from them, be careful about choosing colors that are hard to read.

While you're at it, keep in mind that some people have various forms of color insensitivity. The most common form makes it difficult to distinguish midrange shades of red from midrange shades of green, so you may want to avoid using such combinations when the distinction is important to your presentation.

Watch the Line Endings

Sometimes, PowerPoint breaks a line at an awkward spot, which can make slides hard to read. For example, a bullet point may be one word too long to fit on a single line. When that happens, you may want to break the line elsewhere so the second line has more than one word. (Press Shift+Enter to create a line break that doesn't start a new paragraph.)

Alternatively, you may want to drag the right margin of the text placeholder to increase the margin width so that the line doesn't have to be broken at all.

TIP

Web addresses (URLs) are notoriously hard to squeeze onto a single line. If your presentation includes long URLs, pay special attention to how they fit. And consider using URL shortening services such as Bitly (https://bitly.com) or TinyURL (https://tinyurl.com). (With some of these services, you can personalize the short URL links to maintain your company's branding.)

Keep the Background Simple

Don't splash a bunch of distracting clip art on the background unless it's essential. The purpose of the background is to provide a well-defined visual space for the slide's content. All too often, presenters put up slides that have text displayed on top of pictures of the mountains or city skylines, which makes the text almost impossible to read.

Use Only Two Levels of Bullets

Sure, it's tempting to develop your subpoints into sub-subpoints and sub-sub-subpoints, but no one will be able to follow your logic. Don't make your slides more confusing than they need to be. If you need to make sub-sub-subpoints, you probably need a few more slides.

Avoid Bullets Altogether If You Can

Bullets have become a cliché. If possible, eliminate them altogether from your presentation. A single, well-chosen photograph is often a far better way to communicate a key point than a bulleted list.

Keep Charts and Diagrams Simple

PowerPoint can create elaborate graphs that even the best statisticians will marvel at. However, the most effective graphs are simple pie charts with three or four slices and simple column charts with three or four columns. Likewise, pyramid, Venn, and other types of diagrams lose their impact when you add more than four or five elements.

If you remember only one rule when creating your presentations, remember this one: *Keep it simple, clean, and concise.*

Chapter 25
Ten Ways to Keep Your Audience Awake

Nothing frightens a public speaker more than the prospect of the audience falling asleep during the presentation. Here are some things you can do to prevent that from happening. (Yawn.)

Don't Forget Your Purpose

Too many presenters ramble on and on with no clear sense of purpose. The temptation is to throw in every clever quote and every interesting tidbit you can muster that's even remotely related to the topic of your presentation. The reason that this temptation is so strong is that you most likely haven't identified what you hope to accomplish with your presentation. In other words, you haven't pinned down your *purpose*.

REMEMBER

Don't confuse a presentation's title with its purpose. Suppose you're asked to give a presentation to a prospective client on the advantages of your company's new, improved, deluxe model ChronSimplastic Infindibulator. Your purpose in this presentation is not to convey information about the new Infindibulator, but to persuade your client to buy one of the $65 million beasties. The title of your presentation might be "Infindibulators for the 21st Century," but the *purpose* is "Convince these saps to buy one or two."

Don't Become a Slave to Your Slides

PowerPoint makes such beautiful slides that the temptation is to let them be the show. That's a big mistake. *You* are the show — not the slides. The slides are merely visual aids, designed to make your presentation more effective, not to steal the show.

Your slides should *supplement* your talk, not repeat it. If you find yourself just reading your slides, you need to rethink what you put on the slides. The slides should summarize key points, not become the script for your speech.

Don't Overwhelm Your Audience with Unnecessary Detail

On November 19, 1863, a crowd of 15,000 gathered in Gettysburg to hear Edward Everett, one of the greatest orators of the time. Mr. Everett spoke for two hours about the events that had transpired during the famous battle. When he finished, Abraham Lincoln rose to deliver a brief two-minute postscript that has become the most famous speech in American history.

If PowerPoint had been around in 1863, Everett probably would have spoken for four hours. PowerPoint practically *begs* you to talk too much. When you start typing bullets, you can't stop. Pretty soon, you have 40 slides for a 20-minute presentation. That's about 35 more than you probably need. Try to shoot for one slide for every two to five minutes of your presentation.

Don't Neglect Your Opening

As they say, you get only one opportunity to make a first impression. Don't waste it by telling a joke that has nothing to do with the topic, apologizing for your lack of preparation or nervousness, or listing your credentials. Don't pussyfoot around — get right to the point.

The best openings are those that capture the audience's attention with a provocative statement, a rhetorical question, or a compelling story. A joke is okay, but only if it sets the stage for the subject of your presentation.

Be Relevant

The goal of any presentation is to lead your audience to say, "Me, too!" Unfortunately, many presentations leave the audience thinking, "So what?"

The key to being relevant is giving your audience members what they need, and not what you think is interesting or important. The most persuasive presentations are those that present solutions to real problems rather than opinions about hypothetical problems.

Don't Forget the Call to Action

What would a sales presentation be if you never asked for the sale? A wasted opportunity.

The best presentations are the ones that call your audience to action. That may mean buying your product, changing their lifestyles, or just being interested enough to do more research into your topic. But the opportunity will be wasted if you don't invite your audience to respond in some way.

If you're selling something (and we're all selling something!), make it clear how your audience can buy. Tell them the toll-free number. Give them a handout with links to websites they can go to for more information. Ask everyone to sing "Sweet Home Alabama." Do whatever it takes.

Practice, Practice, Practice

Back to good ol' Abe: Somehow a rumor got started that Abraham Lincoln hastily wrote the Gettysburg Address on the train, just before pulling into Gettysburg. In truth, Lincoln agonized for weeks over every word.

Practice, practice, practice. Work through the rough spots. Polish the opening and the closing and all the awkward transitions in between. Practice in front of a mirror. Videotape yourself. Time yourself. Practice.

Relax!

Don't worry! Be happy! Even the most gifted public speakers are scared silly every time they step up to the podium. Whether you're speaking to 1 person or 10,000 people, relax. In 20 minutes, it'll all be over.

No matter how nervous you are, no one knows it except you — that is, unless you tell them. The number-one rule of panic avoidance is to never apologize for your fears. Behind the podium, your knees may be knocking hard enough to bruise yourself, but no one else will notice. After you swab down your armpits and wipe the drool from your chin, people will say, "Weren't you nervous? You seemed so relaxed!"

Expect the Unexpected

Plan on things going wrong, because they will. The projector may not focus, the microphone may go dead, you may drop your notes on the way to the podium. . . . Who knows what else may happen?

Take things in stride, but be prepared for problems you can anticipate. Carry an extra set of notes in your pocket. Bring your own microphone if you have one. Have a backup projector ready if possible. Bring two copies of your presentation on flash drives, and don't put them both in your briefcase.

Don't Be Boring

An audience can overlook almost anything, but one thing they'll never forgive you for is boring them. Above all, do *not* bore your audience.

This guideline doesn't mean you should tell jokes, jump up and down, or talk fast. Jokes, excessive jumping, and rapid speech can be unimaginably boring. If you obey the other instructions in this chapter — if you have a clear purpose and stick to it, avoid unnecessary detail, and address real needs — you'll never be boring. Just be yourself and have fun! If you have fun, so will your audience.

Index

A

accent colors, 158
Action Buttons (Shapes gallery), 245
Add Animation button (Advanced Animation group), 180, 184, 304
Add Assistant option (SmartArt), 290
Add Bookmark button (Playback tab), 304
Add Chart Element button, 273
Add Effect button (Advanced Animation group), 177
Add Section, 209
Add Shape Above option (SmartArt), 290
Add Shape After option (SmartArt), 290
Add Shape Before option (SmartArt), 290
Add Shape Below option (SmartArt), 290
Add Shape button, 290
Adjust group, 228, 232
Adjust section (Picture Format tab), 230
Adobe Acrobat, 337
Advance Slides area, 96
Advanced Animation (Animations tab), 175, 176-179
Advanced Animation group, 177
AI (artificial intelligence), 103, 134, 168. *See also* Copilot
Align Bottom (Align button), 255
Align button (Shape Format tab), 255
Align Center (Align button), 255
Align Left (Align button), 255
Align Middle (Align button), 255
Align Right (Align button), 255
Align Top (Align button), 255
alignment commands, 150-151
All at Once (animation), 181
Amazon, as source for audio files, 294
Amount setting (Advanced Animation), 178
animated puzzle, 185-188

Animation (Animations tab), 175
Animation gallery, 175, 176
Animation icon, 236
Animation Painter, 185
Animation pane, 178-179, 180, 181
Animation Pane button, 179
animation settings dialog box, 182, 183
animations
  applying, 175-188
  commandment for, 349
  for customizing slides, 14
  previewing, 181
  timing of, 185-188
Animations tab, 175-188, 304
Anyone with the Link Can Edit, 328
Apple Music, as source for audio files, 294
Apply Only to This Picture option (Compress Pictures dialog box), 232
Apply to All button, 201
area charts, 260, 262
Arrange group, 199, 252
Arrows (shape outline option), 251
artificial intelligence (AI), 103, 134, 168. *See also* Copilot
artistic effects, 226
Artistic Effects button (Picture Format tab), 226, 227
Artistic Effects command, 226
aspect ratio, 163
Assistant boxes, 289
Audacity, 172
audiences
  commandment for, 349
  don't overwhelm your audience with unnecessary detail, 358
  ways to keep your audience awake, 357-360
Audio (Record tab), 342
Audio button (Insert tab), 296

Audio button (Media group), 295
audio clips, 296, 297, 298–299
audio files, 294, 295
Audio on My PC, 295
audio options, 297–299
Audio Options group (Playback tab), 298
AutoCorrect dialog box, 79, 80
AutoCorrect feature, 73, 79–81
AutoFormat As You Type tab (AutoCorrect feature), 81
auto-layout, commandment for, 349
automatic word-selection option, 52
AutoSave feature, 26, 241
AutoShapes, 288
Axes (chart element), 261, 273
Axis titles (chart element), 273

B

Back button, 28
Background (Slide Master), 193
Background Removal tab, 228
background styles, 164–167
Background Styles control, 195
backgrounds
  keeping background simple, 354
  removing picture backgrounds, 227–229
  as slide feature, 13
backing up, commandment for, 349–350
Backstage view, 32–33, 37, 41, 92–93
Bandcamp, as source for audio files, 294
Banded Columns check box (Table Design Options), 312
Banded Rows check box (Table Design Options), 312
bar charts, 260, 262
Basic Shapes (Shapes gallery), 245
Bevel (shape effect option), 225, 252
Bevel (Text Effects Menu), 153
Bing, using Copilot in, 115–116
bitmap picture, 214–215
Blank (slide layout), 57
Block Arrows (Shapes gallery), 245, 246

Blur (artistic effect), 226
body text (of slide), 14
bookmark (video), 303–305
Border (picture formatting), 225
borders, 224, 225
Borders (Table Styles), 313
boring, don't be boring, 360
Both Hanging (chart layout SmartArt), 291
box & whisker charts, 263
brightness, changing on pictures, 230, 231
Bring Forward command, 254
Bring to Front (Shape Format tab), 254
Browse icon, 41
Bullets and Numbering dialog box, 145–146, 147
Bullets button, 145, 147
bullets/bullet lists
  avoiding altogether, 354
  Convert to SmartArt, 284–285, 287
  default bullet characters tied to themes, 51
  defined, 145
  limiting levels of, 354
  limiting number of, 352
  picture bullet, 147
  recommendations for using, 146
By 1st Level Paragraphs (animation), 183
By 2nd Level Paragraphs (animation), 183

C

call to action, don't forget it, 359
Callouts (Shapes gallery), 245
Cameo (Record tab), 341
Can Edit or Can View (OneDrive option), 328
capitalization, 73, 78–79
Capitalize Each Word option, 78
Capitalize First Letter of Sentences (AutoCorrect feature), 80
Capitalize Names of Days (AutoCorrect feature), 80
case options, 78
Cement (artistic effect), 226
centered tab, 149
Chalk Sketch (artistic effect), 226

Change Case command, 78
Change Chart Type button (Type group), 267
Change Shape, 246
Change the data range (Select Data Source dialog box), 269
channels (Teams), 331–332
character-formatting commands, 141
Chart (as placeholder in slide masters), 195
Chart button (Illustrations group), 265
Chart Data Range text box, 269
Chart Design tab, 267, 270, 272
Chart icon, 262
chart layouts, 260, 270–271, 291
Chart Layouts group, 270
chart style, 271–272
Chart Style gallery, 271, 272
Chart Styles group, 272
Chart titles (chart element), 274
charts
    adding boxes to, 290
    adding new slide with chart, 261–265
    adding to existing slide, 265–266
    adding to presentation, 261–266
    axes on, 261
    changing data selection, 269
    changing layout of, 270–271
    changing style of, 271–272
    changing type of, 266–267
    datasheet for, 260
    defined, 260
    deleting boxes in, 290–291
    editing source data, 269–270
    embellishing, 273–275
    flowcharts, 288
    Increasing Arrows Process chart, 283
    keeping charts simple, 355
    layouts of, 260, 270–271, 291
    legend on, 261
    map charts, 278–279
    organization charts, 289–291
    pasting chart from Excel, 266
    refreshing, 270
    series of, 260
    as slide element, 14
    styles of, 260
    sunburst charts, 276–277
    treemap charts, 276–277
    types of, 260, 262–263
    understanding, 260–261
    working with chart data, 267–270
ChatGPT, 109, 110–111
Cheat Sheet, 3
Choose a SmartArt Graphic dialog box, 285
circles, drawing, 244
Clear Recording (Record tab), 342
Click and drag, for selecting objects, 48
Click to Add Title placeholder, 23
clip art, 194, 216
Clip Art (as placeholder in slide masters), 195
Clipboard, 53, 54, 266
Clipboard task pane, 55
Close (Slide Master), 193
Close button, 26
Close Master View button, 193, 195, 197
collaboration
    on OneDrive, 326–330
    on presentations, 319–335
    in real time, 333
    on Teams, 330–332
    understanding, 319–321
    using comments, 334–335
collapsing, in outline, 71
Collated (printing), 94
color. *See also* color schemes
    accent colors, 158
    adding to text, 143–144
    avoiding unsightly color combinations, 353
    changing color of bullet characters, 146
    hyperlink colors, 158
    text/background colors, 158
    using theme colors, 158–161
Color (on Color/Grayscale options), 50
Color (printing), 94
Color (shape outline option), 250

Color button, 230
color depth (of picture), 214
Color drop-down list, 146
Color menu, 230
Color Saturation (Color button), 230
color schemes, 158, 159–161, 164, 241, 349
Color Temperature (Color button), 230, 231
Color Tone (Color button), 230
color variant, applying, 158–159
Color/Grayscale options, 50
Colors dialog box, 160, 161
column charts, 260, 262, 264, 265
columns, making, 151
Columns button, 151
combo charts, 263
comments, using, 334–335
Comments group, 334
Comments pane, 334
Comparison (slide layout), 57
Compress Media icon, 305
Compress Pictures command (Adjust group), 232
Compress Pictures dialog box, 232
compressed audio files, 294
Compressed Windows Enhanced Metafile (EMZ), 216
Compressed Windows Metafile (WMZ), 216
compression options (media), 305
computer, inserting pictures from, 219–220
computer gurus, commandment for, 349
Configure (presentation), 96
Content placeholders, 47, 57, 195, 261–262, 307–308
Content with Caption (slide layout), 57
contrast, changing on pictures, 230, 231
Copilot
　accessing free version of, 114
　choosing between free and paid versions of, 112–113, 123
　creating picture with, 119–121
　described, 110–112
　as explaining King James Shakespeare theory, 51
　getting content from into PowerPoint, 118–119
　getting started with, 109–121
　as goal-oriented, 132
　for help in creating slides/presentations, 28
　perfecting your prompts to, 131–136
　as providing footnotes to document factual sources of answers, 134
　refining responses from, 117–118
　reply to "Who in the Sam Hill was Sam Hill?," 9
　using Copilot app, 114–115
　using Edge sidebar, 117
　using free version of, 113
　using in Bing, 115–116
　using in PowerPoint, 123–129
Copilot dialog box, 124
Copilot icon, 124, 127
Copilot sidebar, 124, 127–129
Copy command, 53–54
Copy Link (OneDrive option), 330
copyright materials, commandment for, 348
Correct Accidental Use of cAPS LOCK Key (AutoCorrect feature), 80
Correct TWo INitial CApitals (AutoCorrect feature), 80
Corrections command (Adjust section), 230
Cortana, 112
Create Graphic group, 291
Create New Theme Colors dialog box, 160
Create New Theme Fonts dialog box, 162
Crisscross Etching (artistic effect), 226
Crop button, 223
cropping feature, 223–224
Ctrl key, when selecting objects, 48
Ctrl+Z (Undo command), 56, 59, 70, 79, 229, 241–242, 311, 312, 350
Current slide (main screen), 16, 17
Current slide (Presenter view), 97
Curve Shape tool, 248
curved line, drawing, 248–249
curved shape, drawing, 248–249
custom dictionaries, 77
Custom Dictionaries button, 77
Custom Path (Motions Paths), 184
Custom Range (printing), 94
Custom Show (Set Up Show dialog box), 96

custom shows
    printing, 94
    using, 104–106
Custom Shows dialog box, 104, 105, 106
Custom Shows feature, 104
Custom Slide Show button, 104, 105–106
Custom tab, 161
Customize (Design tab), 156
Customize Colors, 159
Customize group (Design tab), 163
Customize Slide Size, 163
Cut command, 53
Cutout (artistic effect), 226, 227
Cycle (SmartArt diagram), 281, 285

D

Dashes (shape outline option), 251
Data group (Chart Design tab), 267, 269
Data Labels (chart element), 274
Data Table (chart element), 274
date, adding to slides, 200–201
Date and Time check box, 200
Date area (as placeholder in slide masters), 200
decimal tab, 149
Decrease Font Size button, 142
Define Custom Show dialog box, 105
Delay (Animation group, Timing tab), 188
Delete button, 58
Delete Mark button, 229
demote (paragraph), 68
Design Ideas feature, 168
Design Ideas pane, 168, 217
Design tab (Ribbon), 21, 155–156, 168
Designer (Design tab), 156
Designer button, 168
Designer feature, 168, 217
Designer task pane, 20, 22
Diagram (as placeholder in slide masters), 195
diagrams
    creating SmartArt diagrams, 284–286
    editing SmartArt text, 287–288
    example of simple SmartArt diagram, 282
    keeping diagrams simple, 355
    as slide element, 14
    tweaking SmartArt diagram, 286–287
    types of SmartArt diagrams, 281, 285–286
dictionaries, custom, 77
direct formatting, 162
Display Drawing Guides on Screen check box, 256
Display Smart Guides When Shapes Are Aligned, 257
Distribute Horizontally (Align button), 255
Distribute Vertically (Align button), 255
Don't Show on Title Slide check box, 201
double-headed arrows, 46
Draw Borders group (Table Design tab), 310
Draw button, 255
Draw Custom Path (Advanced Animation), 178
Draw Table button, 311
Draw Table command, 310
drawing
    complicated picture, 254–257
    displaying rulers, gridlines, and guides for, 240–241
    general drawing tips, 239–242
    other shapes, 244–250
    rectangles, squares, ovals, and circles, 244
    simple objects, 242–244
    on slides, 239–257
    sticking to color scheme, 241
    straight lines, 243
    tables, 310–312
Duplicate command, 54
Duration (Animation group, Timing tab), 188
Duration drop-down list, 172

E

Edge sidebar, 117
Edit Data button (Data group), 268, 269
Edit Master group, 203, 205
Edit Master tab, 193
Edit Shape button, 246
Edit Theme (Slide Master), 193

editing
　entire slide, in outline, 67
　header and footer placeholders directly, 202
　paragraph, in outline, 67
　presentations, 325
　slides, 45–63
　text, 19–21, 52–53
　text objects, 51–52
Editing group (Playback tab), 302
Effect Options button, 181
Effect Options drop-down list (animation), 175, 181, 182, 183
Effect Settings dialog box, 183
Effects (picture formatting), 225
Effects (Table Styles), 313
effects, adding of to animate object, 179–182
Effects Option drop-down list (transitions), 171–172
Emphasis effect (animation), 177, 180
EMZ (Compressed Windows Enhanced Metafile), 216
End Time box (Trim Audio dialog box), 299
Enter, to move from slide to slide, 25
Entrance effect (animation), 177, 180
Equation Shapes (Shapes gallery), 245
Eraser button (Draw Borders group), 311
Error Bars (chart element), 274
Excel, pasting chart from, 266
Exit effect (animation), 177, 180
expanding, in outline, 71
expect the unexpected, 360
Export options (File tab), 338
Export to Video (Record tab), 342
Eyedropper tool, 144, 250

F

Fade In control (sound), 298
Fade In control (video), 302
Fade Out control (sound), 298
Fade Out control (video), 302
Fade style (Animation gallery), 176

file formats
　High-Efficiency Image File Format (HEIF, , HEIC, HIF), 215
　.m4a, 294
　.mp3, 172, 294, 295
　PowerPoint's bitmap picture, 215
　PowerPoint's vector drawings, 216
　Tag Image File Format (TIF, TIFF), 215
　.wav, 172, 294, 295
File menu, 42
File tab, 338
filenames, picking meaningful ones, 37
Files (Presentations channel), 332
Files tab (main screen), 16, 17
Film Grain (artistic effect), 226
Find command, 59–60
Find dialog box, 59–60, 61
Find Next button, 60, 62
Find What box, 60, 61
Find Whole Words Only check box (Find What box), 60–61
First Column check box (Table Design Options), 312
Fixed radio button, 200
Fixed text box, 200, 201
Flip Horizontal, 252
Flip Vertical, 252
flipping, 252
Flowchart (Shapes gallery), 245, 288
flowcharts, creating, 288
Fly In entrance effect (animation), 180
Fly In style (Animation gallery), 176
flyout button (Animation group), 181
Font Color button, 143
Font control (Ribbon), 143
Font dialog box, 140, 143
Font drop-down list, 184
Font group (Home tab, Ribbon), 140
fonts
　changing size of, 142
　choosing, 143

controlling font settings, 140
using theme fonts, 162
Footer area (as placeholder in slide masters), 200
Footer check box, 201
Footer text box, 201
footers, 200–202
Format Background button, 166
Format Background pane, 166, 167, 199
Format Data Labels pane, 274
Format Data Series pane, 278, 279
Format Shape pane, 251
Format tab, 272
formatting
character-formatting commands, 141
commandment for, 348
direct formatting, 162
picture formatting, 225
of slides, 13–14
free-form shape, drawing, 246–248
Freeform Shape tool, 247, 248
From Beginning button (Start Slide Show group), 25
From Beginning (Record tab), 341–342
From Beginning (slide show), 97
From Current Slide (Record tab), 342, 343
From Current Slide (slide show), 97
Full HD (1080p) (compression option), 305
Full Page Slides (printing), 94
funnel charts, 263

G

General channel (Teams), 331
generative AI, 110, 111, 115, 134
generative pre-trained transformer (GPT), 111
Glass (artistic effect), 226
Glow (shape effect option), 252
Glow (Text Effects Menu), 153
Glow, applying to picture, 225
Glow Diffused (artistic effect), 226
Glow Edges (artistic effect), 226

Go to Section, 210
Google Play, as source for audio files, 294
gradient fill, 165–167, 250
Gradient Fill radio button, 166
Graphics Interchange Format (GIF), 215
graphs, use of term, 260
Grayscale (on Color/Grayscale options), 50
Grid and Guides dialog box, 256
gridlines, 240–241, 256–257, 275
Gridlines button, 275
Gridlines check box, 240
Group command (Shape Format tab), 257
Group Text drop-down list (Text Animation tab), 183
guides, 240–241, 256–257
Guides check box, 240

H

hallucinating, 134
Handout master, 190, 195–197
Handout Master button (Master Views group), 196
hardware graphics acceleration, 96
HD (720p) (compression option), 305
HDMI connection, for slide show, 99
Header & Footer button (Text group), 200
Header and Footer dialog box, 200, 201, 202
Header area (as placeholder in slide masters), 200
Header Row check box (Table Design Options), 312
headers, 200–202
Help feature, 27
Hide Background Graphics check box, 199
Hierarchy (SmartArt diagram), 281, 285
High-Efficiency Image File Format (HEIF, HEIC, HIF), 215
histogram charts, 263
Home button, 28
Home page (Backstage view), 42, 43
Home tab, 22
hyperlink colors, 158

I

I-beam (cursor shape), 20
Icon (ICO), 215
icons, explained, 2–3
illustrations, 14
Illustrations group, 245, 265
images
   adding style to, 224–237
   adding to slide master, 194
   cautions in overdoing them, 216
   compressing, 232–233
   correcting sharpness, brightness, contrast, and color, 230–231
   creating of with Copilot, 119–121
   inserting, 216–222
   removing backgrounds from, 227–229
   resizing of, 222–223
   use of for bullet characters, 146
   using Copilot sidebar to change, 128–129
In Click Sequence to Automatically (Audio Options group), 298
Increase Font Size button, 142
Increasing Arrows Process chart, 283
indents, 148–149
Insert Audio dialog box, 295, 296
Insert Chart dialog box, 262, 263, 265
Insert Layout button (Slide Master), 193
Insert Layout (Edit Master group), 195
Insert Picture dialog box, 219
Insert Shapes group, 246
Insert Slide Master button, 193, 203
Insert tab (Ribbon), 242, 249
Insert Table dialog box, 308
Insert Video dialog box, 300
interface, navigating PowerPoint interface, 16–17
internet, inserting pictures from, 216–218

J

jiggle, making text jiggle, 184
JPEG File Interchange Format (JPG, JPEG, JFIF, JPE), 215

K

Keep Changes button, 229
keyboard and mouse, controlling presentation with, 99–100
keyboard shortcuts, 26, 53, 54, 56, 59, 61, 70, 71, 97, 141, 142, 150, 155, 243

L

landscape orientation, 164
laser pointer, 96, 100, 101, 102, 340, 343
Last Column check box (Table Design Options), 312
layers, changing on drawings, 254–255
Layout button (Create Graphic group), 291
Layout button (Slides section of Home tab), 58
layouts. *See also* chart layouts; slide layouts
   adding new ones in slide master, 195–196
   choosing, 205
   in masters, 190
Learn More (Record tab), 342
Left Hanging (chart layout SmartArt), 291
legend, on charts, 261
Legends (chart element), 275
Light Screen (artistic effect), 226
Line button, 243
line charts, 260, 262
Line Drawing (artistic effect), 226
line endings, 354
Line Spacing button, 149
lines
   controlling aspects of style of, 251
   drawing straight lines, 243
   justifying, 150
   spacing of, 149–150
Lines (Shapes gallery), 244
Link Settings dialog box, 328
List (SmartArt diagram), 281, 285
Loop Continuously, 96
Loop Until Stopped check box (Audio Options group), 298
Loop Until Stopped check box (Video Options group), 302

love handles, 48–49, 50
lowercase option, 78

M

.m4a format, 294
magnifying glass, 35
main screen, 16
map (chart type), 262
Map Area (Series Options group), 279
map charts, 278
Map Labels (Series Options group), 279
Map Projection (Series Options group), 279
Mark Areas to Keep button, 229
Mark Areas to Remove button, 229
Marker (artistic effect), 226
Master Layout button (Master Layout group), 206
Master Layout dialog box, 206
Master Layout group (Slide Master), 193, 195, 206
Master Views group, 191, 194, 195
masters
  applying, 204
  applying themes to, 194–195
  creating new one, 202–204
  defined, 189
  described, 13, 54
  layouts in, 190
  modifying, 191–195
  multiple masters feature, 202–204
  placeholders in, 195, 199
  preserving, 204–205
  using, 198–200
  using headers and footers in, 200–202
  working with, 190–198
Match Case check box (Find What box), 60
Matrix (SmartArt diagram), 281, 285
Media (as placeholder in slide masters), 195
media, compressing, 305
Media group, 300
Message text box, 329
Microsoft 365 (M365), 9–10
Microsoft Copilot. *See* Copilot

Microsoft Office Assistant ("Clippy"), 111–112
Microsoft Print to PDF, 94
Microsoft Stream, 337
Microsoft Support, 28
Microsoft Teams (Teams), 330–332
Microsoft Video Editor, 299
MIDI files, 294
mistakes
  automatic correction of common ones, 73
  fixing ones while drawing shapes, 243
  using Eraser button (Draw Borders group) on, 311–312
Modify ranges and series (Select Data Source dialog box), 269
Monitors group, 88
More Colors, 146
More Colors button, 160
More Images control, 35
More Legend Options, 275
Morph transition effect, 173–174, 235–236
Mosaic Bubbles (artistic effect), 226
motion clip, adding to slides, 299–305
Motion path (animation), 177
Motion Path effect (animation), 180
Motion Paths Draw (Advanced Animation), 178
Move Down button, 70
Move Up button, 70
.mp3 format, 172, 294, 295
Multiple Monitors area (slide show), 96

N

New (in Backstage View), 34–35
New Comment button (Comments group), 334
New Slide button (Slides group), 22, 63, 307
Next slide or animation (Presenter view), 97
nontext objects, selecting, 48
Normal view
  limitation of, 62
  for selecting individual objects, 48
Normal View button, 194
notes. *See* speakers notes
Notes (Presenter view), 97

Notes and Handouts tab, 202
Notes master, 190, 197–198
Notes Master button (Master Views group), 197
Notes Page view, 84–85
Notes pane, 84
number, adding to slides, 200–201
Number area (as placeholder in slide masters), 200
numbered lists, 147–148
Numbering button, 147

O

objects
  animating, 179–182
  changing stacking order of, 254
  defined, 47
  drawing simple objects, 242–244
  duplicating, 54
  examples of, 47
  flipping and rotating, 252–254
  group of, 257
  hiding background objects in slide masters, 199
  inserting audio sound object, 295–297
  lining up, 255–256
  resizing or moving, 48–50
  selecting, 47–48
Office Assistant ("Clippy"), 111–112
On Bookmark (video), 304
On Click Of (trigger), 178
On Mouse Click or After options, 172
One Letter at a Time (animation), 181
One Word at a Time (animation), 181
OneDrive
  AutoSave feature as enabled by default, 241
  availability of, 219
  managing features of, 324–326
  as platform for collaboration, 320
  as private storage system, 322
  saving to, 39–40
  sharing OneDrive presentation, 326–330
  working with, 321–330
Online Pictures dialog box, 216, 217
Online Videos (video source), 300
Open dialog box, 41, 42
Open screen (Backstage view), 41, 42
open shape, drawing, 248
OpenAI, 111
opening, don't neglect your opening, 358
opening screen, 15
Options dialog box, 339
organization charts, 289–291
outline
  adding new slide in, 70
  adding paragraphs in, 69
  calling up, 65–67
  collapsing and expanding, 71
  Copilot as proposing outline for presentation, 126
  important things to notice about, 66–67
  moving text up and down in, 70
  promoting and demoting paragraphs, in outline, 68–69
  selecting and editing entire slide in, 67
  selecting and editing paragraphs in, 67
outline box, 50
Outline View button (Ribbon's View tab), 65
Outlook (OneDrive option), 330
Oval button, 244
ovals, drawing, 244

P

Page Down key, 24, 46
Page Up key, 24, 46
Paint Brush (artistic effect), 226
Paint Strokes (artistic effect), 226, 227
panic, commandment for not panicking, 350
Paragraph group (Home tab, Ribbon), 144, 145
paragraphs
  adding new one, in outline, 69
  alignment commands for, 150–151
  promoting and demoting, in outline, 68–69
  selecting and editing, in outline, 67
Paste command, 53, 54
Paste Options, 54

Pastels Smooth (artistic effect), 226
Pattern Fill, 167
PDF (Portable Document Format), 337, 338–340
PDF/XPS button (Export option), 338
Pen and Laser Pointer button, 102
pen and laser pointer color, 96
Pen Style drop-down, 311
Pen tool, 102
Pen Weight drop-down, 311
Pencil Grayscale (artistic effect), 226, 227
pencil icon, 328
Pencil Sketch (artistic effect), 226
Photocopy (artistic effect), 226
Picture (as placeholder in slide masters), 195
Picture (SmartArt diagram), 281, 286
Picture Border (Picture Styles group), 225
Picture Color Options command, 230
Picture Corrections options, 231
Picture Effects button (Picture Styles group), 225
Picture Format tab (Ribbon), 217, 223, 224, 226, 228, 230
Picture or Texture Fill radio button, 167
Picture Style gallery, 225
Picture Styles group, 225
Picture with Caption (slide layout), 57
pictures
　adding style to, 224–237
　adding to slide master, 194
　applying artistic effects, 226
　applying picture border, 225
　applying picture effects, 225
　cautions in overdoing them, 216
　compressing, 232–233
　correcting sharpness, brightness, contrast, and color, 230–231
　creating of with Copilot, 119–121
　drawing complicated picture, 254–257
　inserting, 216–222
　predefined styles of, 224, 225
　removing backgrounds from, 227–229
　resizing of, 222–223
　types of, 214–216
　using Copilot sidebar to change, 128–129

Pictures button, 216
pie charts, 260, 262
Pin icon, 43
Pin to List (theme), 36
Pinned (Home page), 43
pixel density, 214
pixels, 214
Placeholder drop-down list (Master Layout group), 195
placeholders
　Content placeholders, 47, 57, 195, 261–262, 307–308
　defined, 47
　for headers and footers, 200
　in notes master, 197
　restoring lost ones, 206
　in slide masters, 195, 199
　text placeholders. *See* text placeholders
Plastic Wrap (artistic effect), 226
Play and Pause button (animation), 236
Play button (Animation pane), 181
Play Full Screen check box (Video Options group), 302
Playback tab (Ribbon), 297, 301, 302
polygon, drawing, 246–248
Portable Network Graphics (PNG), 215
portrait orientation, 164
Posts (Presentations channel), 332
.potx file extension, 207
PowerPoint
　defined, 7–8
　exiting, 28–29
　gaining access to, 9–10
　main screen, 16
　navigating interface, 16–17
　opening screen, 15
　starting, 14–15
　templates, 15
　ten commandments, 347–350
　uses of, 8
　using Copilot in, 123–129
　Web App, 327

.pptx extension, 12
practice, practice, practice, 359
Presentation Coach, 104
Presentation tools, 101, 102
Presentation Views group, 62, 202
presentations
  adding chart to, 261–266
  closing, 26
  collaborating on, 319–335
  configuring, 96
  controlling with keyboard and mouse, 99–100
  creating blank presentation, 15–16
  creating of with Copilot, 124–126
  creating one based on template, 208
  displaying yours, 25
  editing, 325
  exporting to other formats, 337–344
  finding video to add to, 299–300
  inserting pictures in, 216–222
  introducing PowerPoint presentations, 11
  media for showing, 11–12
  opening, 41–42
  pinning of for easy access, 43
  practice, practice, practice, 359
  printing, 92–95
  proofing, 73–81
  saving, 12, 26, 29, 37–41, 322–323
  sharing OneDrive presentation, 326–330
  understanding presentation files, 12
  working with presentation sections, 209–210
Presentations channel (Teams), 331
Presenter view (Monitors group), 88, 97, 343
Preserve button, 205
Preserve Master option, 205
Preview (Animations tab), 175
Preview (Record tab), 341
Preview control (Transition tab), 170
Print All Slides drop-down list, 94
Print All Slides option, 94
Print command, 92
Print Current Slide, 94
Print dialog box, 87

Print Hidden Slides check box, 87, 88
Print Preview feature, 95
Print Selection, 94
printers, changing, 93–94
printing
  custom shows, 94
  part of document, 94
  presentations, 92–95
  speakers notes, 87–88
Process (SmartArt diagram), 281, 285
projector, setting up, for slide show, 98–99
promote (paragraph), 68
prompts, 115–120, 124–125, 127–129, 131–136
Proofing, 77
public address (PA) system, for slide show, 99
Publish as PDF or XPS dialog box, 338
punctuation, 73
Pure Black and White (on Color/Grayscale options), 50
purpose, don't forget your purpose, 357
Pyramid (SmartArt diagram), 281, 286

Q

Quick access toolbar (QAT) (main screen), 16, 17
Quick Layout button (Chart Layouts group), 270
Quick Layout Gallery, 270
Quick Print button (QAT), 92

R

radar charts, 260, 263
Recent list, 42
Recently Used Shapes (Shapes gallery), 244
Recolor (Color button), 230
Record Audio, 296
Record button, 296, 342
Record tab (Ribbon), 341–342
recording, slide show, 342–344
Recording dialog box, 103
Rectangle button, 244
Rectangles (Shapes gallery), 245
rectangles, drawing, 244

Redo command, 56
Reflection (shape effect option), 252
Reflection (Text Effects Menu), 153
reflections (style option), 224, 225
Refresh Data button (Data group), 270
Rehearsal feature, 103
Rehearse Timings button, 103
Rehearse with Coach button, 103
relational database, 276
Relationship (SmartArt diagram), 281, 285
relaxation, importance of, 360
relevance, being relevant, 359
Remove Background button (Adjust group), 228
Remove from List (theme), 36
Remove Section, 210
Repeat (Animation group, Timing tab), 188
Repeat button, 103
Replace All button, 62
Replace button (Editing group), 61–62
Replace button (Find dialog box), 61
Replace dialog box, 61
Replace Text as You Type (AutoCorrect feature), 80
Replace With box, 61
Reset button, 223
Reset Graphic button (Reset group), 287
Reset group, 287
Reset Slide, 199
Reset to Cameo (Record tab), 342
resolution (of picture), 214
Rewind when Done Playing (Animation group, Timing tab), 188
Ribbon (main screen), 16–17, 18–19, 21
Right Hanging (chart layout SmartArt), 291
right-aligned tab, 149
Rotate button (Arrange group), 252, 253
rotate handle, 49, 253–254
Rotate Left, 253
Rotate Right, 253
rotating, objects, 253
ruler, for help in lining up drawings, 240–241
Ruler check box, 148, 240

S

saturation, changing on pictures, 231
Save a Copy page (Backstage view), 37, 38, 41
Save As dialog box, 39, 322, 323–324
Save as Show (Record tab), 342
Save button, 37, 241
Save command, 26
saving
   commandment for, 347–348
   doing so frequently when drawing, 241
   presentations, 12, 26, 29, 37–41, 322–323
Scalable Vector Graphics (SVG), 216
scatter charts, 260, 262
Scenes button (animation), 236
Screen Recording (Record tab), 342
scroll bar, 24
scroll box, 46
Search Bing text box, 217, 218
Search box, 27, 35
Search button, 27
Section, 209
Section Header (slide layout), 57
sections, 209–210
Select Data button (Data group), 269
Select Data Source dialog box, 269
Send Backward command, 255
Send Link dialog box, 327, 328, 330
Send to Back button (Arrange group), 199
Send to Back (Shape Format tab), 255
Sentence case option, 78
Series Options group, 278, 279
Series Options icon, 278
Set Expiration Date (OneDrive option), 328
Set Password (OneDrive option), 329
Set Up section (Slide Show tab), 103
Set Up Show dialog box, 95–96
Set Up Slide Show button, 95
Shading (Table Styles), 313
Shadow (shape effect option), 252
Shadow (Text Effects Menu), 153
shadows, 144, 224, 225

Shape (picture formatting), 225
shape effects, applying, 252
Shape Effects button (Shape Format tab), 252
Shape Effects (text box format), 249
Shape Fill control (Shape Styles group), 250
shape fill, setting, 250
Shape Fill (text box format), 249
Shape Format, 239
Shape Format tab (Ribbon), 152, 243, 246, 249, 250, 252, 254, 257
Shape Outline control (Shape Styles group), 250
shape outline, setting, 250–251
Shape Outline (text box format), 249
Shape Styles group, 243, 250
Shape Styles (Shape Format tab), 250
shapes
  drawing, 245–246
  as slide element, 14
  styling, 250–252
Shapes button (Illustrations group), 242, 243, 244, 245
Shapes gallery (Shapes group), 242, 243, 244–245, 247, 248
SharePoint (platform for collaboration), 320, 321
sharpness, changing on pictures, 230, 231
Shift key, holding down while drawing shape, 243
Show AutoCorrect Options Buttons, 79
Show without Animation option, 96
Show without Narration option, 96
single-headed arrows, 46
Size (Slide Master), 193
sizing handles, 49, 244
Slide group (Home tab), 209
Slide Layout task pane, 47
slide layouts, 13, 14, 47, 56–58
Slide master, 190
Slide Master button (Presentation Views group), 194, 195, 202
Slide Master tab, 193, 203
Slide Master view, 143, 144, 191, 192, 193, 202
slide masters
  applying, 204
  applying themes to, 194–195
  creating new one, 202–204

defined, 189
described, 13, 54
layouts in, 190
modifying, 191–195
multiple masters feature, 202–204
placeholders, 195, 199
preserving, 204–205
using, 198–200
using headers and footers in, 200–202
working with, 190–198
Slide Navigator (Presenter view), 98
Slide Number check box, 201
Slide Preview pane, 199
slide show
  keyboard tricks for, 99–100
  mouse tricks for, 100
  recording, 340, 342–344
  setting up, 95–96
  starting, 97
  using custom shows, 104–106
  working in Presenter View, 97–98
Slide Show Name field, 105
Slide Show tab (Ribbon), 25, 88, 97, 103
Slide Size button, 163
Slide Size dialog box, 163, 164
Slide Sorter button (Presentation Views group), 62
Slide Sorter view, 48, 62–63, 170
Slide Thumbnail pane, 209
slide transitions, 13, 169, 170–174
slides
  adding chart to existing slide, 265–266
  adding chart to new slide, 261–265
  adding new one, 22–24, 63, 69–70, 87
  adding tables to, 307–315
  animating, 169–188
  applying background styles, 164–167
  change manually in slide show, 96
  changing size of, 163–164
  deleting, 58–59, 63
  designing, 155–168
  don't become slave to, 358
  drawing on, 239–257
  duplicating, 59

editing, 45–63
formatting of, 13–14
hidden slides, 87, 106
inserting table on, 309–310
keeping them updated, 96
layouts in, 13, 14, 47, 56–58
moving from slide to slide, 24, 46
rearranging, 62–63
rehearsing timings for, 103
scribbling on, 102
selecting and editing entire slide, in outline, 67
selecting ones to show in slide show, 96
tips for creating readable slides, 351–355
using Designer to improve, 168
Slides pane (main screen), 16, 17
Slides-Per-Page control (Page Setup group, Handout Master tab), 196
smart tag, 266
SmartArt
　creating SmartArt diagrams, 284–286
　editing SmartArt text, 287–288
　as slide element, 14
　style gallery, 286
　tweaking SmartArt diagram, 286–287
　understanding, 281–283
　working with, 281–291
SmartArt Design tab (Ribbon), 286–287
SmartArt style, defined, 286
SmartArt Styles group, 287
Snap Objects to Grid check box, 256
Soft Edges, applying to picture, 225
Soft Edges (shape effect option), 252
sound
　adding, 294–299
　commandment for, 349
　controlling when sound is played, 298
　fading sound in and out, 298
　hiding sound icon, 298
　inserting audio sound object, 295–297
　looping sound, 298
　recording audio clip, 296, 297
　setting audio options, 297–299
　as slide element, 14
　when using projector or TV, 99
sound clip, adding to slide master, 194
Sound drop-down list (transitions), 172
sound files, 294
Space category, 233
spacing, of lines, 149–150
speaker notes, overview, 84–85
speakers notes
　adding extra notes page for slide, 86–87
　adding to slide, 85–86
　displaying on separate monitor, 88–89
　printing, 87–88
　using text generated by Copilot on page of, 128
Specific People (OneDrive option), 328
Speed setting (Advanced Animation), 178
spellchecker, 73, 74–76
Spin effect (Advanced Animation), 178
squares, drawing, 244
Standard (480p) compression option, 305
Standard (chart layout SmartArt), 291
standard left-aligned tab, 149
Stars and Banners (Shapes gallery), 245
Start (Animation group, Timing tab), 188
Start after Previous (Start setting in animation), 185
Start on Click (Start setting in animation), 185
Start Slide Show group, 25, 104
Start Time box (Trim Audio dialog box), 299
Start with Previous (Start setting in animation), 185
Status bar (main screen), 16, 17
Stock 3D Models, 233
stock library, inserting pictures from, 220–222
Stock Videos (video source), 299–300
stocks (chart type), 262
Stop button, 296
storage, commandment for, 348
styles
　background styles, 164–167
　for charts, 260
　for pictures, 224, 225

sunburst charts, 263, 276–277
surface charts, 263
Switch Row/Column button, 268
Switch Row/Column (Data group), 267–268
Switch rows and columns (Select Data Source dialog box), 269
synchronization status, 322
Synonyms menu, 77
System Tray, 324

T

Tab key, when selecting objects, 48
Table (as placeholder in slide masters), 195
Table button, 309, 310
Table Design Options group, 312
Table Design tab, 310, 312
Table icon (Content placeholder), 308
Table Layout tab (Ribbon), 313–315
Table Styles gallery, 312
Table Styles group, 312
tables
   adding style to, 312–313
   adding to slides, 307–315
   creating in Content placeholder, 307–309
   drawing, 310–312
   inserting, 309–310
Tables group, 310
tabs, 148–149
Tag Image File Format (TIF, TIFF), 215
Task pane (main screen), 16, 17
Taylor, Jen, 112
Teams
   desktop version of, 331
   as platform for collaboration, 320, 321
   web version of, 331
   working with, 330–332
teams, use of term, 330
templates
   commandment for, 349
   creating new one, 207
   creating presentation based on, 208

defined, 34, 207
suggestions for, 35
supplied by PowerPoint, 15
working with, 207
text
   adding color, 143–144
   adding recurring text, 194
   animating, 182–185
   avoiding excessive verbiage, 352
   avoiding small text, 352
   big picture text formatting, 144–151
   changing look, 140–144
   changing size of characters, 142
   character-formatting commands, 141
   converting of to SmartArt, 284
   creating fancy text with WordArt, 151–153
   editing, 19–21, 52–53
   editing SmartArt text, 287–288
   finding, 59–60
   formatting, 139–142
   making text jiggle, 184
   moving up and down, in outline, 70
   overriding master text style, 198–199
   replacing, 61–62
   selecting, 52
Text (as placeholder in slide masters), 195
Text Animation tab, 183
Text Box button (Text group), 249
text boxes, 14, 249–250
Text Effects button (WordArt Shape Format tab), 153
Text Effects menu, 153
Text Fill button (WordArt Shape Format tab), 153
Text group, 200
Text Highlight Color button, 144
text objects, 48, 51–52
Text Outline button (WordArt Shape Format tab), 153
Text pane (Editing SmartArt), 287, 290
text placeholders, 13, 14, 19, 57, 66, 144, 177, 178, 179, 180, 182, 183, 354
Texture button, 167

Texture gallery, 167
Texturizer (artistic effect), 226
theme effects, 162–163
Theme Effects gallery, 162
Theme gallery, 157
themes
  applying, 21, 157–158
  applying theme effects, 162–163
  applying to masters, 194–195
  components of, 156
  defined, 34, 156, 207
  examples of, 34
  as PowerPoint feature, 13
  predefined ones, 156
  searching for, 35, 36
  selecting, 36
  suggestions for, 35
  using theme colors, 158–161, 162
  as working in Word, Excel, and PowerPoint, 155
  working with, 156–163
Themes drop-down list (Slide Master), 195
Themes group (Design tab), 156
thesaurus, 73, 77–78
Thesaurus button, 77
This Device (video source), 299, 300
3D Model tab (Ribbon), 236
3D models
  defined, 233
  morphing, 235–236
  using animated models, 236–237
  working with, 233–237
3D models button, 233
3D Rotation, applying to picture, 225
3D Rotation (shape effect option), 252
3D Rotation (Text Effects Menu), 153
thumbnails, 24
TIF, TIFF (Tag Image File Format), 215
Timer (Presenter view), 97
timing
  of animations, 185–188
  of slides, 103
Timing (Animations tab), 175, 184

Timing (Transition tab), 170
title (of slide), 14
Title and Content (slide layout), 57, 284
Title Only (slide layout), 57
Title Slide (slide layout), 57
tOGGLE cASE option, 78
Tools (Presenter view), 98
Total Row check box (Table Design Options), 312
touchscreen, moving from slide to slide on, 46
Transform (Text Effects Menu), 153
Transition to This Slide, 170, 171
transitions, 13, 169, 170–174
Transitions gallery, 171
Transitions tab, 169–174
treemap charts, 263, 276–277
Trendline (chart element), 275
Trigger (Advanced Animation group), 178
trigger, in animation, 178
Trigger button (Advanced Animation group), 304
Trim Audio button, 298, 299
Trim Audio dialog box, 298–299
Trim Video button, 302
Trim Video dialog box, 302, 303
true color pictures, 214–215
TV, setting up, for slide show, 98–99
Two Content (slide layout), 57
Type group, 267

U

uncompressed audio files, 294
Undo button (QAT), 242, 243
Undo command, 54, 55–56, 62, 241–242. *See also* Ctrl+Z (Undo command)
unexpected, expect it, 360
Update Automatically radio button, 200
UPPERCASE option, 78
URLs, and line endings, 354

V

Variants gallery, 158
Variants group (Design tab), 156, 157

Variants section (Design tab), 21
vector drawings, 215, 216
video
   adding to slide master, 194
   adding to slides, 299–305
   controlling when it plays, 302
   crafting, 340–341
   fading video in and out, 302
   finding video to add to presentation, 299–300
   inserting, 300–301
   looping, 302
   playing it full screen, 302
   setting video options, 301–305
   as slide element, 14
   trimming, 302
Video Editor (Microsoft), 299
Video Options group, 302
View buttons, 19
View tab (Ribbon), 50, 62, 63, 65, 75, 77, 84, 85, 86, 148, 191, 202, 240, 243, 256, 334
Views tab (Ribbon), 194, 195, 196, 197, 199

W

Watercolor Sponge (artistic effect), 226
waterfall charts, 263
.wav file format, 172, 294, 295

web, inserting pictures from, 216–218
Weight (shape outline option), 250
When Selecting, Automatically Select Entire Word check box, 52
Windows bitmap (BMP, DIB, or RLE), 215
Windows Enhanced Metafile (EMF), 216
Windows Metafile (WMF), 216
Wipe style (Animation gallery), 176
WMZ (Compressed Windows Metafile), 216
WordArt, 151–153
WordArt Quick Styles gallery, 152
WordArt Styles group (Shape Format tab), 152
wording, using consistent wording, 352–353

X

XPS, defined, 339

Y

YouTube Music, as source for audio files, 294

Z

Zoom control (main screen), 16, 17, 184
Zoom slider, 63, 239–240

About the Author

Doug Lowe wrote his first computer book in 1982 and hasn't stopped writing since. Spread out and cut up, that should be more than enough pages to cover the entire route of California's high-speed rail . . . oh wait, never mind. Maybe someday. His most recent books include *Java All-in-One For Dummies*, 7th Edition; *Networking All-in-One For Dummies*, 9th Edition; and *Electronics All-in-One For Dummies*, 3rd Edition.

Although Doug has yet to win a Pulitzer Prize, he remains cautiously optimistic. He is also hopeful that Paramount+ will buy the film rights to this book and turn it into a miniseries. We can get Copilot to write the script! It'll probably be better than most of the TV Doug will be binge-watching now that this book is finished.

Doug lives with his beautiful wife, Kristen Gearhart, in sunny Fresno, California, which is kind of boring but fortunately is really close to a lot of not-boring places. Thank God for air-conditioning.

Dedication

This one is for my dear friend Tedd Lyons. I miss you so much.

Author's Acknowledgments

This year marks the 30th anniversary of the first edition of this book.

I have Elizabeth Kuball to thank for this edition and most of the recent editions of this and my other *For Dummies* books. What an outstanding journey it's been. Elizabeth continues to do fantastic work and in my humble opinion is the best in the biz.

And a huge thanks for all of the other people who contributed, including Ryan Williams for giving the entire manuscript a thorough technical review and making so many excellent suggestions, and all the others whose names I may not know but who do their jobs like the pros that they are. I am filled with gratitude for all of you.

Publisher's Acknowledgments

Associate Editor: Elizabeth Stilwell
Editorial Manager: Sofia Malik
Editor: Elizabeth Kuball
Technical Editor: Ryan Williams
Production Editor: Tamilmani Varadharaj
Cover Image: © Summit Art Creations/Shutterstock.com
Special Help: Kristie Pyles

Leverage the power

Dummies is the global leader in the reference category and one of the most trusted and highly regarded brands in the world. No longer just focused on books, customers now have access to the dummies content they need in the format they want. Together we'll craft a solution that engages your customers, stands out from the competition, and helps you meet your goals.

Advertising & Sponsorships

Connect with an engaged audience on a powerful multimedia site, and position your message alongside expert how-to content. Dummies.com is a one-stop shop for free, online information and know-how curated by a team of experts.

- Targeted ads
- Video
- Email Marketing
- Microsites
- Sweepstakes sponsorship

20 MILLION PAGE VIEWS EVERY SINGLE MONTH

15 MILLION UNIQUE VISITORS PER MONTH

43% OF ALL VISITORS ACCESS THE SITE VIA THEIR MOBILE DEVICES

700,000 NEWSLETTER SUBSCRIPTIONS TO THE INBOXES OF **300,000** UNIQUE INDIVIDUALS EVERY WEEK

# of dummies

Custom Publishing

Reach a global audience in any language by creating a solution that will differentiate you from competitors, amplify your message, and encourage customers to make a buying decision.

- Apps
- Books
- eBooks
- Video
- Audio
- Webinars

Brand Licensing & Content

Leverage the strength of the world's most popular reference brand to reach new audiences and channels of distribution.

For more information, visit **dummies.com/biz**

PERSONAL ENRICHMENT

9781119187790
USA $26.00
CAN $31.99
UK £19.99

9781119179030
USA $21.99
CAN $25.99
UK £16.99

9781119293354
USA $24.99
CAN $29.99
UK £17.99

9781119293347
USA $22.99
CAN $27.99
UK £16.99

9781119310068
USA $22.99
CAN $27.99
UK £16.99

9781119235606
USA $24.99
CAN $29.99
UK £17.99

9781119251163
USA $24.99
CAN $29.99
UK £17.99

9781119235491
USA $26.99
CAN $31.99
UK £19.99

9781119279952
USA $24.99
CAN $29.99
UK £17.99

9781119283133
USA $24.99
CAN $29.99
UK £17.99

9781119287117
USA $24.99
CAN $29.99
UK £16.99

9781119130246
USA $22.99
CAN $27.99
UK £16.99

PROFESSIONAL DEVELOPMENT

9781119311041
USA $24.99
CAN $29.99
UK £17.99

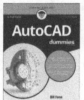
9781119255796
USA $39.99
CAN $47.99
UK £27.99

9781119293439
USA $26.99
CAN $31.99
UK £19.99

9781119281467
USA $26.99
CAN $31.99
UK £19.99

9781119280651
USA $29.99
CAN $35.99
UK £21.99

9781119251132
USA $24.99
CAN $29.99
UK £17.99

9781119310563
USA $34.00
CAN $41.99
UK £24.99

9781119181705
USA $29.99
CAN $35.99
UK £21.99

9781119263593
USA $26.99
CAN $31.99
UK £19.99

9781119257769
USA $29.99
CAN $35.99
UK £21.99

9781119293477
USA $26.99
CAN $31.99
UK £19.99

9781119265313
USA $24.99
CAN $29.99
UK £17.99

9781119239314
USA $29.99
CAN $35.99
UK £21.99

9781119293323
USA $29.99
CAN $35.99
UK £21.99

dummies.com

dummies
A Wiley Brand